VISITING MRS NABOKOV

Martin Amis is the author of eighteen books,
fiction and non-fiction, including *London Fields*,
Money, *The Information*, *Experience*, *The War
Against Cliché* and, most recently, *Yellow Dog*. He
lives in London.

ALSO BY MARTIN AMIS

Fiction

The Rachel Papers
Dead Babies
Success
Other People
Money
Einstein's Monsters
London Fields
Time's Arrow
The Information
Night Train
Heavy Water
Yellow Dog

Non-Fiction

Invasion of the Space Invaders
The Moronic Inferno
Experience
The War Against Cliché
Koba the Dread

Martin Amis

VISITING
MRS NABOKOV
And Other Excursions

VINTAGE

Published by Vintage 2005

6 8 10 9 7 5

Copyright © Martin Amis 1993

Martin Amis has asserted his right under the Copyright, Designs and Patents Act, 1988 to be identified as the author of this work

First published in Great Britain in 1993 by
Jonathan Cape

Vintage
Random House, 20 Vauxhall Bridge Road,
London SW1V 2SA

www.rbooks.co.uk

Addresses for companies within
The Random House Group Limited can be found at:
www.randomhouse.co.uk/offices.htm

The Random House Group Limited Reg. No. 954009

A CIP catalogue record for this book
is available from the British Library

ISBN 9780099461876

Extracts from *Collected Poems* by Philip Larkin, edited by Anthony Thwaite, are reproduced by kind permission of Faber and Faber Ltd

The Random House Group Limited supports The Forest Stewardship Council (FSC), the leading international forest certification organisation. All our titles that are printed on Greenpeace approved FSC certified paper carry the FSC logo. Our paper procurement policy can be found at:
www.rbooks.co.uk/environment

Printed and bound in Great Britain by
CPI Antony Rowe, Chippenham, Wiltshire

To Joe, Isabel, Roland,
Frankie – and Dolores

CONTENTS

INTRODUCTION AND
ACKNOWLEDGMENTS

Warily looking back through these pieces, I glimpse a series of altered or vanished worlds, including those of my younger and much younger selves. Things change. Graham Greene is dead. Véra Nabokov is dead. Salman Rushdie is still alive, and still in hiding: if writing fiction is, among other things, an act of spiritual freedom, then Rushdie is a man who has been imprisoned for the crime of being free. Graham Taylor, one-time manager of Watford Football Club, is now manager of England: for the time being. Monica Seles, whose professional debut I witnessed (she was fourteen), has since won eight Slams; as I write, she is in hospital, recovering from a knife attack at a tournament in Hamburg (her East German assailant was a Steffi Graf fan, and his intention was to pave the way for Steffi's return to the number-one spot). Nuclear deterrence is dead. Or at least Mutually Assured Destruction is dead: this extraordinary edifice – at once massive and notional, and, it appeared, impregnably self-sufficient – was unseamed by three words of diplomacy, from Mikhail Gorbachev (the three words were: 'This isn't serious.' As a planetary arrangement, four tons of TNT per human being wasn't only uncomic. It wasn't serious). The nuclear age has survived its Deterrence period and is entering a new phase, one which we can confidently – though not safely – call Proliferation. John Braine is dead: as a writer, his dream was to make a great deal of money; but he died in penury. George Bush and Dan Quayle are dead, politically. The star interview is dead, as a form. Sent to New York to interview Madonna, I felt no significant disruption in my plans when Madonna refused to see me. The great postmodern celebrities are a part of their publicity machines, and that is all you are ever going to get to write about: their publicity machines. You review the publicity machine. Even the humble literary interview is dying, or growing old: 'It was with dread/detachment/high hopes that I approached X's townhouse/office/potting shed. The door opened. He is fatter/smaller/taller/balder than I expected. Pityingly/perfunctorily/politely he offered me instant coffee/a cigarette/dinner. Everyone told me how modest/craven/suave/vain/charming I would find him, so I was naturally unsurprised/taken aback by his obvious charm/vanity, etc., etc.' Darts is dead. Its decline followed an opposite course to that of nuclear deterrence. It tried to sanitise or detoxify itself (no alcohol, no tobacco, no obesity); but then it transpired that the prospect of messy self-destruction was the only thing anyone liked about it. Isaac Asimov is dead. Topless sunbathing is no longer remarkable. Roman Polanski no longer makes interesting films. V.S. Pritchett isn't ninety any more: he will soon be ninety-three. I have now been doing this sort of thing for more than twenty years. I don't get around as much as I used to.

Not long ago I saw a book of this kind described by a reviewer as 'a garage sale': the writer was selling off his literary junk, in informal surroundings. Certainly it is considered a nice gesture if, in introducing such a book, the writer abases himself for having assembled it. Actually the authorial motive – or vice or weakness – we are examining here is, I think, dully clerical: an attempt at order and completion. John Updike, an obvious hero of the genre, took this tendency too far, perhaps, when in *Picked-Up Pieces* he reprinted a sixty-word citation to Thornton Wilder, together with a fifty-word footnote doggedly justifying its inclusion. All I can safely promise the reader is that, though much has been left in, much has been left out.

After university I worked in an art gallery (for three months), then in advertising (for three weeks), then at the *Times Literary Supplement* (for three years), and then (for four more) at the *New Statesman*. In 1980 I quit going to an office and became a full-time writer. The main characteristic of this way of life, it seemed to me, was that nothing ever happened to you. Being a novelist, in those days, was not in itself a distraction, as it can be now. Now, if you're not careful, you can spend half your life being interviewed or photographed or answering questions posed by the press, on the telephone, about Fergie or Maastricht or your favourite colour. Nothing ever happened to you – except journalism: the kind of journalism that got you out of the house. Getting out of the house is the only thing that unites the pieces in the present book – an unrigorous arrangement, which I didn't quite stick to anyway. *Not* getting out of the house will be the controlling theme of a subsequent volume, one devoted to the lowest and noblest literary form: the book review. Novels, of course, are *all* about not getting out of the house.

And so, equipped with some kind of assignment, you get out of the house! This might mean a fifteen-hour flight or a ten-minute drive to the other side of Regents Park. Things can go well or they can go badly. When things go badly, you are simply an embarrassment to your destination. You return hours or weeks later with half a page of notes and the prospect of much cloistered contrivance. When things go well, the necessary elements come together with little or no encouragement. Writing journalism never feels like writing in the proper sense. It is essentially collaborative: both your subject and your audience are hopelessly specific.

But the excursion itself (the solitude, the preoccupation, the solving of successive difficulties) – *that* sometimes feels like writing.

I am grateful to all the journalists who commissioned, retrieved, subbed, improved, bowdlerised or fact-checked these pieces, but I am especially grateful to the late Terence Kilmartin, of the *Observer*. I think of him as my first and last editor. He started me off and made it easy for me to keep going. Now he too is dead, and I miss his guidance and his friendship; but I will never finish a piece without mentally sending it past his desk.

Special thanks are also due to George Brennan, Emily Read, Pascal Cariss and Chaim Tannenbaum.

GRAHAM GREENE

'All my friends . . . are dead. One finds that one's acquaintances die at the rate of nineteen or twenty a year. That would include only about four that one has known well. I keep a rather morbid list. Yes, with a cross against the ones I knew really well.'

'How do you feel when another one goes? Does it leave the life that remains feeling thinner?'

'I think it does a bit. Evelyn – I was shocked by his death. One is shocked when a bit of one's life disappears. I felt that with Omar Torríjos [the Panamanian leader]. I think that's why, in the case of Torríjos, I embarked on what I hoped would be a memoir but turned into a rather unsatisfactory blend of things.* I felt that a whole segment of my life had been cut out.'

'That list of yours. It must be quite a long list by now.'

'Oh yes.'

It is, I believe, fairly common to feel a tremor of intimate recognition on your first glimpse of Graham Greene. Like most literate residents of the planet, you have known this presence (cool, fugitive, slightly sinister) all your reading life – and now here he is. He stands at the entrance to his Paris apartment, erect and inquisitive. The pale, headmasterly face

---

Getting to Know the General, The Bodley Head, 1984

is impassively well-preserved and, in its outlines, seems no different from the photographs on the three-shilling Penguins of the Fifties: long upper lip, frowning forehead, the moistly clouded stare. His clothes, too, are the expected mixture of greens and browns, the lank tie heavily knotted (with the thin end out-dangling the thick). The only obvious infirmity he suffers is an arthritic little finger; his handshake is gently, and appropriately, masonic.

'Do you have any particular feelings about turning eighty?'

'No, except annoyance at all this fuss and halloo. That business in *The Times* . . . One thing I did enjoy was going up to Bury St Edmunds to the Greene King Brewery and doing a *mash* – the first stage of brewing. By October there will be 100,000 bottles with a special label with my signature on it. It's their strongest beer. They're very good, Greene King. Now *that* I liked . . . Otherwise, well, I get tired more easily, I begin to forget names. I'm in rather better health than I was five years ago, when I had a cancer and an operation. I'm on a plateau. I'm not as manic and I'm not as depressive.'

The flat is spacious but not airy. Through the closed second-floor windows come the usual sounds (triumphant and hysterical) of mobilettes on the Boulevard Malesherbes. The English Sunday newspapers are fanned on the table, along with a copy of the *Spectator*, open at the correspondence page. Greene's accent is now thoroughly European, and the *r*s are candidly Gallic; when he says, 'Belief is *rational* and faith is *irrational*', the stressed words sound exactly the same. He has the demeanour and habitat of a retired civil servant or (just possibly) an exiled spy – a quiet Englishman, a confidential agent, a third man.

Veteran interviewees have a repertoire, and to begin with Greene relied fairly heavily on his anecdotal store. The time he joined the Communist Party with Claud Cockburn 'in hopes of getting a free trip to Moscow', the time he requested electric-shock treatment from a psychiatrist friend, the time

he was deported from Puerto Rico by the American autho-
rities, his experiments with benzedrine while writing *The
Confidential Agent* (in the mornings) and *The Power and
the Glory* (in the afternoons) before the war. Sensing my
familiarity with these stories (I had just read the collected
essays and the two volumes of autobiography), Greene said:
'As you see, I've got nothing new to say. One's said it
all in one's work. It was embarrassing at the National Film
Theatre the other day. I'd just received Quentin Falk's book
about my experiences with film and films, and I had time to
read it beforehand. Luckily it had been published only the
day before. Because every *word* that I uttered in response
to questions at the NFT had been taken from this book. I'd
got absolutely *nothing* further to contribute.'
'You certainly get about a good deal.'
'I haven't much this year,' said Greene, who has visited
Switzerland, England, Italy, Spain, Antibes and now Paris,
all in the last couple of months. 'I've resisted the temptation
of Panama, at least. I love long plane journeys, especially if
I'm being paid for and I'm travelling first class. I used to
go to Panama via Amsterdam to avoid going to the United
States – a fifteen-hour journey, which I loved. I drank a lot
of Bols gin, and I read. And there were no telephones and
no letters. It's like being in a hospital. I'm very happy in a
hospital. Nobody can really get at you.'
The telephone rang. 'Another professor,' sighed Greene.
'You say you avoid going to the United States . . .'
'Well, I don't *like* the United States. And I don't like
New York. I don't like the electricity – I don't *like* getting an
electric shock whenever I touch a door handle. I don't like the
dirt, and on the whole – with many exceptions – I don't like
Americans. They strike me rather as the English abroad strike
me: noisy, and incredibly ignorant of the world. I had a woman who came to see me from Houston the other day, and she
was the most incredibly stupid woman I've ever known. And
she was a graduate. We talked about the Central-American

situation. She'd never heard of it. She'd never heard of any troubles down there. Later she wrote to me saying that she'd talked to her colleagues about what I'd said and she found, to her astonishment, that a lot of them agreed with me.

'Reagan is a menace. I'm very disappointed by the death of Andropov. I had great hopes of him. I preached for some years that any reform in Russia could only come – not from the old men or the army – but from the KGB. A Polish film-director told me that the KGB let the army go to Afghanistan in order to get their feet in the mud ... Despite the obvious noises Reagan has been making he's as extreme as anyone in the Kremlin. I'm amused and interested by the fact that he's meeting Gromyko, but I have a feeling that Gromyko will not be helping the re-election. He will have a clever move to damage it. I don't think he will allow Reagan to pass himself off as a peacemaker.

'I felt the shadow darken when Reagan came to power. But perhaps we're all getting used to the idea. Perhaps the next generation will live under this shadow even more equably than your own. I've got a secret dream that Colonel Gadaffi will get hold of a couple of nuclear bombs and drop them somewhere. America and Russia will come together to extinguish the danger, and might never entirely separate.'

At one o'clock we tiptoed through the *merde de chien* and lunched in moderate bourgeois splendour at a Right Bank brasserie. 'We're stinging the *Observer* for this, are we? Good.' The lordly waiters seated Monsieur Greene with some reverence and listened shrewdly to his request for a '*martini-dry. Sec! Très*, très *sec*.' He added, 'I never do what the doctors tell me. I think the body knows better than the doctor. I never eat vegetables. Castro was shocked. He said – what regime do you have? His was very strict, you see. I said, I don't have one. I eat and drink what I like.'

'So if the body says – have a drink ...'

'Then I drink.'

*

4

Greene was drinking – moderately but with relish – the following night. By a fairly extraordinary coincidence, he has befriended *my* best friend in Paris, a youngish (English) artist who went down to Antibes several years ago to paint Greene for the National Portrait Gallery. So a picnic dinner was arranged at the private wine-cellar of another common friend. Old friends die but new ones are born – and it is clear that Greene has something like a genius for friendship. Friendship is complicated too, however, and nothing about Graham Greene is uncomplicated. There are contrary impressions to be dealt with.

He is an ideologue. You sense that his beliefs are embedded in past struggles and ascendancies. (In Catholic Central America, with its hot and cold wars, the old polarities are still vivid.) His life and work have been grounded on faith, and on its opposites and counterparts: loyalty and betrayal, stoicism and doubt. He is fond of quoting Browning: 'Our interest's on the dangerous edge of things./The honest thief, the tender murderer,/The superstitious atheist . . .'; and he has always been drawn to moral bandit-lands. 'Human beings are more important to believers than they are to atheists,' he has said. But they are less important too, in a sense; and we remember Bendrix's remark in *The End of the Affair*, that even with love we get 'to the end of other people', and must look for something else.

'There is a certain sympathy,' he told mé, 'which the present Pope doesn't seem to recognise, between the believing communist and the believing Catholic . . . I don't feel as though I've changed much since I joined the CP at the age of twenty-seven. Curiously enough there's an Indian woman who's writing a book claiming that I'm the only one of the Thirties group whose beliefs remained unchanged. Orwell changed, and Auden changed. Isherwood changed. I retain this sympathy for the *dream* of communism anyway, though I agree that the record is very discouraging. We're all unbelievers within our own faiths.'

I taxed him with his oft-misquoted remark that he would rather end his days in Russia than in America.

'What I meant was that I would end my days *sooner* in Russia because there they pay writers the compliment of regarding them as a danger.'

'But if it came to it?'

'All right. Yes. I would rather end my days in the Gulag than in – than in *California*.'

'That's a very typical remark, if you don't mind me saying so.'

But he didn't seem to mind at all.

Observer, 1984

Postscript: Geopolitical change has made Greene's opinions and preoccupations sound rather more antique than they sounded in 1984; but I suspect that his legend will increasingly tend towards the nostalgic, the romantic, the regressive. It is, as Communists used to say, no accident that his novels work most powerfully on the adolescent. For my generation Graham Greene was inevitably the first serious writer you came across: he seemed exemplarily adult and exemplarily modern. Now he seems neither. Now *he* seems adolescent, though in the richest and (again) the most romantic sense. It is a commonplace to say that his novels, for all their geographical variety, did not 'develop'. Greeneland stays the same. What happened was that he got older as he wrote about it. His manner changes (the surprising poetry of the early novels, the gaunt and sober maturity of the Forties and early Fifties, the more playful and forgiving later work), but the oppositions, the relationships, the moral trade-offs are all recognisably constant. I do not find this world 'over-schematic' so much as weirdly suspenseless. The faithbreaker must die. The policeman's pistol will tend to be

6

phallic. The adulterer will never be redeemed . . . Greene's influence, none the less, will remain deep and formative. We happened to read him before we read anybody else. He was an awakener.

Two additional memories survive this visit. When we exchanged the man-made earth-colours of Greene's apartment (he *did* look like a headmaster, and his sitting-room looked like a headmaster's study) for the bright lights and tuxed waiters of the prosperous Right Bank brasserie, there was a third person present: Greene's woman friend, whom I had agreed not to mention (and shall not name here, even though her identity is well enough known). As we were being seated by the *maître d'hôtel*, or some comparably exalted personage, the lunchers fell silent; then came a surge of agitated murmurs. This had nothing to do with Graham Greene. It had to do with the removal of his friend's overcoat, revealing: a woman of a certain age but still fiercely gamine, in purple angora sweater and skintight shiny black trousers. Greene enjoyed this frisson, this minor *épatement*, as clearly as he enjoyed his pre-lunch Martini – and his friend's conversation: we had several acquaintances in common, and she proved to be a passionate and talented gossip.

When I returned from the Boulevard Malesherbes to my hotel in the Latin Quarter I entered a scene from one of Graham Greene's darker entertainments. In the lobby people were wielding mops and buckets with an air of resigned and weary lamentation. A member of the staff had just been decapitated in the lift-shaft.

EMERGENCY LANDING

When it comes to flying, I am a nervous passenger but a confident drinker and Valium-swallower. And although I wasn't exactly goosing the stewardesses or singing 'Viva España' (this was a BA flight to Malaga), I was certainly in a holiday mood. In fact I had just called for my second pre-lunch cocktail – having enjoyed, oh, I don't know, a good three or four on the ground – when I began to sense that something was up.

Suddenly withdrawing the half-dozen meal-trays she had just laid out, the flustered blonde stewardess told me that the bar-service had been suspended. In answer to my very anxious enquiries, she told me that the bar-service would soon resume. I was still grumbling to myself about this when the Captain's voice came on the public-address system. 'As you have probably noticed,' he began (I hadn't), 'we have turned full circle and are heading back to Gatwick. For technical reasons.'

Now I saw that the sun had indeed changed places, and that we were flying north over France towards the Channel. Unworriedly I resigned myself to the usual frustrations: the six-hour wait, the free orangeade, the bun-voucher. Now I saw also that the stewardesses were systematically searching the overhead compartments. So. A bomb scare. But this bomb didn't scare *me*.

8

The Captain came on again. In a bored voice he levelled with us about the 'alert'; then, more urgently, he added that, in view of the time factor, it was now thought necessary to make an emergency landing, at Dinard. At this point, still feeling no more than mildly devil-may-care, I took the second half of my Valium 5, helping it down with a swig of duty-free whisky. I offered the bottle to the girl in the window seat, whose clear distress I began, rather grandly, to pooh-pooh. The bottle was taken away from my hand by the stewardess and fondly restored to its yellow bag. We speared down on Dinard, not in the cruising, wallowing style that aeroplanes usually adopt for landing, but with steep and speedy purpose.

Seats upright. Place your forehead on the back of the seat in front of you. There will be more than one bump. Don't be alarmed by the reverse thrust. Leave all your hand-baggage. Move as quickly as you can to the exits and slide down the escape-chutes. When you are on the ground – run.

I glanced, for the first time in my life, at the benign cartoons of the safety-procedure card. Then I hunkered down for the final seconds. I thought of my wife and eight-month-old son, whom I was flying to join. I had escorted them to Gatwick ten days previously, on the same morning that an Air India jumbo had been blown to pieces (or so we then thought) over the seas of south-west Ireland. My apprehension at Departures that day had been far more intense than anything I was feeling now. What I was feeling now was, mainly, relief that my wife and child weren't with me. Had they been, everything would now be different. For a start, I wouldn't be drunk. I placed my wallet on my lap (I had no jacket), and waited.

The 737 landed like a skimmed stone, like a bomb itself, like a dam-buster. The reverse-thrust came on with such preternatural power that the tail seemed to lift, as though the whole aircraft was about to start toppling end over end. In this weird squall of gravity and inertia, my wallet shot off my lap and slithered along the floor, four or five rows away.

Now the plane was quenched of its speed; seatbelts clicked, and immediately a pressing queue had formed in the aisle.

My paramount concern at this point was, of course, to find my wallet. Coolly lingering in a vacant three-pack, I was well placed to watch the passengers flee past me to the end of the aeroplane. As they awaited the stewardess's order (the doors had to open, the chutes had to inflate), the passengers pressed forward, four or five women – perhaps those with children – in the forefront. Physically they showed no more agitation than, say, people in fairly desperate need of a bathroom. But their voices contained an edge of panic. In those few seconds I remember only one word being spoken, and often repeated. 'Please . . . Oh please.' Soon the stewardesses were urgently shooing them down the aisle. I waited. Then, grumbling and swearing, I crawled around in search of my wallet and scattered credit cards, which had themselves been torn loose by the Gs.

At last I strolled to the door. 'Sit and jump,' said the stewardess. Those elongated dinghies are a lot less stable than they look, but down I went – wheee! – and jogged away from the aircraft, which, I saw, had reached the very brink of its runway and had jarred to a halt midway through a ninety-degree turn. Five yards from its nose lay the edge of a lumpy brown field.

Around me was being enacted the formless drama that perhaps invariably succeeds every incident of mass crisis or jeopardy. I can only describe it as a scene of peculiar raggedness, with sights and sounds somehow failing to coordinate. A man keeled over in the grass, clutching his heart and moaning loudly. A girl with a sprained ankle was being helped away three-legged to safety. Busily the stewardesses gave comfort where they could. I myself – with, no doubt, egregious nonchalance – attempted to console a weeping woman. There was a good deal of crying in the air, brittle, exultant. Soon the French security guards were shepherding us tenderly across the field to the terminal.

After a shock (I later learned), the body needs a lot of sweet tea. But the drinks were on BA, and most people drank a lot of brandy, which (I later learned) is the very thing the body needs least. I compromised by drinking a lot of whisky, and remained in capital fettle throughout the five-hour wait. The evening soon became an exercise in maximum *esprit de corps*, with the passengers informally dividing into two camps: those who were saying, 'I've never been so scared in my life,' and those who were saying, 'You think this was bad? This was nothing. Let me tell you about the time I . . .' My position was, I suppose, unusual. I had not felt fear; but I knew that fear would have been an appropriate feeling.

Now, all writers secretly maintain a vampiric attitude to disaster; and, having survived it, I was unreservedly grateful for the experience. Here I sat, not in Gatwick but in Dinard, enjoying a good free dinner and pleasant camaraderie. And when I flopped into bed at five the next morning – replacement aircraft (the original was later searched, fruitlessly), baggage identification on the dark tarmac, the incident-free completion of the journey – I felt like a returning lord, a man who had come through a testing time, without a scratch, without a wince.

And I was wrong. For the next few days, although outwardly cheerful enough, I was pretty sure I was dying – and of natural causes, too. My body was subject to strange tinglings. Throughout my tragic siestas I lay there trembling and boiling, as if a tram station or a foundry had established itself beneath the bed. I watched the world through veils of helplessness. This was no hangover. This was old age. One morning I found a brief report on the Dinard ordeal in the *Herald Tribune*. Incredibly, there was no mention whatever of the quiet and simple heroism with which I had borne it . . .

My wife suggested that I was suffering from delayed shock – which, I admit, gave me quite a turn. Although I had privately diagnosed a brain tumour, I was still reluctant to identify the malaise as an after-effect of something that had bothered me so little. My body, however, continued to insist on the truth. Hoaxers and other operatives in the terror business will be relieved to learn that, when it comes to fear, there's no such thing as a free lunch, or a free dinner.

So much, then, for my valour on the fields of France. I emerge from the incident with another new experience, and no credit whatever. I was as brave as a lord, as brave as a newt. Chemically numbed at the time, my fear – of which there had clearly been plenty – had just burrowed deep and waited. I had sneaked out of the restaurant without settling the bill. The body's accountants had redressed the ledger, with interest. And for nearly a week I was wearily picking up that tab.

Observer, 1985

NUCLEAR CITY: THE MEGADEATH
INTELLECTUALS

Washington is nuclear city. In any imaginable exchange, however 'surgical', 'splendid', 'cathartic' or 'therapeutic', Washington would go (and so would San Diego, Seattle and San Francisco). Washington would be 'taken out'. Its well-forested malls would go, the silver masonry of its imperial buildings would go, its museums and monuments would go; a good deal of such history as America has would go, along with all the random life that any great city contains: the jazz bars of Georgetown, the residential follies of Capitol Hill, the beggars (lobbyists of the street), the graffito saying NO NUKES, the bumper sticker saying NO FAT CHICKS, the National Gallery's Matisse: The Early Years in Nice (and that particular interest in human form and posture), the Rose Garden, the day schools – all would go. Washington stands there, like a king on a tumbrel, awaiting decapitation.

When nuclear weapons become real to you, when they stop buzzing around your ears and actually move into your head, hardly an hour passes without some throb or flash, some heavy pulse of imagined supercatastrophe. Staring at the many-eyed helmet of the Capitol, you see the clouds above on fire, the winter sky ignited, taken out. Now is the time to see this, and your head is the place to see it in. The reality won't be seen by anyone. Certain Virginians,

I suppose, might get to view the lit brain, the scorching shower, the moronic fist of the mushroom cloud. But no one will 'see' the bursting city. To this crime there will be no witnesses; there will just be innocent bystanders, in their millions. Many times the cinema has tried to imagine a nuclear attack upon a city. What the cinema cannot get, what *we* cannot get, is the simultaneity: everything becoming nothing, all at once.

Washington is nuclear city, is Thermopolis, in another sense, too. With famous prodigality and greed, nuclear weapons squander resources, gobble money, hog know-how. But what of the intellectual resources, what of the thought, the acuity, and concentration they hourly consume? In institutes, foundations, committees, endowments, and in a thousand offices along the corridors of power, people are sitting around all day thinking about these man-made objects, nuclear weapons – the strangest subject, with its squalor, profanity and nausea, its addictive fascination and terrible glamour, its unique inclusiveness and complexity. Having read a yard of books on the question, I had come to Washington to read a yard more, to talk and to listen, to peer into the nuclear campus. People came up with all these nuclear weapons, and then nuclear weapons came up with all these people – thinkers, minders – to wonder what to do with them, what to do about them, how to do without them.

'Some of these guys', one expert told me, 'are nukies for life. Only one subject. Nukes this. Nukes that.' Their office walls are sandbagged with nuclear literature, their floors are heaped with nuclear dossiers and printouts. They like maps, graphs, blackboards. They tend to talk with almost inhuman rapidity: you sit there listening to cascades of acronyms, blizzards of abbreviations. In some of their faces you can make out the orbits of strain, of moral care; but many of the boys in the school have the superanimation, the robust esprit of the gratified hobbyist. Two things immediately strike you – or they struck me. There are no women here. And there are no smokers.

This last point exercised me above and beyond the familiar torment of nicotine denial. Halfway through an afternoon of intense discussion, with my lungs starting to sob and plead for their customary half-hourly snack, I would sometimes master the usual feelings of shame and criminality, and say, 'Would you mind if I had a cigarette?' 'Yes, I would, actually' was the standard reply. With shared embarrassment we would then lurch back into our X-ray lasers and hard-kill capabilities. Even if you get them out of the office and into a bar, they cough and gag and fan themselves the instant you get burning. It seems discrepant that these connoisseurs of thermal pulse and superstellar temperatures, these fireball merchants and inferno artists should all go green at the sight of a Marlboro. But you are going to get discrepancies – comic, tragic, pathetic – when your subject is nuclear weapons.

Nuclear weapons are everything and nothing. This is their genius. On the one hand, they are bargaining chips, pawns in a propaganda contest, peace-keepers – mutually cancelling, a double bluff we all go along with. They are nothing. How can anyone get hurt by an 'umbrella'? On the other hand, nuclear weapons are what they are and do what they do: they multiply matter by the speed of light squared; they deal in tons of blood and rubble; they are instruments of mass destruction. They are everything, because they can destroy everything. It's just as well, for their sake, that they sometimes look like nothing.

Marcus Raskin, who is now at the Institute for Policy Studies in Washington, tells the following story about his time with the 'strategic community' under Kennedy. This was 1961. Word came through that the Soviet Union was about to test a fifty-megaton hydrogen bomb. Everybody reached for their circular slide rules. 'Fifty thousand tons,' people were calmly muttering. 'Four times Hiroshima.' It took several minutes before they realised what they were dealing with: not the equivalent of fifty thousand tons of TNT, but the equivalent of fifty million tons of TNT. And these were experts who thought about little else. As Raskin says, if you stare at nuclear weapons long enough, you start to lose your grip on what they are, what they do.

Actually, it was more like *sixty* million tons of TNT: fifty-eight megatons, the biggest bang ever. A train carrying the Hiroshima yield in TNT form would take up four miles of track. A train carrying the equivalent of the Soviet H-bomb would put a girdle round the earth at the latitude of London with a three-thousand-mile overlap. Military strategists, of course, have a special contempt for such Believe-It-or-Not formulations. And that contempt is understandable. For at moments like these, nuclear weapons edge out of their shadowland; they edge out of nothing and start heading for everything. We see them, but do we really believe them? Believe it or not. Believe it or else. Luckily for them (but not for us), nuclear weapons are unbelievable: they defy belief, they are beyond belief. Do we really see the train – do we really see the preposterous savagery of fifty-eight million tons of TNT?

The atom bomb, said J. Robert Oppenheimer, who put the first one together, 'is shit'. It's just 'a big bang'. He had felt rather differently after the Alamogordo test: 'I remembered the line from the Hindu scripture ... "Now I am become death, shatterer of worlds." ' Both intuitions are quite accurate. Everything and nothing. If they become everything, we become nothing. If they become nothing, we become everything, all over again. So which is it going to be?

One flight down from Marcus Raskin at the Institute for Policy Studies you will find William Arkin, who describes himself as America's 'most troublesome nuclear weapons expert'. His office resembles that of an ecstatically disciplined academic – the room is information-crammed, yet orderly, alphabetical, fingertip. Behind the cover of his beard and glasses, Arkin seems at first to exude the brusqueness and glaze of the far-gone nukie: you feel you are keeping him from higher things. And so you are.

There is a kind of nuke chat that sounds like masochism – amused, collusive, cheerfully scandalised. You talk about government policies as if you were talking about your children, their pointless delinquencies, their cute inanities. (You know what they did? Have you heard what they're doing now?) For a while Arkin and I did this kind of nuke chat. He told me about the $6,000 nuclear-hardened coffee pot, the 'readiness to test' facility at Johnston Island, south of Hawaii. Then his manner changed, and I sensed what I was to sense many times in Washington: a desire to escape complexity, to escape detail and the proliferation of detail, a desire to change the language, to edge back toward first principles.

'What you have to understand, what you have to make clear, is that the nuclear arsenal is a living organism, constantly adjusted, refined, alerted, programmed, mobilised. Under Reagan we have shifted from prevention to preparation. They're not interested in World War III. They're interested in World War IV. The nuclear war plan spans 180 days. It's a confession of inevitability – "it can't not happen" – though it's so fucking complicated that they can't even see it ... Nuclear war is not just an idea. The whole planet is wired up for it.'

Nuclear geography – or cosmology – is a pressing theme in Arkin's work. You read him and listen to him with scepticism, with trepidation, because he is telling you that the nuclear arsenal is not nowhere – it is everywhere. Every minute, in thousands of locations, in the oceans, in the heavens, there are reports, readings, dispatches, exercises, posturings, provocations. The Defense Mapping Agency has 'digitised' one third of the earth's 39 million square miles;

scientists monitor the weather, the upper atmosphere, sun spots, meteor trails; they study 'gravity intensity profiles' and cloud-particle characteristics (for 'nose-cone erosion testing applications'). The highest detection spacecraft is a third of the way to the moon; even the innocent quasars, among the most distant objects in the universe, are pressed into service (Very Long Baseline Interferometry) for superaccurate readings of the earth's rotation and polar motion. Meanwhile, planners of postwar 'reconstitution' call hotels 'strategic locations' and wonder whether the cable-TV network meets 'national security specifications'. Meanwhile, the National Weather Service feeds wind data into civil-defence computers twice daily to update fallout forecasts. Everything and nothing (but mostly everything), a pullulating reality dependent upon thousands of assumptions, all of them untested, all of them untestable.

Military science is deeply interested in the planet, in nature. But what kind of interest is it? It is national interest. Let us look further. (Leave no stone unturned: it might have a weapon under it.) Volcano activation, hurricane manipulation, tidal-wave initiation, quicksand generation, ice-cap liquefaction, ozone depletion, asteroid diversion: all have been looked into as possible means for getting the most out of nuclear weapons. Other weird shapes hover and beckon in the realm of speculation. The antimatter weapon, which would yield forty-three megatons for every kilogram expended. The heat bomb, a gigaton (or thousand-megaton) device exploded outside the atmosphere: there would be no fallout, no blast – and no oxygen either, so that survivors of the continental firestorm would soon succumb to asphyxiation. Finally, for now, there is the black-hole weapon. A small black hole could be electrically restrained and thus deprived of fresh material; it would explode, and at last we would be up there in the million-megaton range.

Some people, you might reasonably conclude, are never satisfied. 'You've heard about *smart* weapons? Well, now they have *brilliant* weapons.' Around the corner from the Institute for Policy Studies is the Committee for National Security – situated, appropriately enough, above a pizza parlour called Vesuvio's. My interlocutor was Robert English, mustachioed, bright-eyed, casually dapper: another young expert in another smokeless zone. 'There's this "deep-interdiction" or assault-breaker weapon called Skeet. You fire a missile deep into enemy lines, and it dispenses submunitions about the size of hockey pucks that will seek out enemy tanks.' If there are no tanks around, the brilliant weapon will brilliantly hang around until some enemy tanks show up. Robert English smiles and shrugs and shakes his head.

'It's the saddest story. With Gorbachev things are *really* different. Look at the moratorium on testing. Instead of an American response, you just get a series of excuses. They say that the Soviets had just finished "an orgy of tests". They say that because we don't have a "command economy" our scientists will go off and make toys unless they get a regular blast. It's always *toys*, for some reason ... Recently there was some bilateral agreement on a new emphasis on "imprecisely located weapons": small, mobile, land-based missiles. Crisis-stable. A good idea for both sides. It's now becoming clear from the Department of Energy figures that money is being spent on an enhanced electromagnetic pulse weapon that would release electrons over a wide area. What would this weapon be directed against? "Imprecisely located targets." It happens again and again. It really is the saddest story.'

If history is a nightmare from which we are trying to awake, then the Reagan era can be seen as an eight-year blackout. Numb, pale, unhealthily dreamless: eight years of DO NOT DISTURB. This was the Reagan Sleep, when America crashed. Now, perhaps, we have started to come to, at last. Now we notice the state of the linen and feel the airlessness of the room. We look in the mirror and see the patchy beard, the spiked hair, the crimson eyes.

During the early years of the decade, the fresh faces in Reagan's apparat began talking about nuclear weapons in a new tone, a tone of subhuman frivolity.

'Soviet leaders would have to choose between peacefully changing their Communist system ... or going to war.'

'Nuclear war is a destructive thing, but still in large part a physics problem.'

'It would be a terrible mess, but it wouldn't be unmanageable.'

'Dig a hole, cover it with a couple of doors, and then throw three feet of dirt on top ... If there are enough shovels to go around, everybody's going to make it.'

'I do not think the real danger of the situation is nuclear war and mass destruction; I think the danger is political coercion.'

'I've always worried less about what would happen in an actual nuclear war exchange than about the effect that the nuclear balance has on our willingness to take risks in local situations.'

One would have thought that there was nothing more 'worrying' than an 'actual nuclear war exchange'. But Richard Perle evidently managed to come up with something even more worrying: American prudence. When a powerful man bandies such discrepancies, he is sure to get himself mythologised: 'Dr No', 'The Prince of Darkness'. We fictionalise him, we send him off to nothingland with his nuke pets, his nuke familiars. Perle is gone now, and to hell with him; but he was real, and the policies were real. They brought people out into the streets in their hundreds of thousands.

In 1983 came the President's 'vision', the Strategic Defense Initiative, soon to be nicknamed Star Wars; a different fiction, a kind of science fiction, was consolingly emplaced.

Most of us believe, incorrectly but with good reason, that we live under the auspices of Mutual Assured Destruction. In fact, the Soviet Union has never subscribed to MAD; and neither has the United States, except for a brief period in the Sixties (when McNamara briefly allowed the notion to hold sway as a means of heading off military procurements). The underlying strategy has always been something else: preemption, counterforce, escalation dominance, prevailing, denying victory to the Soviet Union. Or, if you prefer, *winning*, which in turn means *going first*. Why then does MAD continue to loom in the public consciousness? Because it is an accurate description of reality. Whatever the policy, whatever the plan, MAD will be the result. Mutual Assured Destruction is not an arrangement between the US and the USSR. It is an arrangement between human beings and nuclear weapons.

Strategic thinking always rotates and loops back on itself, as it must. The ballistic missile defence idea, for instance, has been around since 1946, long before there were any ballistic missiles to defend against, and has popped up every ten years or so. Predictably, the *winning* idea is a year older and has gamely survived the appearance of thirty thousand nuclear warheads on the other side. Nuclear-war fighting, 'prevailing', has normally been kept at the think-tank, worst-case level, wheeled out in times of crisis or belligerence – and wheeled back in again when the planners saw the 'collateral damage' or when the public saw the planners. But the Reagan emphasis, the Reagan candour, was a new phenomenon. After the incautious remarks of 1981–3, everyone was told to shut up while SDI seized 'the moral high ground'. Momentarily revealed as being everything, nuclear weapons quietly went back to being nothing.

And what about Ronald Reagan? What about the blinding, the terminal discrepancy that *he* represents? Here is a forgetful old actor with a head full of Armageddon theology and Manichaean adversarialism, interspliced with war movies and scraps of *Reader's Digest*, an old media man who has foreclosed one arms treaty (Comprehensive Test Ban), broken out of a second (SALT II), and is whittling away at a third (ABM); a babbling, bloopering illusionist who now bestrides the spoils of the biggest buildup, or spend-up, in the history of the planet. 'We may be the generation that sees Armageddon.' 'We have a different regard for human life than those monsters do.' 'Israel is the only stable democracy we can rely on as a spot where Armageddon could come.' Washingtonians talk about 'the Caligulan possibility' – with the President somehow going solo on nuclear war – but we may be more worried, these days, about the President's celebrated talent for delegation. Imagine a Soviet leader who laid aside his Marx and Lenin in favour of Revelation and Ezekiel. Ideology is something the *enemy* is meant to be contaminated by. But what about *theology*, and 'end-time' theology at that? How would the alarmists, the procurers, targeters, and contractors of the Pentagon feel about General Secretary Reagan?

To get some idea, I arranged to meet a diplomat from the Soviet embassy. It was a morning of such deracinating wind chill that I for one could have used a toasty little nukelet, groundburst on Dupont Circle. Some of the tramps shivering in the doorways are Vietnam vets, frantic, melancholy. For all the wrong reasons, the Reagan story is their story, too. A story of humiliating memories and willed resurgence. I had been told by a friend that my Russian contact would probably have a tail on him and there was a certain amount of eyeing and frowning before we identified each other among the fronds and fountains, the antebellum splendour of the Mayflower Hotel. Absolute weapons require absolute enemies (inhuman, superpowerful – mass destructors), but Sergei and I got along fine. He didn't want to kill me. I didn't want to kill him. We drank a lot of coffee and smoked up a storm.

US–Soviet strategic relations, said Sergei, work as a kind of 'body language'. The disposition of forces sends messages to the other side, which responds with various bristlings and squirmings of its own. At the moment, Reagan's body language seems to consist of a reversible V-sign: V for victory, together with an obscene gesture. Briefly we mention 'ethnic targeting', a tactic that is now falling out of favour, even in the Pentagon. The aim would be to concentrate on the Russians and spare all the Uzbeks and Kazaks. 'That is also not very nice,' said Sergei. His dusty face is sardonic, put-upon, long-suffering. No doubt there are Soviet 'options', somewhere or other, for an America consisting entirely of blacks and Hispanics. How dwarfed we are, how belittled we all are by nuclear weapons.

'My father was chief of staff of the strategic bomber division in Siberia during the Fifties,' says Sergei. 'This was when the Americans were talking about the "bomber gap". We knew that our planes couldn't reach *Japan*.' After the bomber gap came the missile gap. There was no bomber gap. There was no missile gap. Now up springs the SDI gap, the Star Wars gap. 'In the Fifties, America suffered a loss of innocence [the end of nuclear solitude]. SDI is a way of restoring the lost virginity.' So perhaps we should not imagine SDI as a shield over America. We should imagine it as a nice new hymen. 'About war, America *is* innocent. Send the boys overseas. They'll be back by Christmas. In the USSR, war is a disaster, a cosmic tragedy, a holocaust. Families, children. Something that can't be rationalised.'

Reagan is said to hate the cognomen 'Star Wars'; he thinks it trivialises his proud dream. But it was the Great Trivialiser himself who, in his historic address of March 1983, invoked the George Lucas money-spinner: 'If you will pardon my stealing a film line, the Force is with us.' In conclusion, Sergei and I pondered three further curiosities in the President's speech. If the US merely *added* the defensive systems to the offensive systems, Reagan conceded, the Soviets would consider them aggressive, and 'no one wants that'. Want it or not, *that* is what we are getting. One also wonders why, if Star Wars is just a logical response to a clear Soviet advantage, the 'initiative' caused such consternation in the President's strategic apparat? And why, if the Soviets already had the technology, did Reagan offer to share it with them?

Currently Reagan's lawyers are inspecting the ABM Treaty, which prohibits ballistic missile defence, in search of a 'broad' reading, a reading so broad that it will, remarkably, permit ballistic missile defence.

'What next?' I asked Sergei.

'They need Soviet violations. They *must have* Soviet violations.'

Washington is a society: a debating society. The debaters have been called Hawks and Doves, Warriors and Disarmers, Generals and Paediatricians. I will call them Recruiters and Pressed Men, for this straightforward reason: nowadays, we are all in the military; we are all in uniform. The old and the young are in uniform. Our babies are born, not in their birthday suits, but in uniform (in little sailor suits, perhaps). Although the full militarisation of space is still only a 'vision', the planet has already been militarised, digitised. We are all on the front line.

Someone new to this subject, someone innocent of it – an extraterrestrial, a pre-nuclear Rip Van Winkle – would have no trouble choosing between the arguments of the Recruiters and the Pressed Men. There is, emphatically yet ironically, no contest. In their styles of discourse the Pressed Men are as varied and distinctive as all human discourse is. The only unquestionable achievement of nuclear weapons is the goaded eloquence of their opponents: the moral inerrancy of Jonathan Schell, the elegant historicism of Solly Zuckerman, the sensitive hardheadedness of Freeman Dyson, the witty tenacity of Robert Scheer and Daniel Ford. Passion, humour, memorability, appositeness – against all this, against this everything, the Recruiters offer precisely nothing. What else can they offer? What else have they got to give? They can field the desk-job manliness of George Will and Norman Podhoretz, the prideful frigidity of Colin Gray and Keith Payne; the rest is a desert of business language, euphemism, and cliché, with an occasional chant or whoop from the school yard or the rumpus room. It is the voice of the technophiliac, the tough guy, and the toady. With the Recruiters you are not in the presence of active thought; you just sit there and watch the laborious bolstering of stock response, the steady fattening of prejudice. Besides being called 'war criminals' and 'mass murderers' (phrases used with surprising freedom here in Washington), the Recruiters are referred to as 'the megadeath intellectuals'. But the term is a contradiction. There is no intellectual content in megadeath. There never has been and there never will be. The mind can do nothing with it.

Addiction is a resilient theme in the story of nuclear weapons, and many a Pressed Man has got hooked on the hardware, the beautiful physics, the undoable Rubik's cube of nuclear strategy. 'There's nothing worse', the writer Andrew Cockburn said to me, 'than listening to some Freezer going on about – I don't know – the Circular Error Probable of Trident II.' But there is something worse. There is something worse than listening to a Pressed Man going on about hard kill and blast over-pressure, PACFLT and AFSATCOM, choke points and back-fit cancellations, FROLIC and SIZZLE and PINCHER and BROILER. And that is listening to a Recruiter going on about them.

This little guy in the three-piece suit is just coming out of his twenties. ('You look a bit older than that.' 'It must be the beard.') On the other hand, he *sounds* a lot younger; at moments of emphasis his vocal cords twang with an adolescent yodel. His name is David Trachtenberg. On his desk are scale models of intercontinental ballistic missiles (look at the size of those Soviet SS-18s!). On the wall behind his chair is a customised poster, jokingly accusing David of being a wanted man, 'convicted of supporting the SDI program'. Next to the poster is a cartoonish watercolour of an unreservedly grinning David, straddling the globe while missiles squirt this way and that; to his right is Uncle Sam, to his left the Russian Bear. David's pals or loved ones evidently felt relaxed enough to present David with this picture, and David evidently felt relaxed enough to hang it on his office wall.

David works for the Committee on the Present Danger ('Present Danger?' sings the lady on the phone), the Recruiter think tank that has supervised Reagan's nuclear policies. Reagan is a member of the board, and close to sixty fellow directors have found work in his administration. Though fairly eerie in its own right, talking to David is not as bad as reading the Present Danger literature, namely a buxom volume called *Alerting America* ('What Is the Soviet Union Up To?' 'Has America Become Number 2?'); with David, at least, there is a human dimension, however subdued. On the other hand, you can smoke while you're reading the literature, and you can't do that while you're talking to David.

'The public has been misled by arms treaties ... It was good to call attention to Soviet cheating, bad not to follow it up ... Menacing violations ... Krasnoyarsk ... The Soviet moratorium on testing is a completely empty gesture ... Height of folly ... Combat environment ... Some kind of limited scenario ... But yet ... If we so choose to do so ...' The language is notable for its sobriety and caution, with few descents into the colloquial: 'making the rubble bounce', for example, Recruiterspeak for overkill or 'undeconflicted targeting'. Otherwise, talking to David is like talking to your accountant. But I will certainly never forget the expression on David's face, one of saintly forbearance, as he told me that the US had decreased its overall megatonnage in recent years.

I kept wondering what his friends were like, what his human dealings were. I kept wondering how it went, humanly. Perhaps David was wondering about the same sort of thing, beneath his flat smile of fastidious scrutiny. How flaky was he finding me? Had I shaved properly that morning? What about the width of my tie? David is no keener on a nuclear holocaust than I am. But he is less fearful — that's the difference. Like Perle, a fellow Dangerman, he is 'more worried' about other things. Hang around too long at this end of the nuclear weapons business, and you lose the knack of imagining what nuclear weapons are, what they can do. I asked David if he ever dreamed about his work, if he ever dreamed about nuclear weapons. But David wasn't going to discuss his dreams with a *journalist*. He assured me that he had 'no problems' on that score. He slept the sleep of the good.

'The Soviet Union', David had said at one point, 'is only a superpower militarily. Not economically, not politically, not ideologically. Only militarily.'

At the time I wondered what *ideologically* was doing in David's sentence. After a while I realised that I had simply been listening to mainstream Reaganism. If the Soviet Union isn't 'really' a superpower, then how many superpowers does that leave?

Meanwhile, or later the same day, Dr Allan Mense is pacing hungrily around his office in the Pentagon. To get in here you need to go through a door marked SURVEILLANCE, ACQUISITION, TRACKING AND KILL ASSESSMENT. People stride in from time to time with documents stamped TOP SECRET (which, in these leak-prone days, means little more than mildly confidential: the top-secret stuff is designated BLACK). On the large wall chart there is a magic-marker diagram showing the earth, the atmosphere, and an incoming missile being briskly zapped by some smart rock, laser beam, or death ray. Dr Mense is tall, florid, early-middle-aged; he sports brogues and braces and a ballpoint-crammed shirt pocket, but the face is wild. He looks like a cop in a Boston precinct station. His barnstorming energy is likable (you feel he would make a fun uncle) and very necessary, too, for Dr Mense is chief scientist on SDI.

'Okay,' he said. 'You tell me. What is the purpose of SDI?'

I hesitated and searched my mind for whatever buzz phrase was currently serving as national policy. 'To, er ... enhance deterrence.'

Dr Mense was astonished. 'That's the right answer! Hardly anybody gets it right. Most people seem to think it's some kind of peace shield.'

I could have said that 'most people' would include the President of the United States, who in June 1986 was still talking coaxingly of 'a shield that could protect us from nuclear missiles just as a roof protects a family from rain'. But I didn't. Any argument I would have with Dr Mense about SDI would be over in ten seconds. He is about Can Do. I am about Don't Do. One's objections to Star Wars need never get as far as the usual haggling points of expense, technical achievability, and so on. One objects to Star Wars because it is just another firebreak. It is just *more*. And more will mean *more*. The President's idea sounded appealingly simple, but it has brought no simplification with it. It has brought only more of the same – more bitter complexities. On every level it will merely add to the epic fairy tale of cry-wolf, brier-patch second-guessing on which, for some strange reason, our existence now depends.

A well-grooved simplifier, Dr Mense gave me his pitch: up-front, down-home, frenziedly, cravenly demonic. Once a fusion-energy expert at McDonnell Douglas, he is now mainly a coordinator. He translates technical data 'into eighth-grade English for the guys on Capitol Hill' and goes out 'to debate the critics with my anti-tomato shield'. Linguistically, this is the jock end of the market. Robust simplicities are delivered like slaps on the back.

'Protection? No. Hey, folks, you're playing the wrong game! If deterrence fails, we're all out to lunch. We'd all be gone. No more Americans! And we don't think, "Gee, by having this system we can just ride out a nuclear war." All we're really doing is planting doubt in the mind of the Soviet offensive mission planner. All we're doing is denying him a free ride.'

'Then why are so many Americans against it?'

'I don't think I'm talking out of school here, but . . .' (And this was before the Tower Report and the palpable sapping of the Reagan momentum.) 'It's not that they're against SDI. They're against the President. You know, here's this bad guy. Food stamps, abortion. All we're saying is, Come on! Jee*sus*: we don't have the data yet!'

'Then why are the Russians against it?'

David, at Present Danger, had given me the Gap answer to this question: 'Because they've done the research. They know it works.' Dr Mense didn't have an answer. He didn't seem to think there *was* an answer. He shrugged hugely, spread his arms, and bulged his eyes, as if to say, 'Go understand people.'

I made my way out of the Pentagon, or I tried. When I stopped every few yards and asked directions, I was proudly told how easy it was to get lost in here. They were right. Getting lost is not a problem. The Pentagon is one of the largest edifices on earth. Its corridors are as wide as boulevards, but they point nowhere, they double back, they leave you where you were before. Signposts and billboards told me everything except how to get away from them. PENTAGON PRAYER BREAKFAST (CONTINENTAL $2). PRAY FOR AMERICA. SPECIAL MUSIC: ARMY CHORUS. My requests for help became more querulous and self-pitying. Bobbing uniforms, dog-tired secretaries, bales of paper, split cardboard boxes, proliferating doorways: the minute administration of an inconceivably vast concern. At last I walked weepily through the shopping malls to the Metro, telling myself that there was no chance whatever, no hope at all, of ever starting to unpick the dreamlike complexity of *this*.

Since 1979 US arms policy has been avowedly 'dual track'. New deployments have been combined with new negotiations; America has rearmed so that she may disarm. Under Reagan, dual track has become a cruder matter of saying one thing while doing another. Dual track is often clearly visible, it seems to me, in the President's face, in the President's eyes. One part of him likes the idea of dramatic reductions (or likes the idea of making speeches about them); what the other part of him wants can best be called nuclear free enterprise, with the American system naturally 'prevailing', naturally 'winning'. Star Wars is the technological fix to his dilemma, his confusion, his imposture.

It is also, incidentally, the missing link in first strike. Useless as a peace shield (and useless against bombers, cruise and low-trajectory missiles, suitcase devices, et cetera), it might yet mop up a 'degraded' retaliation. This among other things is what the Kremlin worst-casers fear; and in a worst-case world, intentions and capabilities are indistinguishable. What do you do with a first-strike capability? You don't go ahead and strike first, unless the Russians look like they're doing it (and, in a crisis, they will look like they're doing it). No, you coerce, you play hardball. Thus you gamble the future to serve local and temporary ends. You show American willingness, American 'resolve' to bet the planet. The weapons improve until they are capable of anything. And, in a crisis, people deteriorate until they are capable of anything. Perched on a twanging ladder of instability, the President will have 'options' unlimited. Humanly, morally, politically, militarily, they will all be zero options. That's what nuclear options are: zero options.

On the nuclear issue, as on so many others, Ronald Reagan has deceived the American people. 'Ronald Reagan has deceived the American people,' I was told, more than once, not just by Pressed Men but by analysts and onlookers in federal buildings, sitting there with their computers and their cherry Coke. 'Don't name me – I'll lose my job.' The hidden aim was broad superiority (only one superpower); the intention was to outbuild and outspend the Russians, while throwing lopsided offers their way to keep public opinion quiet. To the administration's fuddled alarm, Gorbachev called the bluff.

Now, owing to a world-historical fluke, we may get the first arms-reduction deal ever (but watch out for those Soviet violations). The prime mover in this reduction is not Ronald Reagan. The prime mover is Oliver North, with the help of some pillow talk from Nancy, as she attempts to spruce up a tousled presidency for the history books. Reagan's avowed policy was to negotiate from nuclear strength. In 1987, he must negotiate belly-up, from domestic impotence. 'You hear that, Ivan?' Colonel North used to shout during his lectures on geopolitical strategy. Well, you hear that, Ollie? Such are the cosmic jokes, the astronomical cheap shots, that fashion our destiny in the nuclear age.

After forty years of concerted thought, no one has got anywhere with nuclear weapons. No one has discovered what to do with them; no one has discovered how to do without them. The story of their management is a story of repetition, false summits, the retracing of steps. Nuclear technology changes, the procurements change, but the situation does not change. By a radiant paradox, public opinion has changed only that aspect of policy that directly concerns the public: it has killed off civil defence. (Remember the films and drills, the blast-shelter singsongs, the pathetic docility of the human actors?) Public opinion is there, however, and it is waiting. Imagine nuclear weapons as sentient beings: there they are, preposterously savage, stupidly inert, yet not quite fearless. For they fear what they most threaten, ordinary people, people who have felt their mortal insult, people who have grasped a simple truth: that there is something wrong with the planet.

Fred Kaplan is among the more recent nuclear chroniclers. He completed his classic study, *The Wizards of Armageddon*, at the age of twenty-eight. Four years later, his young face bears the orbits of care and strain; but these I partly attributed to his two-year-old twin daughters, who swayed and staggered around the lunch table as we ate. 'You go into this subject with certain feelings and instincts. Then you're confronted by endless complexity. The complexity has no limit, and you can take on as much of it as you want. But when you come out the other side, you're left with the same feelings and instincts. They're completely unchanged.' Although Fred will talk about nuclear weapons, and talk well, his eyes are resigned and long-suffering. 'He wants to give them up,' says his wife, 'and just write about hi-fi or something.' Fred nods and sighs. We all want to give them up. We are all long-suffering. We all want to give them up and get on to something else.

Seeing the Kaplans' children made me anxious to see my own. If you spend too much time with this subject, if you spend too much time in nothingland, you begin to feel marginal, spectral, insubstantial. You want to get away from the death-ubiquity; you want to get back to life. And when I took my seat in the smoking section of the 747 at Dulles, I realised I was flying back just as I had flown in: with extra sadness, bitter complexity, with extra nuke fatigue – but unchanged. However far you go into nuclear weapons, there is no understanding to be had, only more knowledge. This is as it should be, because nuclear weapons are nothing.

And everything, also, at the same time. In *The Fate of the Earth*, Jonathan Schell stressed the need for sobriety in the nuclear debate; the Pressed Man must be civil to the Recruiter, despite the enticements of exasperation and anger. I have always assented to the justice of this tenet, while often wondering why I find it so hard to abide by. I genuinely don't *want* to be civil to, or civil about, the Pentagon handyman, the peanut at Present Danger, the charm-school colonel on the phone with his *You betcha* and *That's what we're here for* (but what *else* are they here for?), the princes of darkness, the foolish and complaisant President. How strictly do civilised rules apply to civilisation's enemies? This is a human story, and human pressures, human mobilisations, can be brought to bear upon it.

The answer to a predicament must be of the same size as that predicament. It must have congruence. The nuclear debate is a debate conducted with our fathers – but it is *about* our children. If the Recruiters are to be isolated and eventually pathologised – if the planet is to grow up – then our children will have to act in self-defence. We must fix our kids so that they will have nothing to do with anyone who has anything to do with anyone who has anything to do with nuclear weapons, with instruments of blood and rubble. The process will begin at that moment of mortal shame when we acquaint them with the status quo, with the facts of life, the facts of death. So come on. In an inversion of filial confession, we will have to take deep breaths, wipe our eyes and stare into theirs, and tell them what we've done.

Esquire, 1987

WATFORD IN CHINA

In 1983 Watford Football Club paid an off-season visit to China. A modest, obscure, suburban team, Watford were newcomers to the higher ranks of the sport — where they have not remained. Their controversial 'long-ball' game (the midfield punt towards the big blokes in the opposition's penalty area) lifted them from the Third Division to the First. Star player: John Barnes (now of Liverpool). Manager: Graham Taylor (now of England). Chairman: Elton John.

Fearing the worst — and hoping for the best possible copy — I expected Watford to play the China card. That is to say, I expected half the squad to play pontoon and drink beer in their hotel rooms, while the other half would play pontoon and drink beer out by the pool. I expected the players to eat steak and chips, do *Sun* crosswords and make frequent calls home, to the wife, the girlfriend, the agent and the bookie. I expected the team's only cultural concession to their historic tour would be the odd racist taunt, the occasional self-destructive experiment with rice wine, and one or two requests for a Chinese takeaway. How would these stormy individualists fare, how would they cope, in the unsmiling termitary of Red China?

Wearing a Billy Bunter suit, a banded boater, purple sunglasses and a diamond earring, Chairman Elton John gazed down fondly at his protégés. Kippered and sallowed by the twenty-hour flight, in regulation blazers, flannels and club ties, the players impassively awaited their baggage in the chaotic kiln of Peking Airport. For a moment they looked far more inscrutable and regimented than the quacking Chinese who bustled about them ... I knew then that all my expectations were misplaced. And so it proved.

The Press has often been blamed for the poor image of footballers and football in general. There *is* a tacit conspiracy in Fleet Street – but it is a conspiracy of silence. The world of the athlete – where unnurtured youth is confronted by adulation and money – provides opportunities for yahooism rivalled only in the rock-music business (of which more later). Off the field, and especially away from home, footballers behave so outrageously that it's a full-time job looking the other way.

And yet, one by one, the Watford squad approached the Hall of Preserving Harmony, peered into the Pavilion of Universal Tranquillity and passed through the Gate of Benevolence and Longevity. Somewhat reluctant, homesick and disorientated, they broached the Forbidden City, and emerged as creditable ambassadors.

The man responsible for this, as for so much else at Watford, is the manager Graham Taylor. Six years ago Watford were a nothing club in the dregs of the Football League. Elton John, a fan since his schooldays in Pinner, took over the chairmanship, injected a good deal of money (the usual estimate is £1.6 million) and hired Taylor from Lincoln City. In 1983 Watford finished runners-up to Liverpool in the First Division. But Taylor wants more than success from his players: he wants to form them as individuals. It is a little-known fact, for instance, that the Watford team are contractually obliged to do seven hours of community work each week. Footballers are often no more than chattels to their clubs; and when the game is finished with them, they blunder out into the world like stranded adolescents. But Watford remains a paternalistic, smalltown outfit, as I saw for myself. The stands and terraces are dotted with women and children, not with National Fronters and bald hooligans. Compared to most other grounds in the First Division, Vicarage Road is a vicarage tea-party.

The day after our arrival Watford turned out for a joint training session at the Workers' Stadium, the 80,000-seater where they would play China the following night, the first of two meetings with the national side. Taylor was wearing full strip and throwing off as much sweat as anyone in the ninety-degree heat. 'Work! One touch and go! *Give* it. *Go. Give* it. *Go.*' Stocky, grinning, intense, Taylor puts his men through their hoops with a spurring candour, a flattering brutality. There is intimacy in his bellowed orders: he is the canny schoolmaster who knows your vanities and soft-spots, who forces you beyond your limits and then sues for peace with a slap on the back. Taylor told me that he had had to gear himself to use the hefty obscenities of the footballing idiom – that he wasn't accustomed to 'the industrial language' that is the language of the game. Well, he seems accustomed to it now, jovially effing and blinding as he stokes his players to the boil.

Elton John (also present, in Humpty Dumpty outfit, baseball cap and purple shades) would later admit that it was Taylor who had saved him from the traditional immolation of the rockstar life. Elton had showed up to a Watford match, looking more like Big Ears than usual, and bearing all the signs of bodily abuse. Taylor summoned him to his house that night and offered him a pint glass brimmed with brandy. 'Here. Are you going to drink that? What the fuck's the *matter* with you?' Elton mended his ways, and not before time. All superstars, it seems, must get off the fast lane before they crash. Some find religion, some find family life. But Elton has found Watford F.C. He delights in his team; and he also enjoyed the anonymity of China, where his music is unknown

36

and he is no more than an exotic curiosity, like a video game or a Beefeater. Only the tourists recognised him.

As Taylor set about exhausting the China goalkeeper ('Catch and roll. Catch and roll. Again. Again. Again.'), I strolled across the pitch and talked to Shen Xiang-fu, the team's number eleven and major star. In what looked like size-two boots, with his square, vigilant face (and with that strange, glassy distance between eye-surface and lid), Shen answered all questions with the same laconic caution.

He was unmarried, like all the China players. He was a student and instructor at the Peking Sports Institute. He earned 75 yuan a month (£25, a fraction above the national average) plus 20 more for dietary expenses (steak, butter). Did he enjoy travelling with the team? Yes, he did. Would he like to play in England one day? Yes, he would. Which British players did he admire? This time the response was immediate: 'Cheega!' The interpreter looked at me helplessly, but I knew who this must be: none other than Keegan Ke-vin. I told Shen how much Keegan earned in a month. He giggled – in embarrassment, as an Englishman might giggle at the sudden mention of sex – and then reassumed his blank and watchful stare.

That night Watford dined at the Great Hall of the People, where their quivering chopsticks negotiated the usual menu of fish stomachs, sea-slugs and ancient eggs. Lustrously dinner-jacketed, Elton John was introduced as 'the world's greatest superstar' by the General Secretary of the China FA. Elton did his stuff, very nicely, and silver salvers and plastic footballs were exchanged. When it comes to banqueting, the Chinese have something else to teach the West: speeches come first, at which stage sobriety and greed can be relied upon to keep them short.

The star guest at my table was the manager of the Workers' Stadium. (His groundsman was seated at the next table along.) He looked like a handsome Thai pirate out of a documentary about the Boat People. From accounts of the West Bromwich Albion tour of China in 1978, I had gathered that the Peking football crowds were as hushed and respectful as a first-night audience at Covent Garden. No 'oooooh, wanky wanky'. No 'you'll ne*AGH*ver walk alone'. I asked the chainsmoking, *mao-tei*-quaffing bigwig about this, and his reply was reassuringly serene.

That's right – Chinese crowds do not indulge in partisanship, and why should they? If your team is winning, you're happy. If your team is losing, you're even happier – because the superior team is schooling you for the future. I wondered how this line would go down with the Anfield Kop, say, as Liverpool trailed 0–4 to an Albanian eleven in the European Cup. How thrilled were the Chinese, I asked, when their team so narrowly failed to qualify for the World Cup in 1982? But my interlocutor's face had closed and hardened. He was as relieved as I was when a voice abruptly announced: 'That's all for the banquet. Goodnight!'

From the outset the Watford Group had been split into three parties, each served by its own coach and guide: Players, Directors and Tourists. This last contingent was made up of businessmen associated with the various club sponsors, and included a cadre of epic drinkers (known as the Gang of Four) who were clearly destined to become the true heroes of the long march. Due to some administrative whim – or to Taylor's protectiveness of his players – it was with the Tourists that the small Press corps was initially billeted.

So while Watford repaired to the luxurious mosque of the Fragrant Hill Hotel, I took my chances at the musty Yan Jing on one of the great avenues of downtown Peking. Here in the bar, the Gang of Four began its nightly skit on the comic Britisher abroad. Soon their table was a float of dead beer bottles. The volume, treble and bass controls all turned steadily upwards. They sang songs, and verbally goosed the passing girls. Thus did they strive to convince themselves that they were not in a coffee shop in Fu Xing Street but in the Butcher's Arms back home.

On the way to the match, through the half-industrialised loops of urban Peking, a Tourist paused in his passionate accompaniment to 'My Way' on the coach Muzak system and said, in a tone of grieved bewilderment, 'Look at the state of that excavator. Where is the maintenance? Where is it?' But there were other things to catch the eye. The crowd, as it approached the Workers' Stadium, resembled an entire ecology on the move: squirming busloads, open lorries from the outlying factories carrying their human freight, the furtive touts at the intersections, and 50,000 bicycles soon to be stacked like forks at the stadium gates. (The match would have been a sell-out twenty or thirty times over, and was being televised live to an audience of 350 million.) We disembarked on the trampled concourse and writhed through the crush. It was only when I reached my seat that I realised, with another kind of disquiet, how little menace such massed humanity could generate.

But during the game the anthill buzzed. Despite the squawked chidings from Big Sister on the PA system, there were regular cries of 'Suit! Suit!' (shoot), *'shou-qiu'* (handball), even a cautious chant (translated for me as 'More grease! More grease!' – more fuel, more work), as well as the ceaseless groundswell of coughed and spluttered comment: Ay! Tsk! Ayuh! *Eehyahah*!

The female voice-over sounded scandalised. 'The Department of Public Security asks the audience on Platform 20 to sit down . . . Strive to become a peaceful and civilised audience.' But the applause for the Watford goals, when they came, was immediate, spontaneous, containing a hint of stoic humility. From then on, moments of weird silence punctuated the game, and you could hear Taylor's hoarse ballockings from the bench – 'Hit the goal, Nigel! BE ACCURATE!' – right across the length of the field.

Weakened by the heat, and by the absence of their four key players (still on domestic duty in the Home Internationals), Watford struggled to contain the swift and skilful Chinese – particularly my pal Shen Xiang-fu, who ran them ragged on the right. A sun-helmeted Elton quit his throne in the stands and frolicked on the pitch as Watford plodded off, 3–1 winners. They could have lost 3–4, as Taylor was quick to admit. 'Do not molest or beat up the performers or referees,' cautioned the loudspeaker. As the tame multitude quietly siphoned itself into the night, the advice sounded unnecessary, even sarcastic. It would sound deeply pertinent after the return match, but that was still a week distant, by which time the mood of the crowd would inexplicably worsen.

The easiest way to get to know the players, I reckoned, was to get to know their nicknames – not for my personal use so much as to shine a light into the dark frat-house which all teams erect around themselves. A footballer's nickname takes any of three forms: a handy diminutive of the surname (as in Greavesy, Mooro, Besty, etc); a TV tie-in based on some fancied resemblance to a small-screen star; plus a third alias of a physical, usually offensive tendency. The players showed a cunning readiness to fill me in, and I was especially indebted to David Johnson, the reserve player whose almost ludicrous charm has long established him as the team mascot.

Goalkeeper Steve Sherwood is called Shirley or Concorde ('because of his nose'). His deputy Eric Steele is called Steeley or Hadley (TV tie-in). Captain and senior player Pat Rice goes under the names of Ricey, Stoneface, Anvil Head and Father Time. Wilf Rostron – Wilfy, The Dwarf. Steve Terry – The Big M, Frankenstein. Richard Jobson, or Jobbo, is remorselessly teased about his effeminate good looks: aka Curlers and Boy George. Paul Franklin – Gower (after David Gower). Ian Bolton – Webby ('he's got webbed feet'). Jan Lohman, who is Dutch, is called Herman (the German), Adolf, and Psycho ('because he's barmy. He is. He's mental'). Nigel Callaghan – Cally, Stump ('his hair') and Beaver ('his teeth'). Les Taylor – Little Legs or Rampant. Ian Richardson – Richo or Shaky (non-existent resemblance to Shakin' Stevens). Steve Sims, Simsy, is called Plug. 'No I'm not,' he said. 'They call me Male Model.' 'No we don't. We call him Plug.'

The nicknames of the four internationals I learned later. They are more respectful in timbre, but only marginally so. Kenny Jackett: Jackdaw or Chinaman (because of his sloped eyes – he was guyed about this almost as much as Rice was guyed about rice). Gerry Armstrong: Your Man ('Your what?' I asked. 'Yuhmahn.' 'Your what?' 'Yuh*mahn*.' 'Sorry. Your what?' 'Jesus Christ. *Y,E,R,M,O,N*'). Luther Blissett: Luth or Black Flash. John Barnes: Barnesy, Digger (TV tie-in: *Dallas*'s Digger Barnes) and Caramac (a reference to the light-hued chocolate bar). As for David Johnson himself: 'They call me DJ. Or Abdul. Or Gupta – that's G,u,p,t,a. Or Elephant Boy. Anything to do with Africa.'

But were Watford having anything to do with China? The day after the match they tackled the Great Wall. The section open to tourists splays off in two excitingly steep ascents, and the players confronted the challenge as a macho hangover cure. 'Gor. I hope the Boss doesn't use this for pre-season training,' said a player, from beneath the antennae of his Sony Walkman. Elton puffed his way to the top in his Humpty Dumpty suit, his startling pallor unaffected by the heat. It was left to one of the Gang of Four to leave a distinctive calling-card on the only human artefact visible from outer space: he vomited down the parapet, as over a ship's side.

After lunch Watford checked out the Ming Tombs. We paced down a lavatorial stone staircase into the arched tunnels and vaults. A Tourist drew a learned comparison between the featureless rust-coloured casements and the creosote used on truck undercoats. Interest was in danger of flagging entirely until an interpreter weighed in with some salacious accounts of the premature burial of imperial concubines. 'When's the next train to Cockfosters?' cracked a Director, not inappositely. If there had been a train to Cockfosters passing through, the suggestion was that he would have been on it.

'Fpall?' said the elderly lift-operator, and kicked a leg in the air like a chorus-girl: '*PSAIOW!*' The scene now briefly shifts to Shanghai, though Watford's points of comparison remain wistfully homebound. The harbourfront Bund 'is like Liverpool'. The near-slums which the Bund conceals 'are like Glasgow'. The dock itself 'is like Tyneside'. The yellow and shoreless Yangtze 'is like the Mersey'. The players settle on the deck of Special Class for the three-hour cruise up the Huang Pu. 'Row, row, row your boat,' says one. 'Slow boat to China,' says another. 'Don't rock the boat ... Banana boat ... I am sailing ... Sailing along ... Riding along in my automobile ...'

From Peking's Yan Jing I check into Shanghai's Jing Jiang, and for the first time I am on the same menu as the players. Bacon and eggs, chicken and chips, steak and chips. At lunch the four internationals fly in from their stopover in Hong Kong. England's two black strikers, Blissett and Barnes, glisten with youth, power, muscle-tone. They look like racehorses – in shocking contrast to the Gang of Four, toiling through the paste and smog of their daily penance.

That night we went to see the Chinese Acrobats, and witnessed their otherworldly feats of strength, balance and artistic contortion. Not for the first time since my arrival in China, I felt assailed by the evidence of Earthling variety: the players, the Gang, the Chinese, with their abstract humour, their ritual courtesy disguising unknown restlessness – and all this so fully expressed by the controlled tension of the acrobats ... Back at the hotel an American party had just arrived. An exhausted 20-stoner awaited service from the

flogged lifts. Shot to pieces gastrically, he looked as though
his own weight was about to drive him into the ground like
a tent-peg. 'Come on, Duane,' said his friend, 'it's only one
floor up. Let's walk it.' But Duane had few options. 'I, uh,
believe not,' he said firmly.

Of the three coaches, Players', Directors' and Tourists', the
Players' is by far the most restfully taciturn. The Tourists'
coach booms with rugby songs, business talk and hangover
boasts. The real nerve-frayer, though, is the Directors' coach,
a rumpus-room of almost psychotic good cheer. It was in
this charabanc of Laughing Policemen and Jimmy Tarbuck
soundalikes that I made the journey to the Shanghai ground,
past lean-tos and go-downs, bamboo department stores and
buses packed with waving arms and beaming, steel-flecked
dentition, through streets latticed by plane-tree fronds, tram
cables and wet washing.

The stadium was an elegant ruin, a shallow bowl of
bleached and flaking stonework. The ballboys sat slumped
beneath their sleepy coolie hats. 'Shanghai audiences are
good audiences and this is a Shanghai audience,' cackled
the loudspeaker. This was a Shanghai audience all right,
but it wasn't such a good one. When the home team went
one up, there were fire-crackers and cherry bombs -- practically a counter-revolution. When Watford equalised and
then took the lead (both goals created out of nothing by
the Shanghai goalkeeper), there was an experimental riot in
one bank of the stadium -- fomented, it turned out, by the
Gang of Four, who were feeding Watford souvenirs through
the steel netting. Like the crowd, however, the game soon
fizzled out in the impossible humidity. At half-time Taylor
marched into the dressing-room. He drew in his breath to
denounce his team, then burst out laughing. Several players
sat with icepacks on their heads and jets of steam billowing
from their ears.

*

43

China now toils through her sixth Five Year Plan, and is rolling up her sleeves for the seventh. There are smiles, handshakes, spurned gratuities; there are the new incentives of the Responsibility System, the crusades of Social Public Morality; there are colour TVs. You also sense a hidden life of impatience and frustration, a resented exclusion from the world of freedom and reward. (Recent attempts at Western marketing show the full gulf of naivety: a lipstick called 'Fang Fang', a type of battery called 'White Elephant', a range of men's underwear called 'Pansy'.) Football is part of this interchange, and China seeks inclusion here as feelingly as she seeks it elsewhere.

China only just missed out on qualification for the 1982 World Cup. They now have a four-year plan on the go, looking to Mexico in 1986. The national side performed well in its first match against Watford, and hopes were high for the second game in Peking. Yet China played a spoiling game, and were thrashed 5–1. Towards the end, the climbing anger of the crowd took a surprising form: Watford's black stars were booed whenever they touched the ball. One tried hard to resist this conclusion, since it attacked everything one wanted to believe about China. 'No, no,' said our suavest interpreter. 'They're just trying to put them off because the black players are so good.' But the aggression was selective and unmistakable, an incensed submission to the worst instincts.

Out on the concourse I searched anxiously for the Tourists' coach, which had taken the precaution of killing its lights as the hoards swirled sullenly round the ground. Cursed, barracked and gestured at, the humble motorcade of the China squad crept abjectly through the gates.

'I wanna go home,' sang the Gang. 'I wanna go home. This is the worst trip, I've ever been on . . .'

The tour now petered out in pleasant anti-climax, with celebrations, sightseeing and some predatory shopping. Elton

John spent forty times the local per-caput income in a single spree. His purchases included replicas of the stone lions beneath Mao's portrait, which gaze across the square at the Great Hall of the People. That night, with eyes like two lumps of sweet-and-sour pork, Elton mastered his exhaustion and took to the piano to crown the farewell shindig. When Elton sang (not for a multitude but for his team) you felt the force, and proximity, of his talent; you didn't want it to end. The high point of his tour, he said, had come at the Children's Festival in Zhongshan Park, when a ten-year-old girl prodigy presented him with a painting of a flock of gambolling kittens. Elton was moved – 'well chuffed'. This would give him more pleasure than anything else he intended to bring back from China. Money isn't everything, he pointed out. And China, however reluctantly, would be forced to agree.

On the flight home the 747 made its first stop in Hong Kong, arrowing in through the genie-clouds above the bay, past the golden cigarette-lighters of the skyscrapers and sparkling hotels – a Manhattan, a Mammon, a vast duty-free store, perched on the very tip of the East, and destined to be dismantled and flattened out into the Chinese fold. One couldn't escape the impression that most foreign visitors make the trip to China chiefly for the shopping. In hotel lobbies, in airport lounges, one was always hearing elderly and prosperous Americans talking lecherously about the latest Friendship Store they had plundered, or planned to plunder. It was said of one press photographer in our party, on the day before our return, that 'his *room* looked like a Friendship Store' . . . While the Directors sprawled in First and Business, the players dozed with their manager in Economy, their faces set in scowls of discomfort. But the team roused itself for the transit lounge (where they have cameras and gadgets, as well as silk and jade), and we all trudged out for one more crack at the loot.

Observer, 1983

Postscript: In terms of cultural responsibility the Watford footballers behaved even better than this account admits – especially when you compared them to certain elements in the press corps. I remember encountering Wilf Rostron, the young defender, in the hotel lobby in Shanghai. He was on his way from the ballet to the opera. Accompanied by the *Sun*'s Voice of Sport, John Sadler, I was on my way from the bowling alley to the snooker room . . . The esprit of the players was a tribute to Graham Taylor. Late at night, ensconced in an armchair, with the pressmen gathered piously at his feet, Taylor would talk of the deeper mysteries of the sport, and would air his dream of a management job somewhere in his native North-East – Sunderland? Newcastle? As far as I remember he never mentioned the possibility of managing England. I write these words on the eve of England's World Cup qualifier against Holland at Wembley: Taylor's watershed, or his Waterloo. But it doesn't surprise me that he seems physically undiminished by the job. Bobby Robson, if you recall, was a shot-faced spectre after about six months. Taylor is made of stubborner stuff. As for the 'enigmatic' – i.e. bafflingly ineffective – John Barnes: there probably isn't any upper limit for bodily splendour in a footballer (look at Ruud Gullit), but Barnes struck me as someone close to being overwhelmed by his own attributes. He appeared to spend much of his free time examining various portions of his person (his forearms, his calves), not from any concern about injury but in simple admiration. Often his hand would rest proprietorially on the prow of his skimpy white shorts. When he arrived he made quite a speech about the need to respect Chinese culture. The next day he turned down his only chance to visit the Great Wall (the much more ebullient, Anglicised and squeaky-voiced Luther Blissett went off alone in a taxi). Taylor said: 'How can you pass up the Great Wall, talking like you were talking yesterday?' Barnes didn't answer, but fell to the contemplation of some neglected highpoint of his physique – his collarbone, his elbow.

JOHN UPDIKE

I met up with Updike at Mass. General – that is to say, at the Wang Ambulatory Care Center of Massachusetts General Hospital, in Boston. The brilliant, fanatically productive and scandalously self-revealing novelist had been scheduled to have a cancerous or cancer-prone wart removed from the side of his hand at 9.30 that morning. It was 10.30 when we eye-contacted each other in the swirling ground-floor cafeteria. 'You know what I look like,' he had said on the telephone. And there was no mistaking him (apart from anything else, he was the healthiest man there): tall, 'storklike', distinctly avian, with the questing curved nose and the hairstyle like a salt-and-pepper turban.

'How *are* you?' I said with some urgency.

'They didn't take it out. It's still here!' He raised his hand to the light. It seemed a gratifying intimacy, after ten seconds' acquaintance. John Updike, warts and all. Most writers need a wound, either physical or spiritual. Updike's is called *psoriasis*, 'skin disease marked by red scaly patches', as my COD unfeelingly puts it. He has written about the condition himself, rather more feelingly, in the *New Yorker*. Actually the growth seemed quite inoffensive, like a sizeable and resolute freckle.

'How frustrating. You must be . . .'

'Yes, I'm very sad,' he said, and looked – as he would

continue to look for the next two hours – like a man barely able to contain some vast and mysterious hilarity. This generalised twinkliness has been much remarked. It is almost the demure expression a child has when gratified to the point of outright embarrassment – but with an extra positive charge, flowing from hyperactive senses. 'No, apparently it's more complicated than I thought. They're going to do it later in the year. The incision will go from there to there. I'll have to wear a support for a while. I won't be able to play golf. I won't be able to type! But listen. How are *you*?'

This, too, was said with unusual concern. Updike ducked and briefly grappled with the *Boston Globe*. He pointed to a piece that I had read, with quivering fingers, half an hour earlier. The previous evening I had flown in from Provincetown: fifteen minutes in a Wright-Brothers seven-seater. That same day, according to the *Globe*, one of these little aeroplanes had lost height and come skimming in over Boston Bay. Sunbathers had dived into the sea from their rafts. The article ended with a reassuring review of the airline's safety record: it was grounded, quite recently, after a series of accidents, all of them rich in fatalities.

'You flew! I warned you not to.'

'Yes, and I'm flying back. After I've done you.'

And he said to me what I had been planning to say to him: 'You're very brave.'

The hospital cafeteria was bright, airy, oceanic; there was foliage, a sun-trapping terrace, a smoking section: it seemed positively fashionable. The atmosphere differed from its British equivalent in many ways – most crucially in that its patrons were, of necessity, on some kind of spree, pushing the boat out, spending big. We joined the queue with our tray. I had coffee, while Updike bemusedly dithered over the half-dozen kinds of tea on offer.

'The ordeal of choice,' I said, suavely enough – though one should stress that these occasions are not suave at all. However genial, they are always anxious and exhausting,

48

with the interviewer fielding about 80 per cent of the nerves. 'Have you read Saul Bellow's new novel?' I went on. (The novel was *More Die of Heartbreak*.) 'He says that in the East the ordeal is one of privation, in the West one of choice.'

'Yes, I keep meaning to get it. There's just something about forking out the twenty bucks. Why don't *I* carry that?' he said, and smoothly commandeered the trembling tray. The gesture was protective, courteous, very *able*, above all. 'So the *Observer* is paying for my tea. How nice.'

The tea cost fifty cents. Nor was this the extent of the moneys I would disburse on Updike's account. Later, when we drove to Harvard, I gave the novelist a quarter for the parking meter. He fanned a handful of change at me, but I told him that Tiny Rowland would pick up the tab. Throughout he showed, not a sensitivity, but an *awareness* about money. 'I was raised in the Depression,' he has said, 'when there was a great sense of dog eat dog and people fighting over scraps.' This feeling has partly survived two decades of book-a-year bestsellerdom and the fact that 'Reagan has turned *America* into a tax haven'. Nowadays Updike could probably hold his own with the other Midases of the age: the arbitrageur, the greenmail raider, the arms dealer, the video vicar.

'My God,' he enthused as we sat, 'we're surrounded by all kinds of sick Americans.' The breakfast crowd in the Wang Center were wary in step and gesture. They were trussed in trusses, braced in braces, coated in powerful lotions, creams, elixirs. 'Bending and bowing in a variety of friezes', to quote from *The Poorhouse Fair* (1959), John Hoyer Updike's youthfully solemn first novel.

All the illness on view had a tonic effect on me. After three weeks of holiday 'parenting' (Updike's word: his speech and prose are permissively sprinkled with modernisms like 'frontal', 'focusing', 'conflicted' and 'judgmental'), I felt like checking into Mass. General myself.

'It makes a change', I said, 'from the triumphalism of the beach.'

'My *actinic caritosis* is a *result* of the triumphalism of the beach. The sun exacerbates it. Look at that woman's glasses!' A lady groped by in what could have been a pair of welder's goggles. 'I guess she really doesn't want any light in her eyes. My God, look at him!'

As Updike feasted his senses on the scene, I reached grimly for the tape-recorder. He hesitated. 'We're not really going to do this, are we? We're just going to have a nice chat,' he said, prophetically enough, 'and then you're going to go home and write a long piece about me and my work.'

Lauded, harassed, honoured, microinspected, Updike is by now simply stoical about the 'attention' his work attracts. And he is a gentleman, and a good old pro. The enemies of promise – or of reasonable productivity – used to be Hollywood, fancy journalism, alcohol, and so on. These days the main enemy is being interviewed. Updike could spend his life doing little else. In a recent *New Yorker* he published a story (and it is a full-time job keeping up with Updike: everywhere you look he is blurting out essays, poems, memoirs, reviews) in which a dissident Czech poet yearns to be rearrested and put back in jail, so that he can write some verse and stop being interviewed.

'A Korean professor might come and torment me for an hour. German TV keeps thinking it wants to stop by. A number of American universities are willing to pay a tempting amount to pinch and poke an author for a day or two. Once a year or so I rise early and do *Good Morning America*. It's kind of a raffish experience. You go in all groggy and sit in the Green Room with Mel Tormé or the father of seventeen girls or some such celebrity of the moment.

'Writers can get over-interviewed. The whole performance indicates that you are quite a swell fellow just by being *you*, whereas we know that what merit we have, if any, resides elsewhere. It rots a writer's brain, it cretinises you. You say the same thing again and again, and when you do that happily you're well on the way to being a cretin. Or a politician.'

Updike can hardly complain – and he doesn't complain – about the abrasions of self-exposure, because he has taken care of all that in his stories and novels. For some reason (won't anyone tell us why?), modern fiction tends towards the autobiographical, and American fiction more than most, and John Updike more than any. The tendency is still regarded as a 'flaw', in Updike and in general; but one might as usefully accuse Shakespeare for having, in his tragedies, a 'weakness' for kings and noblemen and warriors. The dominance of the self is not a flaw, it is an evolutionary characteristic; it is just how things are now.

Yet the case of Updike is unquestionably extreme. The textural contrast between your first and second wife's pubic hair, for instance, is something that most writers feel their readers can get along without. The novelists of yesteryear would gallantly take leave of their creations at the bedroom door. Updike tags along, not only into the bedroom but into the bathroom. Indeed, he sends a little Japanese camera crew in there after them. Humbert, in *Lolita*, wishes that he could turn his nymphet inside out and gorge himself on her very organs. Updike unpeels and vivisects his characters in this way. (If humans do it, it's fair copy.) And so it is with all the other intimacies of thought and feeling. 'It's all in *Couples*,' he will concede. Or: 'The novels are a fair record of what I felt.' Or: 'It's all in the books.'

It is also all in the *New Yorker*. When I was a student, living on the Iffley Road, Oxford, I sometimes wished that E.B. White would call by, in a chauffeur-driven limousine, to offer me a job on the *New Yorker*. It never happened. But it happened to Updike. He was at the Ruskin; the call came on the strength of early stories and proven versatility on the *Harvard Lampoon*. He was already married ('hand in hand, smaller than Hansel and Gretel'), already a father. Pictured with his first child, he looks to me like an oddjobbing baby-sitter, willing and gentle enough, no doubt, but far too young to be of much use. He was twenty-three.

'I left New York after only two years there. The place proved to be other than the Fred Astaire movies had led me to expect. The literary atmosphere struck me as ugly, and still does. Resentful, poisonous, a *squeezed* feeling. I came up here to be out of harm's way: inaccessibility is the best way of saying no. But Boston is becoming an honorary borough of New York.'

Under the enlightened patronage of the magazine – an unbroken relationship – Updike established himself in Ipswich, Mass. 'There was space here. We raised the children – or they seemed to raise themselves.' And so did the poems, stories and novels: earnest, gawky, forgiving, celebratory. He did his 'secluded and primitive' childhood in *Olinger Stories* and elsewhere, his dad in *The Centaur*, and his mum in *Of the Farm*. Fame, sophistication, modernity and wealth arrived with *Couples* (1968), when Updike did Ipswich.

Every writer hopes or boldly assumes that his life is in some sense exemplary, that the particular will turn out to be universal. *Couples* struck enough people this way, and was soon labelled 'the anatomy of a generation'. Its broad success also depended on a combination of the intensely literary and the near-pornographic. A cat's-cradle of vigorous adultery, as filtered through the sensibility of a modern James – or a modern Joyce. What Joyce did for the residents of Dublin, Updike recklessly offered to do for the dreamy dentists and Byronic building-contractors of 'Tarbox':

. . . the neighbours' boy linked to her by a handkerchief, lithe. Lower classes have that litheness. Generations of hunger. Give me your poor. Marcia brittle. Janet fat. Angela drifty and that Whitman gawky, resisting some-thing, air. Eddie's Vespa but no Ford, Carol's car. He home and she shopping. Buying back liniment. I ache afterwards

... Death. Hamster. Shattered glass. He eased up on the accelerator.

Didn't ease up. Pressed on. Five hundred pages like this. *Couples* is littered with brilliancies; but the smile and the flinch alternate too rapidly for the reader's comfort. The book seemed to be Updike's pinnacle at the time. Now it looks more like a shimmering false summit.

Meanwhile, as *New Yorker* readers must have been only too aware, all was not well with the Updike marriage. The annual damage-checks were arriving in the form of the Maples Stories, worldly comedies of disintegration with titles like 'Waiting Up', 'Sublimating', 'Separating' and 'Divorcing: A Fragment'. Sample home truth, sample gallantry (the subject here is 'guilt-avoidance'):

> 'I've decided to kick you out. I'm going to ask you to leave town.'
>
> Abruptly full, his heart thumped; it was what he wanted. 'O.K.,' he said carefully. 'If you think you can manage.'
>
> ... 'Things are stagnant,' she explained, 'stuck; we're not going anywhere.'
>
> 'I will not give her up,' he interposed.
>
> 'Don't tell me, you've told me.'
>
> 'Nor do I see you giving him up.'
>
> 'I would if you asked. Are you asking?'
>
> 'No. Horrors. He's all I've got.'

Soon, young David Updike was publishing his account of the divorce, in the *New Yorker*. Then Updike's mother ('I'm in a writer sandwich,' says Updike warily) weighed in with her version, in the *New Yorker*. 'I've gotten used to being written about,' says his ex-wife Mary, quoted (for a change) in the *New York Times*. Open marriages are not often as open as this. The loop, I mean to say, the circuit or the food chain, is shockingly brief. There is something predatory or vampiric in it – a hint of domestic cannibalism. It represents a kind of love to set these things down, as Updike has always claimed ('loving if not flattering'), and a kind of fidelity too. But a writer's kind, and therefore quite ruthless.

The literary interview won't tell you what a writer is *like*. Far more compellingly, to some, it will tell you what a writer is *like to interview*. A personality is more palatable than a body of work, so all the faceting and detail of the life and writing is subsumed into thumbnail approximation. Who is John Updike? A garrulous adulterer who lives near the sea? By rights, he should have turned up at Mass. General with lipstick on his collar, and then disappeared every ten minutes to supervise abortions for Mabel and Missy and Charity and Hope. For the record, he was charm incarnate. But as for what Updike is *like* – in his head, in his private culture – I knew all that already.

In his perceptions he is almost dementedly sensual: tactile, olfactory. He cowers under a cataract of sense impressions. His fascination with the observable world is utterly promiscuous: he will address a cathedral and a toilet bowl with the same peeled-eyeball intensity. The brain itself is serendipitous and horrendously encyclopaedic: he knows about home improvement ('twenty feet of 2″ pine, quality knotless stock, a half pound of 1½″ finishing nails'), music ('the gigue was marked *allegro*. It began with some stabbing phrases – dit-*duh* (*a–d*), dit-*duh* (*b–c*)'), cars ('padded tilt steering wheel, lumbar support lever for adjustable driver comfort, factory-installed AM/FM/MPX'), trees ('the sapling sugar maples and the baby red oaks'), computers ('rotate (molecule (protein 293)) (angles (from alpha) (to delta) (steps (*0.001 (– delta alpha))))'), painting ('she halts in the pose of Michelangelo's slave, of Munch's madonna, of Ingres' urn-bearer'), boats ('Arthur's newly bought gaff-rigged Herreshoff 12½''), photosynthesis ('the five-sixths of the triosephosphate pool that does not form starch is returned to ribulose 5-phosphate'), pornography, theology, nuclear physics, lino-typing, gold futures, aerodynamics, Africa, cookery, cosmogony and I don't know what-all. The unblinkingness of his eye is opposed to the mighty wooziness of his heart. He is a romantic, an Arcadian, a tremendous (and not always a tasteful) yearner for purity, innocence, the cadences of goodness. He is greedy, androgynous, devout, determined, intolerably sentimental and unforgivably bright.

What makes this chaos meaningful, and what lifts the work from the merely phenomenal, is the way time is acting on it. Countervailingly, and increasingly, Updike's prose is sour, withering, crafty, painfully comic. Such an immersion in the physical world, it seems, will tend not towards nostalgia but towards an invigorating and majestic cynicism. Mortality and its terrors were the fount of much of the early mawkishness; now they form the backing for a new robustness, a humorous pessimism that Updike has fatalistically embraced.

'Yes, it's another part of me, isn't it?' he says. 'Maybe it's the best part of me. It's funny that I can be so sour when I'm such a sunny, cheerful individual. But when I get going on it . . .'

'It comes.'

'It comes. It comes.'

It comes in the revitalised form of Harry Angstrom, Rabbit, the vulgar bohunk he left behind in Pennsylvania. Rabbit is not the 'Updike who never went to Harvard', as some commentators claim; he is part of Updike's mind and always has been, part of all our minds, the material man who sulks and gloats about sex and money. With *Rabbit is Rich* (1982), the third in the sequence, the hitherto fruitless homage to Joyce finds a truly modern application; at last Updike is elaborating and not just annotating *Ulysses*, urging it further into the twentieth century.

It comes in the form of Henry Bech, the eponym of

Bech: A Book (1970) and *Bech is Back* (1983). 'I keep meaning to kill Bech,' says Updike, viciously; but he won't go away. Rabbit differs from Updike the man. Bech differs from Updike the writer: he is highbrow, cosmopolitan, single and Jewish, thus allowing Updike, through a feat of empathic daring, to arrogate a culture that has 'kept the secret of its laughter a generation longer than the Gentiles, hence their present domination of the literary world'. Updike echoes Malamud: 'By developing a Jewish persona I was saying something like: "Look, I'm really Jewish too. We're all Jewish here." ' But he was also challenging that domination, typically demanding more than his fair share. Another voice, another 'third person', witty, wounded and historically central.

Then there is mainstream Updike, the fiction from the horse's mouth. Or (it must be said) from the horse's backside, in the case of *The Witches of Eastwick* (1984), which has just been filmed. The movie is so preposterous that critics have been protective about its source, forgetting that the book is preposterous too: crammed with beauties, but winsome, whimsical, haloed in a seamless futility. It would appear, though, that Updike is the better for the occasional holidays from merit (or therapeutic indulgences), because his most recent book is the near-masterpiece *Roger's Version*. A meditation on death and creation in the pale light of a modern city, it is the richest, funniest and gloomiest book that Updike has yet written. To him, the future may not look as bright as it once did, but to his readers it has never looked brighter.

'Shit,' said Updike. It was his one profanity of the morning. He had just led me into the wrong carpark. We were leaving Mass. General and proceeding to Harvard, where Updike had a lunch.

'You once wrote a novel, or a "romance", called *Marry Me*,' I said. 'Your new book of stories is called *Trust Me*. But maybe you should have called it *Divorce Me*.'

For the book is riven with divorce and its aftermath. Brave ex-wives and their watchful replacements, half-grown children seldom seen, possessions divided, houses scoured and then abandoned. 'They don't call them orphanages any more, do they?' asks one character. 'They call them normal American homes.' I put this to Updike, and quoted the line: 'In the pattern of his generation he had married young, had four children, and eventually got a divorce.'

'A pattern, that's right. Marriage was very erotic when I was growing up. You got married in college and had kids when you were still kids yourselves. Four children in two-year notches. It was the same for everybody we knew. The marginal couples stayed together. The ones who were any fun all broke up. In my case we'd just had enough of each other. It was terrible for the children, having to become grownups overnight.'

This turned out to be the third time Updike and I had met. He couldn't remember the second time, when I had shaken his hand at a London publishing party. And I couldn't remember the first time, when I was a nine-year-old resident of Princeton, New Jersey. 'I spent an evening with your mother and father and some other people. Were you there? You might have been in bed. We played cards. We were all drunk but no one, I think, was as drunk as your father.'

'Those were wild times. Everyone was at it.'

'So I've read,' said Updike. 'So I've read. It was a revolution for all of us – not just for Abbie Hoffman. Kind of a dark carnival. We were all wearing love-beads, in a way.'

Three years later, my parents duly divorced. Divorce, in those days, was like a dreadful disease that everyone's parents kept catching. It occurred to me for the first time that this had determined the pattern of *my* generation. The children of these divorcees, we married late, had children late – too late, perhaps, for the body's good. Updike was delighted to hear about our strained backs and spongy knees, our pleading ankles.

We left the hospital grounds and drove to Cambridge in Updike's powerful Audi. We drove from American sickness to American health – Harvard Yard, in July sunshine, and the student body, muscular and tanktop, yelling, jogging, frisbeeing, cartwheeling, and necking and quarrelling and breaking up. Updike's kids passed through here some time ago. Whereas my first born will be three in November. Sprawled here on the lawns, this particular batch seem to be oddly poised. Seventy-five per cent of them think that they will die in a nuclear war. Probably even more of them believe that they will meet their fate in a singles' bar. Marriage has been re-eroticised for them, whether they like it or not. 'Nature is hard to outsmart,' as Updike said. 'It's always one jump ahead. Nature doesn't really care about us at all.'

He was dropping off some paperwork at the Widener Library: correspondence, the galleys of *Trust Me* – no sooner published than filed away, the decks cleared for the next thing. We parted, and then he called me back, telling me to give his best to my parents. Watching him strut away, head in air, I felt – suddenly and ridiculously – what it was to have been one of *his* children, and how I would have hated to see him go.

I sat on the grass and looked again at one of the new stories. The passage verges on the sentimental (the weakness for the word 'little', the cutely agrammatical 'that' towards the end); but then I was verging on the sentimental myself.

Though Foster was taller, the boy was broader in the shoulders, and growing. 'Want to ride with me to the dump?' Tommy asked.

'I would, but I better go.' He, too, had a new life to lead. By being on this forsaken property at all, Foster was in a sense on the wrong square, if not *en prise*. He remembered how once he had begun to teach this boy chess, but in the sadness of watching him lose – the little furry bowed head frowning above his trapped king – the lessons had stopped . . .

Seeing his father waver, he added, 'It'll only take twenty minutes.' Though broad of build, Tommy had beardless cheeks and, between thickening eyebrows, a trace of that rounded, faintly baffled blankness babies have, that wrinkles before they cry.

'O.K.,' Foster said. 'You win. I'll come along. I'll protect you.'

Observer, 1987

TENNIS: THE WOMEN'S GAME

The emerging women's game can be imagined – perhaps with literal accuracy – as a transcontinental jumbo, with three classes. In First Class you find the top ten ladies (or bobbysoxers or nymphets), with footrests up, harassed by the courtesies of the cabin stewards: Steffi is playing backgammon with her dad; Gaby is hunched under a Sony Walkman. In Club World, together with the shrinks and physios of the top ten ladies, are the second-string ladies, all of them quite well attended, and wearing those special pairs of Club World slippers. In the chaos of Coach, wedged together in blocks of three and four, are the 'gym rats', the eternal aspirants of the modern tour, on yet another leg of their frazzled quest for ranking points, sponsors, backers. Nearly every girl on board has entrusted her schooling to the correspondence course. They are all enduring, or developing, a variety of injuries: 'always *something* hurts.' And they all have jet-lag.

It is raining in Boca Raton, to the disgust of the entire resort. The PR machine is reshuffling flights, drivers and schedules; and the ladies are in the clubroom, playing snap and Scrabble. When the action resumes, Jo Durie will go out in the first round, foreclosing British interest in the event. But that's where all similarities to Wimbledon end. The crowd isn't cringing under umbrellas, smelling of damp dog. It is strolling the landscaped grounds, lightly clad and gorging itself on ice-cream and gooey pretzels. For we are in Florida, the global nursery of the women's game, where the girls can conveniently flit from condo to sports ranch to tournament, and to the stratospheric tendrils of mammoth Miami Airport. The county is still mopping its brow from Prince Charles's recent visit to Palm Beach; but lots of locals are rich and idle enough to turn out for the tennis. The heavy sun gives the young flesh of the players a sumptuously toasty tang, and turns the rest of us into various shades of peanut butter and hotdog mustard.

'Nice place, don't you think,' said my driver as we approached, and then added, before I got any ideas, 'You have to be a millionaire to live here, though.' I believed him. Chris Evert lives here, or has a 'home' here anyway. This is polo-club America, with shaved grass, caddycarts, rows of identical modern villas, and fanatical security. I look in on the sodden press tent to collect my ID tag. But there is hardly time to sample the free Danish ('For MEDIA Only!'), and to be disabused of the idea that tennis journalism is a glamorous job, before we hear the rumour of play. The clouds clear and the voluptuous raindrops cease to fall. Soon the sky is wearing an outfit of faded denim; at dusk it will don a watermelon T-shirt. This is Florida, and even the sky is in questionable taste.

In the absence of Martina Navratilova (either injured or conserving herself for 'the Slams'), and in the absence of any hard gossip about burnout, grasping parents or lesbian molestation, there was only one big story, one big question, at the Virginia Slims of Florida. The question was: can anybody beat Steffi Graf, who nowadays seems to be losing about one match a year? Pat Cash recently called women's tennis 'rubbish'. Yet many well-informed observers believe that the women's game is now more interestingly poised than the men's – as well as being better fun to watch. The men have entrained a power struggle of outsize athleticism, machismo and foul temper. It's all *rat-a-tat-tat*, or *rat-a-tat*, or, on fast courts, simply *rat*. Where is the pleasure in witnessing an ace? The women's game has become just as powerful while remaining significantly slower, so that the amateur has time to recognise the vocabulary of second-guessing and disguise. Although it's still a fight, it's a woman's fight, settled not by the muscles but by the subtler armaments with which women wage their wars. Women's tennis is *Dynasty* with balls, bright yellow fuzzy ones, stroked and smacked by the Fallons, Krystles and Alexises of the lined court.

The crowd wants something to talk about, and the press must have something to write about; so for the first few days attention fixes on the Latest Sensation – the latest double-fisted infant to be groomed for stardom, Monica Seles from Yugoslavia, who has just turned fourteen. The older girls hate playing the child wonders, and Helen Kalesi, the Canadian number one, is having a terrible time with Monica. 'Better than Steffi at that age,' a coach informs me. 'Look at her nerve. She *loves* the ball.' The contest looks elegant but sounds barbaric. Helen is a 'grunter', and Monica is a 'whoofer', emitting a duosyllabic shriek with each contact of ball and racket. 'Uhh!' 'Ugh-*eh*!' 'Uhh!' 'Ugh-*eh*!' Jimmy Connors started the grunting, with his legendary 'Hworf!' Then, as Clive James noted, Bjorn Borg responded with his own nordic variant: 'Hwörjf!' The idea, supposedly, is to incorporate the strength of the stomach muscles; but the strength of the women áll derives from their *timing*, in at least two senses. Prodigies can't happen in men's tennis because the physique develops later. Hence the money trap of the women's game, and one of its peculiar cruelties: as an earner, a girl can peak at puberty and be 'history' by the age of sixteen.

At the press conference after her shock win Monica looks like a startled elf in a Disney cartoon. Her charmingly nervous laugh reveals a garrison of orthodonture. 'What do you

feel?' 'Very happy.' 'What is your goal?' 'To be number one.'
Later, Steffi Graf strides into the tent, having briskly lunched
on her first opponent. Asked about the child wonder, Steffi
concedes with a shrug that Monica, while 'very skinny', is
'a good player'. She is especially haughty about Monica's
reliance on the two-handed groundstroke, which Steffi clearly regards as a contemptible anachronism, like using your
knickers to store the ball for the second serve. As befits a
number one, Steffi is visibly impatient with questions about
her rivals, and generally shows little interest in disguising her
feelings. She quite lacks the PR burnish of the American girls,
all of whom have impeccable media manners and a nice tidy
image. It makes sense: they might want to diversify later on,
like Pam Shriver. If you retire at twenty-five there are a lot
of years ahead, and sportscasting may fill some of them.

The next evening, under the lights, little Monica plays
Chris Evert, who knows a thing or two about child prodigies,
having traumatised them by the dozen year after year. She
was also one herself, and remains the only player in the modern game who has paced her hunger over two decades. Given
a big build-up by the PR witch with the mike ('Ladies and
gentlemin! . . . Wimbledin . . . the US Opin' etc, plus details
of her career earnings), Chris steps forward, sternly smiling,
as straight and crisp as the pleats in her skirt, and shining
with money dignity and hardened achievement. 'Mm,' says
Chris as she strikes the ball (for Chris is no whoofer: more
a gentle moaner). 'Mm.' 'Ugh-*eh*!' 'Mm.' 'Ugh-*eh*!' 'Mm.'
Monica cuts a chastened figure at the post-match conference.
She broke Chris's serve three times, but she failed to hold any
of her own. No laughter now, poor mite. She looks as though
she is longing for a refreshing weep with her mother, or five
hours with her coach, rewiring that drive volley.

Now that the Latest Sensation is history for the time
being, the public eye greedily swivels and fixes with an
incredulous leer on Gabriela Sabatini. As she unveils herself for the first match, under the sun's spotlight, a sigh of

admiration and yearning wafts through the crowd. Sabatini looks like a human racehorse, a (successful) experiment in genetico-aesthetics, engineered, cultured and conditioned for optimum gorgeousness. Her beauty alone scares the life out of her opponents – because tennis is above all an expression of personal power and, in the women's game, is closely bound up with how a player looks, and how she feels she looks.

Up against Gabriela is the noble veteran Wendy Turnbull, with her gym knickers and boyish bob. It is, perhaps, not too great a trespass against gallantry to point out that Wendy is shaped like a Prince Pro tennis racket. She plays a stubby game, too, while Gabriela, of course, is pure motion sculpture on the court, with her balletic delay in the service action and her bravura – her toreador – backhand. It looked like a deeply thankless hour for Wendy, facing this bronzed hallucination of fluency and youth. She tried her 'old tricks' (block return, chip-and-charge), but Gabriela's topspin was a torment to her ageing legs. 'Time,' explained the umpire, every five minutes. 'Time. Time.' And it's the operative word. To Monica it says, 'Not yet'; to Wendy, 'No longer.'

Soon, the Sabatini charisma is devastating the press tent. 'Still got the red BMW, Gaby?' asks one tennis expert from the floor. 'This Argentine singer friend – what's his name?' 'Elio Roza.' 'How do you spell Elio?' 'E,l,i,o.' 'Great. How do you spell Roza?' What did you feel? What will you buy? At the best of times the press tent is hardly a fortress of shrewd inquiry, and when a superstar is near, the Sports Department quickly collapses into Features or Lifestyles. All week the girls troop in and tell the corps that they're crazy about their new coach and are now doing ten thousand pull-ups a day and eating nothing but alfalfa. It is an obligation, and a ritual. 'Have you dreamt of this moment all your life?' 'Yes.' This exchange will go into the paper as follows: 'I have dreamt of this moment all my life.' Thus a cliché is thrown up by the press, and printed by the press. The closed circle suits everybody. And if you put in a 'request' and secure a private interview, if you try to look 'behind the scenes', then all you'll find is another scene, another layer of press patter. This shouldn't surprise anyone. And besides, it has never been a particularly fruitful business, asking teenage girls *what they feel*.

'5 to 11 – Complimentary Champagne FOR ALL LADIES,' says the sign, rather desperately, in the bar of the official hotel. Needless to say, Gaby and Steffi are not to be seen here, enjoying six hours of complimentary champagne. There used to be a few ravers among the better-known players; but tennis girls are compulsive types, and once they started raving, they soon stopped being among the better-known players. All that is of course out of the question these days. Fun and boys and free champagne, like everything else, is scheduled to happen 'later'.

Steffi and Gaby are not to be seen in the hotel. They are cordoned off elsewhere. Only the Coach Class players dwell here in Park Place. They wander around with their sausage bags. They drink milk with breakfast (suggesting childish tastes as well as sensible nutrition). They sleep three to a room and talk worriedly about how they will split the tab. They are not yet – and may never be – on the other side, the place where everyone is suddenly dying to give them money. Their numbers remorselessly dwindle as the week goes on.

For things are getting serious. The plucky underdogs and the eyecatchers are all falling away: Gigi Fernandez, with her vociferous flair and fecklessness; Rafaella Reggi, the glamorous grunter; squawlike Mary Joe Fernandez, the unforgiving baseliner; Sandra Cecchini, dynamically butch and spivvy; the Czech pylon Helena Sukova, borne everywhere on the shoulders of two little bodybuilders (which turn out to be her legs): the shriekers and whoofers and hworfers step aside, revealing the handful of players who are capable of winning it – or of worrying Steffi Graf. All week, as tickets get pricier, the seat allocations for the press have become more and more disadvantageous. For the final, a further spasm of sponsorial greed lofts us up into the bleachers. It is the match everyone wants to see: Graf *v*. Sabatini. Fräulein Forehand meets Bonita Backhand.

On the big day I breakfast within eavesdropping distance of the TV crew that has flown down for the match. 'Do we do a *pre*-match interview?' one of them asks. 'With Steffi? I don't know. She goes into like a trance before the start.' The upside of interviewing Steffi in mid-reverie – or of at least televising the trance – is briefly discussed. Can they *get* the pre-match interview? They think so. In no other sport will two individuals be given up to three hours of screen time, and TV is the fount of all the real tennis money. It is why each square inch of Steffi's shirt is worth a million dollars.

'Ladies and gentlemin!' Seen from on high, the demeanour of the show court clearly reflects the narrowing gap between top tennis and show business. The flags, the floodlights, the VIP boxes, the camera gantries, the officials in candy stripe (pompous Pancho Gonzalez lookalikes, fully convinced, like the TV people, of their vital contribution to the spectacle), the rockhard PR girl with her interminable plugs and mentions and personal thanks to all the allegedly wonderful Dekes and Duanes and Sharons and Karens who have made all this possible. The crowd, too, is participatory in the American style. What kind of clothes do Americans wear when they watch tennis? Tennis clothes. And they join in with their aggressive questioning of calls, frequent demands to be reminded of the score, and continuous and deafening cries of '*Quiet!*'

Steffi Graff is something unbelievable on the tennis court, a miracle of speed, balance and intense athleticism. She looks like a skater but she moves like a puck. During changeovers she gets up early from her chair, and she is always exasperated (hands on hips, head bowed) by any delay from opponent or ballboy. After a great shot she doesn't wait for the applause to start, let alone stop, before she is striding back to the baseline, twiddling her racket like a sixgun. She never smiles.

66

She wants to win every set to love and get on with the next one. You feel that the only player she would enjoy facing is herself.

Today she is facing Gabriela, who has never beaten her in eleven meetings. And it looks like the same old story. Steffi's forehand is booming, and she is slicing her backhand under the breeze. Instead of retreating twenty feet for the high topspin (as Evert had done in the semi-final), Steffi adopts the ploy of jumping waist-high to make her drives. Steffi is one set up and serving at 3–2 in the second. The crowd (strongly Hispanic, or strongly Jewish and therefore anti-German) groans and sweats for the wilting, shamefaced Gaby. Then something happens. And we'll never know what. Steffi collapses in a blizzard of errors, losing all but one of the next eleven games. An instant after the last point Gaby has the snout of a TV camera in her face. Then a microphone in her hand ('It's hard to talk right now'). Soon she is in the press tent, being asked what she feels ('It's hard to say'). And then she is packing her rackets and heading down to Key Biscayne for the Lipton, where she will lose to Mary Joe Fernandez in the quarters, and where Steffi, as tennis writers say, will return to her winning ways.

The person to ask about modern tennis stardom is not a modern tennis star, who will probably be seventeen and speak little English, and who will have attended a course on how to handle herself with – or, more simply, how to handle – the media. The person to ask, if you can get past her agent, is Tatum O'Neal, who is married to John McEnroe and, more importantly, was herself a prodigy, a thoroughbred of the star system. The system prescribes a life of unique enclosure, in which every contact is featherbedded, insulated, mediated. Fixers, helpers, PR people, guys with guns everywhere: these extras are just part of the scenery for the gazelles and snow-leopards of modern tennis, a protected species – priceless specimens – in their bijou theme park. Of course, for the virgin millionairesses there will be life after tennis. But there was no life before it – before they sank into the strange obscurity of stardom.

Vogue, 1988

ST LUCIA

St Lucia – land of contrasts! Patched, mottled, sickly-looking white people sprawl on the fronded patios. Meanwhile, beautiful young black people hover in attendance, making snacks, making drinks, making beds. It is the West Indian reality, obvious and inescapable: the Catering Society. Charming youths with charming nameplates on their breasts (Bently, Regis, Hillary, Justas) fondly anticipate your needs and whims; in the distance, the pretty maids flap and chatter like birds of paradise. With their security guards and pest-controllers, the hotels are townships, fortresses of inflation and entropy. They are protectorates. But what do they protect you from?

The gulf between holidaying and travel is a wide one, and gets wider every day. The big hotels were a part of travel, once upon a time. Yet who uses them now? Who are the five-star people? The prestige of St Lucia is at present undermined by an association with the British package holiday. Some of the older waiters have been known to walk off the set when they saw the people they would have to be waiting on. The typical five-star couple will never stray from the premises, except on some Jolly Roger Buccaneer Bar 'B' Q excursion or chaperoned shopping tour. After lunch it's Limbo Demonstration by Vince; before dinner it's Reggae with Ronnie. Against an attractive spattering of palms, they sit and drink by the pool, frowning at buxom paperbacks or miming along to the canned pop. How can they afford the five-star prices? Are they all betting-shop nabobs or coin-op kings? Have they scrimped and saved for that 'holiday of a lifetime' canvassed in the brochures? After a while I developed the fantasy that they were all highly successful criminals. I moved among train-robbers and jewel-thieves, among industrious burglars. I imagined that an extradition agreement between the UK and the West Indies would, at a stroke, bring the tourist business to its knees.

Cunard La Toc, near the capital of Castries, has recently spent $6 million to 'redefine luxury vacationing in the Caribbean'. This costly redefinition, it turns out, is an attempt to emulate the 'villa' holiday that has effectively preempted the role of the big hotels. The main difference is room service. Anyway, the experience has the authentic torpor of brochure prose. Your suite, ideally designed for comfort, offers plunge pool, personal bar and a panoramic view of the ocean setting. In the restaurants you sample genuine Creole or continental cuisine, together with the island's finest entertainment. Here sports abound: snorkelling, tennis under the sun or the stars, golf on a challenging course cooled by easterly tradewinds. An oasis of natural beauty, created for those who want to 'get away from it all', to relax and unwind . . . In the meantime you wonder whether Paul Theroux would be satisfied by this elegant breachfront resort set in over 100 acres of unspoiled magnificence. Would James Fenton or Bruce Chatwin? Would *V.S. Naipaul*?

Time to travel, or to attempt it. Shrugging off the beach fatigue, bidding farewell to Regis and Bently, my wife and I were driven through Castries to Vigie inter-island airport, to collect our hired car. Castries is described in the brochures as 'bustling'. The people lying flat out on the main street seemed to be questioning this epithet. Also, a not particularly restful-looking spot was signposted 'NO IDLING. NO SLEEPING'. There were, at any rate, two men beneath the awning. One was sleeping. One was only idling. At Vigie, despite all kinds of reservations and confirmations, there was a mood of mission-impossible at the car-hire kiosk. The two uniformed ladies, Denise and Michelle (I would later see Michelle in a Castries bookshop, purchasing a Western), squabbled like love-hate sisters over our voucher, which lay there, scorned, gestured-at. Suddenly I was told that we would need a St Lucian driving licence. I saw myself taking St Lucian driving lessons in Castries, or at least joining a queue in the bustling town hall. My wife and I experienced our first panic attack, our first wave of hotel-need. Regis! Bent*ly*! We told the girls to forget it. We demanded rehotelisation. A few dollars later, though (the licence was no more than a levy), and the car was ours. Having read that there were 'as yet' no traffic lights on the island, I groped for my seatbelt. There was no seatbelt either, as yet. We drove on to Vigie Peninsula – a distance of about fifteen yards – and parked. According to the brochure, the Peninsula 'boasts one of the finest beaches on the island'. The boast was an empty one. It didn't look nearly as nice as the beach at La Toc, where I now saw myself reclining, with Bently hurrying towards me over the smartly raked sands.

But it transpires that St Lucia, for now, is both beautiful and innocuous, like its people. In the small towns (and small towns are the only kind of towns there are here) you sense a strange air of poverty and prettiness. Most of the 'traditional' timber houses, while inconceivably tiny, are primped, made much of, tirelessly adorned. You pull up for a soft drink and find that the Coke and 7-Up signs are there for decoration. The children lining the rural roads are trimly uniformed, healthy-looking, well-ordered – and above all numerous. Dennery and Micoud, the more neglected townships on the island's battered Atlantic coast, lie soaked and puddled in rainy-season boredom. There is much unemployment, and no welfare. People are poor, but nature is rich; it would be hard to starve. The street-wanderers of Micoud regard us with ambiguous levity. We stop for a can of orange juice and are unsmilingly overcharged. Although you wouldn't call them hostile, they are no more friendly than I would feel, if a stranger drove down my street in a car the size of my house.

Even at its most rank and jungly, St Lucia has a kiddy-book harmlessness. The leaves and palms seem greased with baby oil. You expect to encounter Babar the Elephant, smiling tigers, naughty monkeys. Even the real dangers ('minor only!') are Disneyish: poison apples, falling coco-nuts. Swooningly the vegetation topples into the bluer green of the sea. The Pitons, twin larval peaks, look elemental – a land that time forgot – but cinematic too; King Kong would feel at home with them, clambering from one to the other. At the 'unique' drive-in volcano our gaptoothed Rasta led us through the smells and steam of Sulphur Springs. Now here was blackness and menace. The dark cauldrons bubble at 300°F. Fall in there and you would be dead five times over in a couple of seconds. Everywhere the ground fizzed and simmered (busy counter-space in hell's kitchen), containing with effort the fury of its nethers. With its salty gusts, its splattings and eructations, the strangeness and danger of Sulphur Springs underline the absence of such qualities else-where. As we returned to town the locals waved at the car or gazed at us with languid scepticism. In your capacity as a tourist, you feel tolerated as something crucial to the health of the economy. You sometimes feel like a banana trader, a banana planter, a banana expert. Indeed, you sometimes feel like a banana.

Feeling like a banana, however, is not quite what the traveller has in mind. What *does* he have in mind – strange meetings, close encounters, freedom from the usual transac-tions? At Gros Inlet, on the northern tip, we had made our first entrance into the prettiness and poverty: a bluesy bar at noon, the talkative bargirl, the gorgeous baby, the youth wanting a light for his six-paper joint, the spent fifths of rum, a view of the changeless lagoon. On Friday night we returned, as invited, for the weekly Street Party – once a spontaneous carouse, now an island institution. (Spies from gimmick-weary, disco-infested Barbados have visited Gros Inlet, to see how it's done.) This is *rural* carnival: there is no sense of coercion, of enforced high spirits and inter-racial cheer. In the excited miscegenation you gamble and drink and dance. You needn't worry if one of the brothers tries to cut in on you and your wife. The mean-dude persona has yet to arrive, has yet to seep out from untamed Trinidad or feral Jamaica. There is no violence. There is innocence, in fact – and how terrible it would be if one could no longer recognise it. Money is clumsily at work on all this (the high prices, the preposterous odds of the dicing games), and one joins in the informal redistribution of wealth. Money is working on the innocence too; but the people are new at it, for now. Which way will things go?

Late the next morning we began the drive from Castries to Soufrière. It is the worst main road in St Lucia. We were advised to allow at least two hours for the 29 km journey; it might be quicker, they said, to circumnavigate the entire island. The road meanders and so does the car, as you weave between puddle and pothole. Half an hour and a couple of miles later, we were stopped by a young man who stood carelessly in the middle of the road, flagging us down with some show of condescension, as if this was a duty he must reluctantly discharge. Suddenly his head was in the car. After briefly praising his own skills and credentials, he began to give us a guided tour of our destination. He spoke uninterruptably, like a machine-gun. 'The-trop-i-cal-for-est-it-like-a-bot-an-i-cal-garden-it-have-all-kind-of-spec-i men-there-they-got . . .' I can't tell you how long this seemed to go on for. Gravely hungover from the Street Party, my wife and I stared at each other, thinking of the patio, the plunge pool. 'The-St-Lu-cian-par-rot-does-be-fly-ing-a-bout-all-o-ver-the . . .' Every time I urged the car forward he appeared to wriggle in deeper; by now he was practically sitting on my lap. With bulging eyes he told us of the dangers we faced if we went on to Soufrière without him. Youths would harass us, would chase the car, would try to pass themselves off as guides. In other words, we should hire someone like him: otherwise we would have to hire someone like him – and who could possibly want that?

We didn't, but two hours later I was beginning to wonder. I had another head through the window now (bobbing, panting), telling me the same things. And it made no difference that we were travelling at thirty miles an hour.

The sights got seen in the end, under the auspices of Jeremy, one of the boys from Anse Chastenet. After the Diamond Falls he took us to visit his grandparents. A yard zigzagged by chickens, puppies sleeping on the porch, the timber house steaming from the recent rain. We settled in the good-sized room whose balcony gave on to the valley. Out here, in the heat and the wet, you don't fade into the genderlessness of white old age; you stay manly or womanly, to the end. 'I am the oldest driver on the island!' announced the grandfather. I speculated. 'You mean you drove the first car?' 'No! There older drivers than me. But they all dead!' The grandmother swayed and nodded. Now she smiled in judicious assent to the proposition that Bob Marley got cancer because he rolled his *ganja* in newspapers. On the wall were greetings cards, a row of cobwebbed paperbacks, an idealised portrait of JFK at the White House. We went back to the car with gifts of oranges and avocado. We left a packet of cigarettes. And of course Jeremy would be getting an extra big tip.

In the eighteenth century France and England played patball with St Lucia. 'Helen of the West Indies' (beautiful, much fought-over) changed hands a record fourteen times until the English won the Battle of the Saints in 1782. The indigenous Caribs were wiped out; African slaves were imported, then contracted labourers from East India. Universal suffrage in 1951, independence in 1979: the dates are shamingly recent. St Lucia is so young that it makes the visitor feel old (and worn, and sinful). Holidaying is easy here, but travel is harder, more accidental. 'A few more jobs, and it be paradise,' said Jeremy. Like Antigua, St Lucia is on the way up. Capitalism looks on and cracks its knuckles. How far do we want it to go?

The sunsets get a mention, but the brochures undersell the Caribbean sky – its thrilling rapidity of change, the way its brushstrokes seem only a corner of some dreadfully vast canvas, the weird vapours of the grey as the rain moves in off the sea. Often it resembles a thermonuclear explosion, caught in a phase of abstract harmlessness. The skies stimulate travel – mental travel. And unlike the island they will always be there.

Departures, 1986

J. G. BALLARD

England's least conventional writer lives his life against type: in a little Shepperton semi, among the sculpted hedges, the parked Escorts, and the neighbouring houses with their fond appellations – Fairview, Gladecourt. Here in the deep innocuousness of garden suburbia, James Graham Ballard, the glazed SF stylist, the counter-cultural adventurer, the poet-technologian of our modern setting, calmly counts out the days. He has always been a vivid exponent of Flaubert's Law: orderly and regular in his life, savage and original in his art.

'What would you like?' he asked me. 'Scotch? Gin? Vodka?' Actually it sounded more like 'Scotch! Gin! Vodka!' Ballard's voice is strongly musical and resonant, every other word vehemently stressed in the cadences of high sarcasm. It is how I remember him. I'd better explain that I have known Jim Ballard, vaguely, for nearly twenty years. A friend of my father's, he would show up fairly often – affable, excitable, and noisy. He still cuts a pleasantly rounded figure, with his loose shirt and flipflops, his panting laugh. It was eleven o'clock in the morning. There was a time when Ballard used to drink all day (a scotch every hour, starting at nine); postponing that first drink until six in the evening was, he says, an epic battle ('It was like the Battle of Stalingrad'). But he can't take it any more, and neither can I. So he brought coffee to the dusty back room.

'What you see here is a vacuum. Until quite recently it was a happy family house. All these French *Crash*-freaks used to come out here to see me, expecting a miasma of child-molestation and drug-abuse.' (*Crash* was a big hit in France, perhaps because of the Baudelairean waywardness of its theme: the sexuality of the road accident.) 'What they found was a suburban house full of kids and their friends, with a big dog, and me writing a short story in the middle of it all.' Ballard's wife died of pneumonia twenty years ago 'almost to the day', suddenly and bafflingly, during a family holiday in Spain. He raised the three children himself. They're grown up now, all of them thriving professionals. One imagines Ballard as a profoundly tolerant and pragmatic father. None of his children has read a word of his stuff, which delights him. 'No! None of them! Not a *word*. Why should they? They know me well enough as it is. It's a very intimate experience, reading a book. You're as close as you get to anyone – except in bed. No, closer.'

Ballard has already had an unprecedented success with his new novel, *Empire of the Sun*, and now his life is suddenly open to change. That success has been long delayed, and fully deserved; but Ballard doubts whether he can be bothered to gentrify himself at this stage. 'It's very difficult to remythologise one's life. You tell yourself these tales of gold, to sustain yourself, to inspire this one-man team. You need a new set of dreams, landscapes, forests. And what happens? I just sit with a whisky and soda, watching *The Rockford Files*.'

It is a fairly routine irony that *Empire*, as he calls it, is in some ways the most conventional novel that J.G. Ballard has ever produced. Based on his childhood experience as a detainee in Shanghai, it is a survival story, harshly naturalistic, with little of the wicked spin that Ballard usually imparts to time and space. And yet it is also thoroughly Ballardian, a drama of extremity and isolation played out against an 'inverted landscape' which, for all its terror, attracts and compels the actors who move within it. *Empire of the Sun* uses the familiar abstract imagery, the unmistakable lilts ('The Abandoned Aerodrome', 'The Cemetery Garden', 'The Terrible City' are typical chapter headings), and the childlike amorality we find in all Ballard's work. Vanished, ruined, forgotten, disused, drowned, drained – these are the key-words of his lexicon; it is as if, in his landscapes, human life has gone, passed through, absented itself, leaving only icons and totems for the next wanderers to interpret. The new novel shines a light back through Ballard's entire corpus, and in the end the circle is satisfyingly complete. The trauma of Shanghai determined his course as a writer. And now, in *Empire of the Sun*, he gives shape to what shaped him.

'How closely does the book follow your own experience?' I asked him. 'This is what everyone will want to know.'

'Ah, God. Well look. I'm the same age as my hero, I was born in Shanghai as he was, lived in that big house as he did. I *was* interned in that camp but I wasn't separated from my parents – as Jim is in the book. The vast body of Jim's experiences are invented, though psychologically true. You fictionalise to reach the truth ... I've always wanted to write a book about the war and I've always put it off. Oh, I'll do it *next*. Three years ago I reached fifty and felt that the memory might begin to fade. Originally I took it for granted that I would have an adult central character. A doctor, something of this sort. But I couldn't get into the book, nothing came alive, despite the big emotional charge that was waiting, ready to go off, inside my head. Then I thought, what about a thirteen-year-old, someone my age? And – boom! – the cannon went off. I knew it was the only way I could write it. Because of course I don't have the benefit of hindsight. I have no adult response to that experience and couldn't imagine one.'

Later, when I replayed the tape of this interview, Ballard's voice was eerily underscored by two distinct sound-effects: the premonitory surge of airliners as they banked for Heathrow; and the poppings and squawkings of Ballard's swivel chair. He writhed as he talked, partly through natural restiveness, and partly through the difficulty of recalling these times. The memories cannot be assimilated, or purged.

'In the book, I played it all *down*. The beating to death of the rickshaw coolie, for instance – I wasn't a hundred yards away when that happened, I was ten feet away. No, they were very violent times. Executions, public stranglings, disbanded puppet soldiers wandering about, starving armies. You'd have to go to Uganda during the last days of Idi Amin, or the Congo during the civil war, or Cambodia, perhaps, to get some idea of what life was like for the ordinary Chinese. Shanghai was a huge city. Anything could happen. If you fainted in the street from hunger or illness ... you just died where you lay. When I went to school every morning – with chauffeur and governess, to prevent kidnap attempts – I would see a body every two hundred yards. They were just lying all over the place. People brought up in the social democracies of Western Europe have no idea of this kind of savagery. No they don't, actually, and it's a good thing that they don't.'

In 1946, aged fifteen, Ballard sailed to the exotic land that he had only heard and read about: England. 'The culture shock is still with me,' he says. 'I was genuinely stunned. I wasn't prepared for the latitude. The angle of the light, almost as much as the ambient temperature, plays a vital part in one's responses, as if one has a sextant in one's head. I wasn't prepared for the greyness, the harshness of the light, the small, exhausted, shattered community, the white faces, the closed nature of English life. I wasn't prepared for the "furniture" of England. I remember looking down from the ship at Southampton, seeing the little houses and these black perambulators like mobile coal-scuttles. These were English *cars*. I was used to Packards and Cadillacs. It flummoxed me to think that people drove *around* in these things.'

He lived with his grandparents and attended the Lees School in Cambridge – 'just like the camp, only the food was worse'. His mother returned to Shanghai to rejoin her husband, who had stayed on. In 1949 Ballard Sr was put on trial for infringements of the revolutionary code. 'But he knew his Marx and Engels, and talked his way out of it.' Soon afterwards the Ballards returned to England for good. 'They were drained by their experience in the camp. Their view of it was much more sombre than mine. They didn't want to talk about it. Fortunately my sister remembers nothing. She was just too young.'

And so began Ballard's worldly 'career'. But of course he was one of life's surrealists – a natural misfit. He read medicine at King's College, Cambridge. He was interested in Freud, Sartre, Camus: 'My fellow undergraduates hadn't heard of them. Neither had the *dons*.' Thrown out of King's, he read English at London. Thrown out of London, he became a trainee pilot in the RCAF. Thrown out of the RCAF, he ... 'The only thing I wasn't thrown out of was advertising. After I'd been in advertising for a while, I suddenly realised that I hadn't been thrown out of it.' What did this tell him about advertising? 'It told me *run don't walk*. I threw myself out.'

In 1955 Ballard stopped reading SF and started writing it. His early, 'hard' SF stories were as brilliantly imagined and executed as anything in the genre – but it soon became clear that Ballard was *sui generis*, and that SF wouldn't hold him for long. His galaxy was the planet Earth, his terrain that of '*inner* space'. During a three-week summer holiday he wrote *The Wind from Nowhere*. In this novel, since disowned by its author, a global hurricane accelerates until the atmosphere consists of a lateral avalanche. Established as a full-time writer, Ballard proceeded, in his next three books, to subject the planet to death by water, dehydration and mineralisation, but these were *psychological* disaster stories, their landscapes internal as well as actual. At the end of *The Drowned World* the hero heads south, to embrace the terminal heat and insanity of the swamped jungles. 'The American publisher said, "We have a problem with the ending. It's too negative. Couldn't we have him heading *north*?" But it's a *happy* ending. South is where he *wants* to go. Further. Deeper. South!'

The vein of tranced perversity in Ballard's writing found its limits in the late Sixties and early Seventies, with his hard-edge, concrete-and-steel period, an exploration of high-tech atavism, of wound-profiles and sex-deaths, neatly summed up in the first title of the phase, *The Atrocity Exhibition*. *Highrise* begins as follows: 'Later, as he sat on his balcony eating the dog, Dr Robert Laing reflected on the unusual events . . .' The first editor who read *Crash* said in her report: 'The author of this book is beyond psychiatric help.' Ballard was thrilled. 'To me this meant total artistic success. Actually, even I was rather startled when I saw the proofs. But the pornography was used for serious purposes – cautionary purposes.'

'Does the new book signal the end of your hard-edge phase?'

'It probably signals the end of *everything*,' said Ballard contentedly. By now we were having a pub lunch on the riverbank, among the gulls, the launches, the cheerful middle-management of Shepperton. In a more recent novel, *The Unlimited Dream Company*, Ballard imagines the arrival of a sexual messiah who transforms Shepperton into an apocalyptic theme park, igniting all the fantasies of ordinary minds. Like everything he writes, the book is faintly ludicrous, bizarrely logical and deeply haunting. In summer, Ballard finds Shepperton 'lunar and abstract'. I don't see it – but I agree that Ballard has no reason to leave the place. He can look into its ordered streets, its 'airport architecture and consumer landscape', and see anything he likes.

'You seem to be in pretty good nick,' I said, 'considering what you went through.'

'Those were hard times. Don't be deceived by my friend here,' he said, patting his belly. 'By the end of the war the food had pretty well dried up. The Japs could hardly feed *themselves*. Why should they bother about an enclave of Allied detainees? Why? These are the realities. We ate cracked wheat, warehouse scrapings, weevils. You'd shift the weevils to the side and eat them last. I often had three rings of them on the edge of my plate.'

'What do they taste of?'

'They don't taste of anything, funnily enough. Absolutely nothing. We had to eat them for the protein. I remember those years in the camp as a time of high interest and activity. Some of the prisoners behaved with great steadfastness. Most were withdrawn and listless. A few were scrimshankers, petty thieves, or open collaborators with the Japanese. But you'd expect that. I was happy there. It was like having a huge slum family.'

Ballard didn't see as much of the war as his alter ego in the novel. He didn't see the sinking of the *Petrel* on the Shanghai Bund. He didn't see the light in the sky after Hiroshima and Nagasaki (as if God was taking photographs of the end of the world). But he saw every form of human extremity by the time he was thirteen. As a result, nothing can surprise or startle him — except his own fictions. It occurred to me that if I had turned up for the interview three days late with a carload of drunken hitch-hikers, Ballard would not have been displeased, far less disconcerted. He would have said, 'Scotch! Gin! Vodka!' He is a writer for whom anything is possible, as many new readers will soon discover. The way ahead now looks intriguingly unresolved; but we can safely say that J.G. Ballard will go too far — in all directions.

Observer, 1984

CHESS: KASPAROV *v.* KARPOV

The World Chess Championship opens tomorrow in the usual atmosphere of vendetta, scurrility, machination and counterploy. Unquestionably chess is 'the most beautiful game'. Why, then, does it always turn ugly? The principals have been in town for some time. They enjoy the trappings of movie-stars yet they live like ascetics. Hungrily the young Champion works out in the gym and on the football field – even his seconds have been off alcohol for weeks – and continues his campaign against 'the chess mafia'. Meanwhile the Challenger broods and meditates, rebuilding his game, his confidence, and his tattered image. On paper, or on smudged photoprint, it looks like Diego Maradona versus Alex Higgins. Grimly they square up for their strange board meeting. What, exactly, are these characters up to? What are they playing at?

To begin with, Kasparov and Karpov are playing the foremost game of pure skill yet devised by the human mind, a game that is in fact beyond the scope of the human mind, well beyond it, an unmasterable game. Monitored by millions, they are playing this game at a level that they alone can comprehend. Towards the end of some of the games in their last match, world-famous Grandmasters had no idea who was winning. Only in the slow motion of analysis do the lines become clear. To take an analogy from another sport (of which we will need plenty), it is as if Becker and Courier are hitting so hard that not even Connors, craning forward in the front row, can see the ball.

Let us take an average experience of chess. You master the moves, start to play frequently, buy a book or two, learn some ground-rules, some openings, develop a little 'vocabulary', a bit of 'pattern recognition' . . . After a while you notice that you have stopped improving. Your progress, so far, has felt like a slow ascent along rising ground; then you pause, look up, and see a cliff face almost beyond the dimensions of the globe, whose crest is merely a false summit, itself the first of many.

Quickly you relapse into the kind of player who knows one opening to a depth of three moves, who flounders into the middle game hoping for errors more egregious than his own. That is the amateur game: an uninterrupted exchange of howlers. You aren't any good. And the man who always beats you in the pub or the cafe isn't any good. And the man who always beats him in the clubhouse isn't any good. And the man who always beats the man who always beats the man who always beats *him* may just be starting to get somewhere.

Nowhere in sport, perhaps nowhere in human activity, is the gap between the tryer and the expert so astronomical. Oh, I have thrown 180 at darts – twice in a lifetime. On the snooker table I have brought off violent pots that would have jerked them to their feet in the Sheffield Crucible. As for tennis, I need hardly hype my crosscourt backhand 'dink', which is so widely feared in the parks of North Kensington. But my chances of a chess brilliancy are the 'chances' of a lab chimp and a typewriter producing *King Lear*. Even at the most rarefied level, though, chess has a robust universality. The two Ks start a tournament tomorrow, but they will also be starting something else: scores are to be settled, grudges are to be purged. Openly and avowedly, noisily and pridefully, they will be hunting each other's blood. That we *can* understand.

*

Until 1972 the triennial World Championships were quiet affairs – or at any rate Soviet affairs. Then Bobby Fischer emerged, and the fortress of Soviet supremacy felt the challenge of American 'brashness': the histrionic gamesmanship of the stand-off and stalk-out, the tantrum and the sulk. Fischer himself seemed to sense a decline, an air of *ubi sunt?* 'When it was a game played by aristocrats it had more like you know dignity to it.' In retrospect, shaded from the glare of his chess, we can see Fischer as the classic *idiot savant*; he resembles the mental-home chronic who, by some twist of the circuitry, can do cube roots in his head. Fischer had the highest Elo rating – this is the chess computer – of all time. With his contempt for women, his glorification of expensive clothes and what he called 'class' (as in 'he doesn't have any class'), his antisemitism, and his cornball paranoia, Fischer shows that supreme chess genius can ally itself with the paltriest human material.

By 1975 Fischer had gone mad, or gone madder; he was, in any event, too mad to face the defence of his title. (It is said that he suffered a 'panic-fright' at his own achievement.) Anatoly Karpov was thus promoted by default; and the next two Championships took their tenor from the situation and temperament of the challenger, Viktor Korchnoi: Viktor the Terrible, the Leningrad Lip. Disciplined for unsoundness – i.e., near-pauperised for sins of candour – Korchnoi had defected in 1976. He was then boycotted by Soviet players, and his wife and son were refused permission to emigrate. Both these actions were designed not just to punish Korchnoi's treachery but to weaken his game. In his two Championship matches with Karpov – 1978 and 1981 – Korchnoi showed symptoms of what might be called *displaced* paranoia: he *was* being persecuted, but not by hexed swivel-chairs, colour-coded yoghurts, KGB hypnotists evil-eyeing him from the stalls. Karpov, the 'model Soviet', sat through it all, glazed and devout, like a

Futurist poster. And after his victory he obediently cabled Brezhnev, as Botvinnik had cabled Stalin in 1936 ('Dear beloved teacher and leader . . .').

Just before the 1978 Championship I interviewed Korchnoi in London, at the Savoy. At one point, twisting powerfully in his chair, he fell silent, and then grew dreamy. With some wistfulness he confessed that he despaired of ever bringing home, to people in the West, the crawling sliminess, the full squidgy horror, of Anatoly Karpov. 'You know, in Russia we have a fish', he said, 'called a *karp*. A disgusting fish. You wouldn't eat it. That's what Karpov *is*.' I said, 'We've got that fish too. Called a *carp*.' Korchnoi looked startled. 'You have? . . . Good! Good!'

Already, and perhaps over-vividly, Korchnoi sensed that Karpov would not be allowed to lose. The 1978 match was painfully close. Karpov won 6–5; Korchnoi claimed illegal conditions (that hypnotist had returned for the last game) and started court proceedings in Amsterdam; by 1979 Korchnoi's son Igor was in a labour camp. When the players met again three years later, *Tass* was calling Korchnoi a 'calculating huckster', the deserter of his wife and child, whom he hoped never to see again. Korchnoi felt these vast animosities *at the table* – and saw Karpov as their instrument ('Stop squirming in your damn seat, you little worm'). Korchnoi was deflected, tipped over; and in the end he spooked himself.

Karpov wasn't taken to the edge in 1981. But he was taken there in 1984, by Gary Kasparov; and the outcome was the most drastic scandal in the history of the game. Fallout from that 'accident' still poisons the current encounter.

Stressful tales of venue-fixing, spy-planting, rule-bending – or cheating, if you prefer. The outsider, who thinks that chess is pure and cerebral, tends to be shocked by such suggestions. But the insider is not shocked, because he knows that chess, like the human brain, is partly reptilian. This is the game of pins and pincers, of forks and skewers; this is the game of the *spite check* and the *shame mate*. Clearly these psychodramas wouldn't keep happening unless something about the game encouraged them. If, tomorrow afternoon, the World Champion were playing his twin brother, his mirror image, the air between them would still be crackling.

How do you cheat at chess? It strikes one as a contradiction, like cheating at the violin. One of the excruciations of chess is its autonomy; there are no variables; there is no one and nothing to *blame*. Snooker is whisperingly called 'chess with balls' but in chess there is no run of the green ('Dear oh dear, things just aren't going Anatoly Yevgenyevich's way out there'). In tennis you can blame the bounce, the tape, the wind, the glare, the racket, the shoelaces. Even the lumpen simplicity of darts features the loathed 'bounce-outs'. An Argy fullback may break your legs, help you up by tugging on the hairs of your arms, and then, as you start to protest, hawk in your mouth. Now that's cheating. But how do you cheat at chess?

'Sit your opponent with the sun in his eyes,' said Ruy Lopez, who flourished in the sixteenth century. It would seem that cheating at chess is as old as the game; no doubt the languid nawabs and caliphs of sixth-century Asia were kicking each other's shins beneath the table. Alekhine used to cosset his Siamese cats on the board before big games, on the off-chance that his opponent might harbour an allergy. During lightning play, 'chessers' who find themselves a rook down have been known to castle with a piece from the neighbouring board. Nimzowitsch used to smoke an especially noxious cigar. There are further stories of squashed tomatoes, doctor's bleep-gadgets, and eye-contact techniques in the sexual-harassment line.

In his 1977 qualifying match with Korchnoi, Boris Spassky arranged for his 'box' – a curtained booth on the stage, to which the player occasionally retreats – to be positioned *behind* his opponent's chair; and there he lurked, emerging only to make his moves. When he did appear he sported a dazzling sun-visor. It doesn't sound particularly outrageous, but it worked. Korchnoi was on the verge of emotional collapse and threw away four games in a row. He recovered, and won. The intriguing fact is that Spassky, the white knight of Reykjavik, Fischer's courtly and long-suffering victim, had switched colours. Integrity, it appeared, was an anachronism, or an aberration. Fischer was an innovator on the board, but perhaps his main gift to the game was the institutionalising of bad behaviour. This was 'professionalism'. From then on, everyone was playing black.

The Moscow fiasco of 1984 was of a new order of irregularity. Probably domestic Soviet chess has seen greater and more humourless injustices (the reversal of results because of 'faulty' clocks, and so on); but you can't do this sort of thing when the world is watching. Chess insiders *were* shocked by Moscow. Even Bobby Fischer must have raised a hand to check that his wallet was still in place.

During the early games Kasparov showed his only temperamental weakness as a player: hunger. He played with arrogant greed and was soon trailing 0–4 (the winner being the first man to six, with draws not counting). A little later he was trailing 0–5: an abysmal margin. No breather or pep-talk, no pint of lager is going to bring a chess-player back from that kind of deficit, that kind of demonstration. But now Kasparov formulated a remarkable and ruthless strategy. He started to draw, game after game, dull, spoiling, inexorable. His first idea was, simply, to exhaust Karpov, to break Karpov's health. His second idea was to learn how to play him. This was a task that he had skimped in preparation; he was now doing his revision on the board. At twenty-one Kasparov was already a great player. But he was becoming a greater one, in front of Karpov's eyes.

And Kasparov had something else. 'Playing a game against Kasparov is like playing three games against anybody else,' said the British GM Tony Miles, fresh from a 5½–½ drubbing by Kasparov in Basel. 'It's *very* hard to put into words. There are no quiet moves, no simple positions. Everything is *sharp*. But mainly it's his presence. You're constantly aware of his strength, his impatience. He drains you.' Playing a game of high-level chess has been compared to sitting a two-day exam. For Karpov in Moscow, it was five months of Finals.

After 46 games the score was 5–1 to Karpov, with 40 draws. Karpov had had no victory for 21 games. And he had lost 22 pounds. Then Kasparov won game 47; and game 48. 'It was extraordinary,' said a chess writer, and International Master, who covered the match. 'We began in September with great drama as Karpov took his lead. On November 24 he stopped winning. Then – a winter of draws. The band of analysts was dwindling. The press room was like a bunker. Suddenly there were rumours about Karpov's health, and you could feel the political pressures. There were "technical" time-outs – for instance, eight days to change venues. There were meetings with contacts on street corners. Journalists wondered whether they were being followed. Everybody knew that Karpov was in a de luxe private clinic, suffering from exhaustion.' After Kasparov's second straight victory the President of FIDE flew from Dubai to Moscow and ended the match. A new word entered the language: FIDEgate.

It is illuminating to recast the Moscow Championship as a set of tennis, the final set of an imaginary Supergrandslam. The Champion is serving for the title at 5–0. After a game involving 100 deuces, his serve is broken. The next game goes to 300 deuces. By this time the Champion is limping, wincing, howling with fatigue. The Challenger wins the seventh game, and wins the eighth with ease. The umpire now decides that everyone has had enough. 'I wouldn't like to be 3–5 down to Karpov *on his death bed*,' said Nigel Short, the world No. 9. 'People say he looks weedy, but mentally he's very, very tough.' At this stage, however, Karpov was playing like a man with a nagging brain injury: and it is quite clear that

Kasparov sensed victory. The decision still incenses him. For Kasparov it is as if, during an endless rally, with the crowd gasping and shrieking, the Champion's weak baseline lob has gone up, the Challenger ravenously awaits it at the net – and the umpire extends a long hand from his perch, snatching the ball from the air.

The umpire is, of course, Mr Florencio Campomanes, President of FIDE. There is almost something captivating, something blithely Chaucerian, about Campo, with his air of farcical unreliability. If there is no smoke without fire, then Campomanes is a veritable Vesuvius, fizzing and burping with partiality and bad faith. You feel that the world of chess is too small for his talents: he ought to be in arms dealing, or nuclear proliferation.

A Philippino, a one-time Garcia man and now a follower of Marcos (with whom he is said to have many interests in common), Campo was elected to the Presidency in 1982, on 'the Third World ticket'. The extent to which he dominates FIDE is made clear by its recent resolution 'thanking him for his initiative' in aborting the Moscow match, a decision so reviled by the world press that even the *Sun* joined the chorus (RED KING OF CHESS SET TO CRACK UP). 1986 is election year, and Campo has introduced a new 'tax on draws', by which every drawn game diverts 1 per cent of the purse to Campo's chess-development programme in the Third World. Kasparov cleverly preempted the ploy by donating his share of the winnings to the Chernobyl relief fund. Karpov was obliged to follow suit.

Without going too deeply into the intrigues, one can simply say that Campo disports himself like a Third World politician. 'When I ask President Marcos for two million dollars, at worst he wants to know whether he should bring the money straight away or whether I can wait for a cheque.' There are many stories of his intimidation of journalists (threats of denying visas, etc.) and his general admiration for Marcosian strong-arming. Ever since the Moscow row, Campo has cobbled together a defence of this 'unpopular decision' by directing counter-conspiracy charges at 'a small band of journalists' led by Raymond Keene ('skilful', 'cunning', 'forked tongue'). This is the tone of a recent FIDE newsletter, from the disinterested pen of Casto P. Abundo:

> It is no surprise that Keene lies in his book ... in an obvious attempt to *wash his hands* of the affair. Now, in shameless *hypocrisy*, he charges 'incorrect decisions by the President'.

Campo's main adversary, however, is not Raymond Keene. Campo's main adversary is far more centrally placed. He is Gary Kasparov.

Why did Campo do it? Possibly he bowed to pressure from the Soviet Chess Federation, whose officials have a stake in Karpov. But then Campo has a stake in him too. All these careers and ascendancies are interlinked. 'You can't expect to please everybody, or even anybody,' said Campo, with astounding serenity, among the hoots and guffaws of the Moscow press conference. Campo didn't please anybody. Karpov looked sick, up on the podium with the glozing Campo, he looked morally queasy. Soon afterwards he claimed that his 'sports and public reputation' had been 'blasted'. 'By his decision,' Spassky has said, 'Karpomanes' had 'actually destroyed Karpov'.

During the rematch in 1985 Karpov's image took a further tousling. *Der Spiegel* accused him of diverting $½ million through a German agent, who had absconded with the money and was now wanted by the police. It was further claimed that Campo was trying to retrieve the money on Karpov's behalf. The crisis was spectacularly unwelcome. But by this stage, anyway, Kasparov had the whole world behind him. To stamping feet, to cries of 'Gary! Gary!', he surged to victory on a crest of rectitude. Youth, aggression, justice! Only the Chess Federation Karpovites were left muttering in the press room. 'There is nothing we can do,' they said. 'There is nothing we can do.'

So things will stand when White pushes his first pawn tomorrow afternoon. And the question remains: what are they up to? What of the chess itself, the eerie engagement with the 32 pieces and the 64 squares?

'Their styles are so different,' says Tony Miles, 'you can't even compare them. Kasparov is the perfectionist: he analyses to infinity. He likes to establish a tree of complications, say a five-move line with six alternatives per move. He thrives on complexity. You can't out-analyse him. You'll get blasted out of sight. Karpov is more practical and classical, more of an artist in his way. He likes straightforward positions with no forcing continuations. He makes intuitive general assessments and consolidates small advantages. Then he makes them pinch.'

And if you raise your eyes from the board? 'When I played Karpov,' says Nigel Short, 'it took me about half an hour to get over my awe at playing the World Champion. Then it was business as usual, just another game. With Kasparov – it's hard to describe. I found his presence uniquely disturbing. I have never faced such an intense player, never felt such energy and concentration, such will and desire burning across the board at me.'

One can well imagine the exhaustion of playing Kasparov. Watching him do a ten-minute spot on a chat show is exhausting enough. The galvanic giggling, the agitation, the expressiveness: he doesn't sit on his chair – he hovers on it. Recently Kasparov beat ten computers simultaneously, blindfolded. How flattering for the species. There are over 288 billion possibilities through the fourth move (by White *and* Black). Yet the mark of a good chessplayer is not how many moves he considers but how few – as Karpov knows.

Although the betting is on Kasparov, some of the emotional money is tending back towards Karpov, the saddened swat with the Baskerville eyes.

'Chess is like life,' said Spassky. 'Chess *is* life,' said Fischer, who paid the penalty for his obvious mistake. Chess has been called an art, a science and a sport. It can't be an art, because every brilliancy depends on the fuddled collusion of the opponent: even 'the Immortal Game' would have died the death if Black had had his wits about him. It can't be a science, because, simply, it has no content: the singularity of chess is not its readiness but its refusal to serve as a matrix for anything else. And it can't be a sport, not quite, because it is both infinite and precise; every game is recoverable; every game can be re-experienced through the markings on a page. 'It's *definitely* not an art,' said Nigel Short. 'If I have the choice between a beautiful combination and a mundane way of wrapping up the game, then I'll wrap up the game. You must win. It's not an art. It's a fight. It's a fight.'

Observer, 1986

THE ROLLING STONES AT
EARLS COURT

Throughout the entire course of my visit to the first of the Rolling Stones concerts at Earls Court Arena last Friday night, I did not get my eyes spooned out, my teeth stomped in, or my head kicked off. Neither was I deafened, trampled, robbed or maimed. For these small highpoints in an otherwise rather disappointing evening, I hereby give laconic thanks.

Invited to appear promptly for the eight o'clock concert (people who arrived as late as 8.15, one gathered, would be 'turned away'), we joined the panting, aromatic multitude at 7.30 on the hotdog-strewn steps of the Earls Court building. The multitude was also, apparently, a queue: it contracted like a dying amoeba as the semi-circular throng oozed through the doors. Once inside, panic and claustrophobia jockeyed routinely for one's attention; for every hundred-weight of humanity that surged through the doors, a tardy click could be heard, somewhere in the distance, every twenty seconds or so, as the ticketed trickle inched past the two or three turnstiles. Some people fainted, or were haggardly led to the pockets of air at the front of the queue. In the high tradition of all the best rock concerts, you were treated as if you had come to sate some vile addiction rather than simply to exchange cash for entertainment. Beyond the crush at the turnstiles, fans and policemen could be glimpsed moving about in relative freedom. A mere half an hour later, we joined them.

The ante-hall of the Earls Court Arena was a Brobding-nagian underground carpark of remote and overcrowded bars, sweet shops and dirty hot-drinks machines. Normally a token homogeneity obtains at the average rock concert: David Bowie fans all look and behave like David Bowie, Bryan Ferry fans all look and behave like Bryan Ferry etc. But everyone is a Stones fan. On the concrete safari from the turnstiles to the concert area I was impartially menaced by sick junkies, posh druggies, junior droogs, fat suburbanite tikes (who half-tried to lure away the two girls I diffidently squired), elderly men in suits, platformed teenagers – and, I suppose, people like myself, who had quite liked the Stones a few years ago, who had somehow been given or got hold of tickets, and who were now wondering why they weren't somewhere else.

We entered the auditorium. Imagine a hot, dark, sealed football stadium – with people massed on the pitch as well as in the stands. Our tickets said row 'C' (hence the pack of Malleable Muffler Earplugs I had purchased on the way to the show). A T-shirted attendant appeared, frowned at our tickets, scratched his head, and took out a map. In the distance, about 3,000 fans away, a lone ginger-bearded policeman rocked on his heels. Perfect, perfect, I couldn't feel more secure. Our seats were as far away as they could possibly be from the bay through which we had entered, about 150 yards to the right of the podium. We gained them, and sat.

Meanwhile a bad supporting group called the Meters had started up – bad supporting groups being the conventional rock-concert means of (i) sapping your initial high spirits, and of (ii) paving the way for mass hysteria when the star attraction arrives. A coloured New Orleans group, the Meters gave a good indication of what was to come: their steely clatter made short work of what are laughingly known as the 'acoustics' of the venue, sending a torrential wall of sound boomeranging from one corner of the auditorium to the other. Once you were in your seat, too, the real proportions of the place could be gingerly absorbed. As in the Hells of Blake and Doré, the vaultfuls of shadowy supplicants stretch up high into the middle air; along the cornice level are squares of yellow light, where silhouettes of angular figures lean and hover. The Meters packed up their set. People got ready to be hysterical. As quivering roadies groped and blinked about on the stage, I fondled my earplugs. After the usual courteous delay – barely twenty minutes – we were off.

To a 'Dawn of Man'-type prelude from some undisclosed source, the huge leek-shaped tube behind the original stage started to unpeel in segments – and there, perched high on the tip of one of the descending petals, was the awful Mick himself. The stage flattened bouncily out, Mick began jumping up and down on the end of it, and the whopping chords of *Honky Tonk Woman* cracked out into the darkness. Immediately, as is the way at rock concerts, everyone got to their feet. I assume that the first few people to stand up do so out of genuine excitement; the rest do so because they can't see if they don't. People who prefer not to stand up get angry with people who do, and luckily I had a particularly strident and foul-mouthed lot of people behind me to yell at and threaten the lot of people in front of me, who had stood up but soon sat down again. (I turned to see a clump of hate-contorted faces that kept me safely strapped to my seat throughout.)

I was glad I could see the stage, unimpressive though it was from my vantage – and it must have been a flea-circus to the thousands further back. Glad, because it soon became clear that the evening would offer nothing to gratify even the rudest ear. Mick's voice came over as a strangled, monotone holler; the instruments weren't distinguishable from one another; the two percussion men (Watts plus a grinning bongoist) merely provided a basic fuzz on the general cataract of sound. And this wasn't, as they say, just me: a dozen bars of *Get off my Cloud*, easily identifiable on record, passed without comment from the audience, and only when Mick started up did the crowd click, granting the applause traditionally accorded to an ex-number one. Indicatively, too, the two or three new Jagger-Richards creations left the fans embarrassingly cold; only the songs already embossed on the responses could be recreated by the frenzied approximations from the stage. No, it was all too big; there were too many people; you couldn't respond to the music because it couldn't respond to you.

Visually, though, one got some of the point of it – or some of the point of Mick. This well-put-together, vitamin-packed unit of a human being does not really dance any more: it's simply that his head, his shoulders, his pelvis, both his arms, both his legs, both his huge feet and both his buttocks are wriggling, at great speed, independently, all the time. When at one point Mick abruptly fell over, for instance, you couldn't tell whether or not he had meant to; it didn't particularly matter, but you couldn't tell. And when he swung out on a cable over the adoring stalls, I wondered how he could contain his galvanic twitching long enough to stay attached to the rope. No question: Mick is, without a doubt, one of our least sedentary millionaires.

Such energy communicates itself, even to a half-engaged audience. 'My head is really scrambled,' a nearby fan sobbed after *Midnight Rambler*. 'Want some Kit-Kat?' droned another lugubriously to his girlfriend after the same song. But the more vehemently eager-to-be-pleased sections of the audience, having set their hearts on losing their heads, now began to behave as if they actually had. Jumping up and down was the favourite form this activity took, and soon everyone near me was doing it, despite the vicious denunciations from further behind. '*Are you feeling good?*' Mick demanded. 'ARE YOU FEELING GOOD?' No, not at all, I thought, deciding to leave. And having staggered through the forsaken halls into the Earls Court Road, I was obscurely relieved to find that the world hadn't gone mad in my absence. Perhaps I'm too old for this sort of thing now – too old to buy fruitless discomfort at £1 an hour. I shouldn't have gone. I'm never going again.

New Statesman, 1976

PHANTOM OF THE OPERA: THE
REPUBLICANS IN 1988

The Republican Convention is history now, and history didn't look too good down in New Orleans, sapped and battered by eight years of Ronald Reagan. Before I develop that thought, though, I feel it's high time I said a few words about my family. I have a wife and two little boys. Over here to cover the Convention, I happened to miss them very much. Why, just before I left, my three-year-old gazed up at me with those big blue eyes of his and said I was the best daddy in the whole world. My wife and I love our boys. And they love us. Okay?

On closing night it looked like a day-care centre up there on the podium, with the three junior Quayles and Bush's great troupe of grandchildren. They all romped and cuddled among the balloons and spangled confetti. (And what do balloons remind you of? How tall are the people you know who like balloons?) Candidates can't keep their hands off the little ones when they're in public, perhaps because it's the only time they ever see them. The Quayles' first task the next morning, I heard, was to hire someone to mind the kids for three months. This childish spectacle at the Superdome provided a new twist on a familiar image: here were politicians kissing their own babies.

Earlier that evening I was in the Media Lounge eating

complimentary popcorn and watching the TV monitor. One half of the screen was occupied by a white-haired lady wearing four tiers of pearls and an expression of wry indulgence: the other half showed schoolchildren in slow motion, raising their hands to teacher.

A journalist came up behind me and said, 'What's this?'

'It's an ad for Barbara Bush.'

'Jesus Christ, what's going *on* around here?'

Where has he been? Reagan's is a style-setting adminis- tration, and there has been trickle-down. Nowadays, when Chris Evert gets a regular boyfriend, the first thing she does is make an ad about it. On *The Dating Game* the dude will report that his new friend is 'open' and 'communicative' – 'and I admire those skills'. Who is the role model of the nascent media-coaching industry? Forces are working on the American self. Thirty-five-year-olds have spent half their adult lives in the Reagan Era. This has gone on long enough.

'George Bush,' Barbara confided to the camera, and to the cameramen and lighting men and sound men and media consultants who were crouched around her at the time, was 'as strong, decent, and caring as America herself'. She had loved 'this extraordinarily special man', she went on, 'from the moment I laid eyes on him'. Early in the election year the Vice-President had decided that the time was right to tell the public about the death of his first daughter. Now here was Barbara with her side of it, revealing how George's strength ('He held me in his arms') had eventually sustained her. It all seemed to shore up the claim of the Texas delegation which hailed George Bush as 'the best father in America'.

Of course, you feel a bit of a brute going on about all this stuff. But journalists *are* brutalised by modern Conventions – by these four-day ads for the Party. 'This isn't a very interesting Convention so far. It is so well run that there aren't even any lost kids.' That was John Steinbeck in 1956. Dressed in eye-hurting orange blazers,

Uncle Sam suits, and baseball outfits, the pink elephants of the GOP talk about shopping and eating and how the Giants did against the Dodgers. At this corporate outing there was no danger of any politics coming your way, though there was always the possibility of scandal. In fact the media was in for a nice surprise: it would soon be propitiated by the blood of J. Danforth Quayle. But until that story broke – and Quayle broke with it – we took our cue from the piety on display and lapsed into a mood of ghoulish cynicism.

First you inspect the concourse leading to the burger-shaped Superdome and all the conventional Convention junk, with its air of commercial passion and improvisational verve. GO Pork Rinds – They're Republickin' Good. A blizzard of T-shirts and badges and bumper stickers. Don't Du-Ca-Ca on the USA. At one table someone is hawking Oliver North videos. Across the way are life-size cutouts of Reagan and Bush, and beyond them, an outsize mannequin of Reagan as Rambo (or 'Ronbo', as the British tabloids have it): the seventy-seven-year-old sex object is stripped to the waist, a cartridge belt athwart his slabbed chest, and with a giant weapon in his fists. Ronbo is eight feet tall. The slogans and buzz-phrases cruelly harp on the stature gap. Beware of Greeks Wearing Lifts. His Only Platform Is Down in His Shoes. Where oh where is the Democrat with Reagan's inches, his Grecian hair, his Mitchum chest?

Next, one was obliged to traipse around the fringe meetings in a wistful search for repulsive policies. Although I was sad to have missed Phyllis Schlafly's Eagle Forum reception, which featured Robert Bork and Jeane Kirkpatrick ('It was great,' said one journalist, 'Jeane was nuts.'), I reposed considerable hope in Pat Robertson, the one-time TV pastor and tithe mogul. Might Pat talk about Armageddon and Rapture? Might he denounce credit cards for harbouring the Mark of the Beast? Might he heal my jet lag?

At the hotel a phalanx of news-parched media was pressing at the doors of the Robertson reception. No entry until
6.00, said one of Pat's people, because 'everybody in there
has waited a year and a half' to hobnob with the great man.
'*Please* don't turn this into a press conference.' The media
was as good as its word. There was no press conference.
Instead, Robertson was instantly engulfed by a squirming
centipede of mikes and camera tackle; he emerged fifteen
minutes later, with an almost audible pop, and was dragged
off through a side door by his bodyguard. Still newsless, the
newspeople took a few disgusted sips of French cider and
trooped off to the Superdome to cover Ronnie Night.

I lingered among the believers, with their fine hair,
their thick skins, and their low blink-rates. Many of the
women were still shivering from the post-Pat frisson. Their
man hadn't won, but they had the feeling that the GOP
was gathering him – and them – into its bosom. Clearly
Pat hadn't told them what he must know to be the case:
that he's finished. The next night, true, he would get his
prime-time speech (largely ignored by the cameras) and
would thrill the faithful, and the media, with his talk
of 'disease carriers' who place the healthy 'at great risk'.
But Pat's had it: his valedictory press conference was an
ill-attended freak show. He'll just have to go back to his
old job, serving God with his miracle-service TV spot and
stiffing the fuddled and elderly out of their rent cheques and
disability allowances.

Pat Robertson at a national convention, equipped with
delegates, certainly remains a terrible sight. He is a charlatan
of Chaucerian dimensions. To Bush, if not to Reagan, the
evangelicals were probably never much more than a useful
joke, to be kept happy with promises that can't possibly get
past the Senate (like the guff about recriminalising abortion).
Anyway, the video vicarage is now in tatters. Yet another
institution in Reagan's dream city comes crashing to the
ground – and the National Security Council, and Wall

Street, and the Attorney General's office, and the Pentagon. Is it over?

Ronnie Night. First the motorcade and its enthralling expression of personal power: half a six-lane city boulevard sealed off and lined with blinkers and excited cops. Four motorbikes in formation, sirens idling, then six more, then two police cars, then four limousines, then four staff cars (two containing security men, two containing Nancy's helpers and dressers). As soon as the backwash has settled, the cops unplug the bursting sidestreets, and the normal gridlock resumes. No wonder the President looks so young and cheerful: eight years without any traffic.

The time to study Reagan was before he mounted the stage – when he and Nancy took their preliminary seats in the lower gallery. During the imperial entrance, the Reagan face had been divided laterally, the eyes expressing mock alarm, the mouth unqualified gamesomeness. As he settled, a mound of cameras sticklebricked itself into being a few inches from his nose. Reagan jovially waved a hand at the teetering media, as if to say, 'Will you look at all these guys?' Then his smile instantly vanished as he fell into an imitation of a serious man listening to a serious speech. Was it imagination, or did I detect, beneath his mask, the dull throb of astonishment that such modest abilities (plus a few gut instincts) had ushered in, not just a Governorship, not just a Presidency, but an American Era? Apart from that, he looks, he looks . . .

What *does* he look like? He looks like a gorgeous old opera-phantom shot full of novocaine. *Esquire*'s caricaturist Steve Brodner is a longtime student of the Reagan face: 'Ten years ago the face told you a lot about the man. Now that's all gone.' The furtive overlay above the eyes and the wattled dissolution of the jaw have been replaced by clarity and definition. It used to be said that by a certain age a man had the face that he deserved. Nowadays, he has the face he can afford – or the face his handlers decide to go with. One of Dickens's hypocrites has a facial paralysis that gives him a profile of noble immobility; this is the side he presents to his clients, while the hidden half snickers and gloats. With the modern American politician, we must imagine the face *beneath* the face, smarting and flickering with the impostures, the compromises, and the fathomless boredom of public life. Erected by surgeon and makeup man, the face is now the picture window to the soul.

Maureen was there, but Reagan hasn't got any children, or grandchildren, that he can plausibly wheel out and love up. So he goes another way: he loves up Nancy. Reagan has never made any secret of his thralldom to Nancy's talents. With his hints of turbulent nights behind the clipped hedges of Brookline, Dukakis has evidently taken yet another arrow from Reagan's quiver: husbandly romancing has voter appeal. Bush is obviously in a corner on this one with Barbara, who will make TV ads but draws the line at dyeing her hair. Besides, as Bush says with a kind of shrug, it's been forty-three years.

This Convention project of loving up Nancy had begun at a lunch in her honour, where Reagan asked, 'What can you say about someone who gives your life meaning? You can say that you love that person, and treasure her.' On Ronnie Night, Tom Selleck was Reagan's surrogate on the stage; he spoke of cancer surgery, the war against drugs, and that day when 'an assassin nearly took away what she loved most in this life'. After Nancy's little address, we got the ad for Ronnie. You know the one: a fifteen-minute collage of newsclips, Bud and Marlboro commercials, and exquisitely lit home movies. So. An actor, then an actress, then an ad; and then another actor – Reagan, with the Speech.

All morning the hall had rung with the words of ardent glozers and fiery mediocrities, chosen for their sex or their skin colour or their extremes of youth and age. Punctuated by the tinny clunk of the gavel, the clichés of the peanut-faced orators laboured towards you at the speed of sound, chased by the PA echo ... Reagan got up there, and, after one blooper ('Facts are stupid things' – the crowd winced so fondly, so protectively!), a few jokes, several boasts, and a lot of statistics, shared with his countrymen the gift of the trust in a dream of a vision whose brilliant light in a shining moment showed a sweet day of extra love for a special person between the great oceans. 'Here,' he exhaustedly concluded, 'it's a sunrise every day.'

That last revelation can't have been news even in Middle America, which seems to have been in flames all summer. With the Drought, with 50 per cent of all counties declared disaster areas, with the unbreathable city air (not to mention the thirty-foot scum line on the beaches of the North-East), Americans knew all about 'our sunlit new day'. No need to tell *them* 'to keep alive the fire'. Reagan's speech was an apotheosis of a kind: the rhetoric of arcadian green, polluted by reality. Nobody liked it much, even on the floor. Yet the momentum of expectation was so far entrained that the performance somehow passed off as a triumph. This *had* to be the night of rich catharsis, when Reagan's image began its slow wipe, leaving Bush to hurl his first grapple hook across the stature gap.

At lunchtime on the second day the lead local news story was about Convention-related traffic jams. In uniform desperation the media was turning its gaze on the city itself, and duly noting the inevitable contrast between Republicans and New Orleans.

It's true. There is a big difference. Republicans are rich and sober. New Orleans is poor and drunk – and Democrat. Indeed, the city has an air of almost Caribbean laxity. Over Sunday breakfast on my first morning in the French Quarter ('the Quarter'), I watched a teenage girl lurch out of a bar with a beer bottle swinging from her hand. She walked as if she had just come down from Vermont, on horseback; past Big Daddy's Topless and Bottomless Tabletop Dancing she meandered; then she sat on the sidewalk outside a club unceremoniously called the Orgy. No one stared, in forgiving New Orleans. But if I'd had a video camera with me, I could have made a good ad for abortion. In the Quarter, everybody knows about the alternative to *choice*. The alternative to legal abortion is illegal abortion. Just more free enterprise.

There is a little voodoo store a couple of blocks further up Bourbon Street. In the front room there is a tub full of coloured ribbons: 'MOJO'S FOR – LOVE (red and black) stop conFUSSION (yellow and BLACK) FOR a good health (diFFerent colors and stripy BLACK) COURTCASE (BLACK and BLACK)'. In the back room there is a rectangular chest covered in masks and pinecones: 'Pleas do not touch this COFFIN – DANGER – BE WARE of FReddies COFFIN!! PS shit HAPPENing'. The store looked far from prosperous. The potency of voodoo, one fears, is definitely on the wane – except in the realm of economics and, perhaps, in that of prophecy. For George Bush was due in town that day. Soon we would hear the sinister creak of Freddie's coffin lid. And shit would be happening.

Like many of the media I began the day by morbidly attending a brunch thrown by the National Rifle Association, with fingers crossed for a few atrocities from the lips of Charlton Heston and Arnold Schwarzenegger. Resplendently present at the bar, Schwarzenegger no-showed on the podium (as he would later monotonously no-show at the Mississippian, Tennessean, and South Carolinian caucus meetings). In the matinee gloom of the curtainless ballroom, Heston was bland and depressingly centrist; we took what solace we could from the opening blasphemies of a local chaplain ('And now a word to our Sponsor. Heavenly Father . . .') and from Phil Gramm's tribute to capital punishment: 'If they hurt other people we want them put in jail, and if they kill other people we want them put to death.' Hearing this, a couple of elegant young ladies at my table joined in the fierce applause; the palms of their right hands sought their throats in flustered affirmation. Civilised girls. But this isn't civilised. Still, gas chambers and gunslinging aren't news at the end of the Reagan Era. Furloughs are news. The media bitterly decamped to Spanish Plaza to wait for Bush.

Vintage aircraft buzzed the shopping mall, two deejays jabbered into microphones, a fat tug befouled the Mississippi with dyed fountains of red and white and blue, gay protesters took their positions – and into this scene of contemporary pageantry the candidate stepped from the riverboat *Natchez* ... Some minutes later there was this frenzied little blond guy waving his arms around and hollering into the mike, and doing pretty well considering he looked about nine years old. Watching him give his cheek a thorough and astonished wipe after a kiss from Barbara, you might have thought that here was another tearaway Bush grandson. But no: here were three bad decisions (manner, timing, substance) all rolled into one. Here was Dan Quayle.

The TV crews are the Germans of the media. Here they come (watch out), lugging their bazookas and ack-ack launchers, sweating, swearing, and not smiling. They are all elbow and kneecap and have the gracelessness of undisputed muscle. They stand in ranks on crates and platforms, like firing squads. As they focus, their upper lips drag to the left in dead Presley grins. 'They got Channel 56 from Jacksonville, Texas, in here,' said one crewman at the first Bush-Quayle press conference. 'That's how Mickey Mouse it's getting.' I peered through the wires and webbing, the jeans and chinos. When the ticket came on to the stage the cameras phutted like a great flock taking to the air. And there was Quayle, confident, plump-faced, handsome, and stupid, all set to go get 'em.

The process that began in those first few minutes would develop into the detailed recycling of a political being, much of it on prime time. The media chomped him up and pooped him out again. And the contraption that is now being buck-led on to a horse and sent out on the campaign trail is no longer the 'Dan Quayle' to whom Dan Quayle so often, and so robotically, refers. He is a hurried creation of the Bush people: the prepped preppy, wired up for a narrow repertoire of frowns and whoops, wired up for limited damage. Facing his first question about Paula Parkinson (the Washington lobbyist he was alleged to have taken on a golfing trip), Quayle made a gesture of erasure with his hand, said 'No' when he meant 'Yes' and looked like the kind of man who would want to beat you up if you swore in front of his wife. You don't come on to the media like that. Then the bombshell: Quayle – the identikit, join-the-dots militarist – had given Vietnam a miss, staying at home and serving with the National Guard. By the next morning there were rumours that Quayle would be dumped from the ticket. Out of the loop for decades, the media was calling, in effect, for a second ballot. The media wasn't just a crowd, busy dispensing free TV. The media was saying that it was a *player*.

Even before the story broke, one remarkable fact had surfaced: here we had yet another major American politician who was quite at sea in the English language, utterly con-founded by the simplest declarative sentence. Minutes after the press conference, Bush was blooding his young warrior at the California caucus meeting. Before long, Bush found himself standing there with a look of respectful concentra-tion on his face as Quayle hammered out: 'The question today is whether we are going forward, or past to the back.' Even this miserable commonplace was too much for him. Indeed, the only sentence Quayle seemed really comfortable with was 'Let's go get 'em!' The following night he managed twenty minutes of monosyllabic jingoism on the podium, but a day later, in Huntington, Indiana, his syntax was crazily unspooling all over the courthouse steps. 'The Reserve forces is nothing to say is unpatriotic ... By serving in Guard somehow is not patriotic, I really do not subscribe to that . . . And a goal cannot be really a no-win situation.'

Quayle was chosen, supposedly, to help ease Bush's passage to the centre, a position he tried to occupy in his 'soft' acceptance speech, with its Whitmanesque intonations and nudges of moral suasion. Four days later we got a glimpse of the contortions Bush must now attempt, when he addressed the VFW in Chicago and sounded like Spiro Agnew: '[Dan Quayle] did not burn his draft card and he *damned sure* didn't burn the American flag!' No other Veep candidate, no other politician, can ever have won such savage praise for not burning the American flag. Bush chose Quayle, I think, because he responded to and took pleasure in his youth, unaware of the slowly dawning reality that *all* baby boomers are unelectable, by definition (none of us is clean: we've all smoked joints, had sex, worn bell-bottoms, gone to the toilet, and so on). Perhaps Quayle is the fanatically right-wing son that Bush never had. More probably, the young man answered to the young man in Bush, to the frisky kiddishness that remains his central implausibility. By golly. Zip-a-dee-doo-dah. Deep doo-doo. Who does *that* sound like?

One night in New Orleans I fell in with some representatives of the pollster and media-consultant community, people who had worked with Bush, or with 'Poppy', as they call him. ('We think Poppy is a regular guy. Mainly because he says *fuck* a lot.') Here, all values are expedient and professionalised, and politics – fascinatingly – is discussed in strictly apolitical terms. I conflate their voices:

'On Spanish Plaza, Quayle looked like he just did a gram of coke. But they only jerked him off the streets of the Quarter an hour before, and that's what power feels like: you're thinking what you were yesterday, what you might be tomorrow. Their first job then was to calm him down. To calm his ass *down*.

'I think everyone's surprised that he seems so vapid. I mean, we're talking Bob Forehead. There's got to be more there. The Bush people are taking shit now but they're smart guys – they must know that Quayle has moves we ain't seen. Hey. What do you get if you cross a chicken and a hawk?'

'I don't know.'

'You get a quayle. If he's going to help the ticket he's got to bond with his generation. That's the whole idea, right? He's *got* to express more ambivalence about the war. Maybe you'd want to do that with paid media later on, where you can control everything. It could all help Bush. It could release a lot of emotion, as opposed to canned emotion, and the challenge then is to steer that energy in your direction.

'Right now America is button-punching. If Bush looks like everybody's first husband, then Dukakis is looking like a great first date. The point is, Bush has better guys. Someone like Bob Teeter really earns his money when you're three days from a race and the tracking says you're seven points down and wondering whether to go with an attack spot or just keep with the positive stuff. Like Bush-Dole in New Hampshire. Anyone can do the numbers. It's the analysis. It's like on the *Vincennes*. Hey. How do you tell the difference between an Airbus and an F-14?'

'I don't know.'

'Exactly. You don't know either.'

At this point we were joined by a young woman from a news network who had spent the day in fruitless search of a Vietnam veteran willing to denounce Dan Quayle. Later, I heard about one of the more recent techniques in market research. You put sixty or seventy people in front of a videotaped stump speech and hand out dials (marked 1–100) on which the audience plots its undulating level of approval. This information goes into a computer. And out comes a tracking graph that gives you an emotional commentary on the speech. Further equipment is available to measure physical responses.

I left with an image of the American electorate, fitted with heartbeat monitor, peter meter, and armpit humidor dial, and pegged out in the political-science lab of the future.

Not that it appears to matter, but in a sense George Bush is everything that Ronald Reagan only seems to be: war hero, sports star, self-reliant achiever, family man. If George is the best father in America, then Ronnie is the worst (he is also, for instance, a war wimp who lied about his record – to Yitzhak Shamir). Yet Reagan has made it all new: the frictionless illusion of a distinguished life is now far catchier than the effortful reality. The only serious omission in Bush's résumé is thirty years in acting school.

Here are three well-placed comments on the Republican nominee. '[Bush's negatives] are not venal negatives, they're warts negatives.' 'We have a perception problem on some compassion issues.' 'The guy's got no biceps, no tattoos – he's not up to it.' It is evident from his career, and from his autobiography, that Bush has always been prepared to do anything, or anything legal, to get the next job. What the 'anything' is in 1988, apart from the usual low blows of a tight race, is a lot of vulgar bull about family (which is ironic, since Barbara Bush must be one of the few remaining housewives in America). After Reagan, though, the messenger is the message, and this messenger tends to pratfall on the steps to the throne. Poor George, with his warts negatives, his compassion-issues perception problem, and his lack of biceps – and of anchors and songbirds and the bruised names of love . . .

Do we get the feeling that the language has taken a beating over the past eight years? It has been an era of euphemism, during which taxes have become revenue enhancements, accountability has demoted itself to deniability, and the lie has turned into the blooper. Reagan bequeaths an economy so unrecognisably deformed that nobody can get a stethoscope close to its chest. He bequeaths the Debt: just as crucially, he bequeaths an atmosphere in which no politician dares discuss it.

Deep, autonomous, imperishable, Reagan's popularity remains the key to everything, including the election. What *is* this woozy affinity between the American people and a *Bonanza* fan who turns in at 10 pm? Either it is all very simple or it is all very complicated. To adapt the writer Clive James on the singer Barry Manilow: everybody you know despises Reagan, but everyone you don't know thinks he's great. When they see Reagan frowning at his cue cards – instead of wanting less, they want more.

For a decade Reagan has impersonated, with an unguessable degree of sincerity, the kind of American we hear a lot about at election time, if at no other: pious, wise, caring, industrious, independent, and above all *average*. The clear truth that this average American is a vain and shifty prodigal is not something that average Americans are raring to face up to. But then it goes still deeper.

In New Orleans the amplifiers sweltered with that special theme: American exceptionalism. Reagan understands that Americans are 'special' (my candidate for the worst word in the current lexicon). They are special – because they really think they're special. Never content just to be, America is also obliged to *mean*; America signifies, hence its constant and riveting vulnerability to illusion. In elevating Reagan – the average American who was special enough to land the best job in the free world – Americans elevate themselves. So perhaps the Era can be viewed as a narcissistic episode: a time when every American was President. Or not every American. Just every American that we don't know.

Esquire, 1988

VISITING MRS NABOKOV

> He also remembered that the hotel was drab and cheap,
> and abjectly stood next to another, much better hotel,
> through the *rez-de-chaussée* of which you could make out
> the phantoms of pale tables and underwater waiters . . .

These lines from the late novella, *Transparent Things*, came
flooding back to me, as I walked from my own dire hostelry
(fuming radiators, pot-luck room service, a bed like a ham-
mock) to the sparkling citadel of the Montreux Palace Hotel,
where the Nabokovs took up residence in 1961, and where
Véra Evseevna Nabokov has now spent the last four years,
alone, in the sixth floor of the old wing.

Why Montreux anyway, I wondered, and why a hotel?
When the BBC came to Montreux to record what is now
known as 'the last interview', Nabokov remarked: 'I have
toyed on and off with the idea of buying a villa. I can imagine
the comfortable furniture, the efficient burglar alarms, but I
am unable to visualise an adequate staff. Old retainers require
time to grow old, and I wonder how much of it there still is
at my disposal.' The interviewer, Robert Robinson, said of
Montreux that it gives 'a curious feeling of taking a walk in
an old photograph'. Strolling through the sun and mist of
the lakeside, I thought of the lost and innocuous parklands
of an idealised boyhood. The Swiss children are dapper and

immaculate on their skates. The Swiss midges, keeping themselves to themselves, are much too civic-minded to swarm or
sting.

The Nabokovs lived in the thick of the twentieth century –
a shared life of almost novelettish glamour, peril and pathos:
enforced exile from revolutionary Russia (where the young
Vladimir was a teenage playboy, poet and millionaire); the
hysteria and hyper-inflation of Weimar Germany (Nabokov's
father, the great liberal statesman V.D. Nabokov, was assas-
sinated at a political meeting in Berlin); a precarious stay
in France as the country fell to the Germans; and then
last-minute escape (Véra is Jewish) to the hospitable void
of the New World.

In America Nabokov completed twenty hard years on the
literary and academic treadmill. Meanwhile he had the task
of reincarnating himself as (broadly speaking) an English
novelist rather than a Russian one. Irrevocable prosperity –
i.e., freedom – finally arrived in the form of *Lolita* (1959).
Small wonder, then, that the Nabokovs should have chosen
to repair to what Humbert Humbert calls 'my lacquered,
toy-bright Swiss villages and exhaustively lauded alps' and
the suspended playground of Montreux. For all its plotting
and incident, the life of Vladimir and Véra Nabokov has had
a simple theme, that of dedication. They came to Montreux
to put the *oeuvre* in order, to supervise the translations of
earlier work, and to get the last novels safely out of the way.

Mrs Nabokov awaited me patiently in one of the pillared
public rooms of the Montreux Palace Hotel. 'What would
you like?' she asked at once. 'Whisky? Gin? You can have
anything.' At 11.30 am, I found this a tolerant offer. I chose
wine, while Mrs Nabokov requested a 'J & B' – or a 'Chay
& Pee' (her English is strongly accented and still slightly tentative). The smiling waiter bantered and soothed; according
to legend, Vladimir Nabokov was a compulsive tipper, and
his wife clearly remains one of the cossets of the staff. She

sipped prudently at her whisky, which she did not entirely finish. She was, I think, simply being convivial. Whenever I tried to pay for anything Mrs Nabokov would firmly interpose. 'No, this is mine – this is *my* party.'

She has thick white hair and expressive, ironical eyes. She has been rather ill recently – her hearing is a little weak and she uses a stick; but even now, in her seventies, the deeply responsive face is still suffused with feminine light. It is above all a humorous face. 'V.N.' as she sometimes calls him, used to boast that she had the best sense of humour of any woman he had ever known, and it is easy to appreciate this and other reasons for his pride. A combination of modesty and natural inquisitiveness or warmth makes her a ticklish subject for interview. 'But let's talk about yourself,' she will say. 'Are you married? . . . Do you want children? . . . Do you see your family?'

At this point, as arranged, we were joined by Dmitri Nabokov, the Nabokovs' only child and a figure of considerable interest himself – racing driver, mountaineer, international opera singer, as well as the accomplished translator of many of his father's novels. Dmitri is at present living near his mother: in the hospital at Lausanne, to be precise, where he is completing a long convalescence after an awesome car crash last year. It was only a few miles up the road that, following a visit to Montreux, Dmitri's powerful car mysteriously 'left the road'. He forced his way from the flaming wreck and was rushed to the hospital, which was providentially only ten minutes away and contains one of the most advanced burn-treatment units in the world. From there Dmitri coolly telephoned his mother, saying that he had had a minor accident and would be over to see her soon. It was some while before Véra found out that her son had been lucky to survive.

For a time we marvelled at Dmitri's injuries, which are still visible, not to say conspicuous. We talked of the body's remarkable powers of recovery. Staring at Dmitri's scorched fingers, I couldn't help paying tribute to the body's remark-able powers of destructibility in the first place. Halfway through this observation I began to regret having made it. But it seemed to go down well enough. With mock squeam-ishness Véra then asked her son when the 'purple lace' (i.e. the mortified crimson veins) on his arms would disappear. A very Nabokovian formulation. Like his father, Dmitri is tall, balding, athletic, expansive, and innately good-humoured; he defers to his mother with a courtly protectiveness. Mrs Nabokov listened to her son's progress-report with concern and some amusement, and then turned to me. 'Do you drive? ... You drive very carefully, I hope.'

Dmitri and I now moved through into the dining room, while Véra retired to her suite, promising to join us for coffee. 'I'll see you later then,' I said. 'So long,' said Mrs Nabokov ... Over lunch it soon became clear that Montreux has devel-oped into a kind of clearing-house for the Nabokov light industry. Dmitri is currently translating *Transparent Things* into Italian; Véra is translating *Pale Fire* into Russian (for *samizdat*, of course, as is the fate of V.N.'s translation of *Lolita*). There is also constant activity in the subsidiary-rights department. For instance, Dmitri is still licking his wounds over the recent Broadway adaptation of *Lolita*. 'A disaster. Quite a disaster,' as his mother later added.

Dmitri has an especially delicate problem on his hands at the moment. When Vladimir Nabokov died, on 2 July 1977, a novel lay half finished on his lectern. In Dmitri's opinion *The Original of Laura* is one of his father's most daring and pellucid performances; yet Nabokov was inflexibly opposed to the novel being published in its incomplete form. It is a terrible dilemma, and one that the surviving Nabokovs have by no means resolved.

For if there is a greater obligation than the one owed to Vladimir Nabokov, it is the obligation owed to literary history. Dmitri and Véra are profoundly conscious of this, and it is intimately bound up with the tenor of their family pride. I raised the subject of the *Nabokov-Wilson Letters* and the sad, strange dissolution of a friendship which that correspondence records, all ending in bafflement and anger with Wilson's inexplicable attack on Nabokov's translation of *Eugene Onegin*. 'Edmund Wilson,' said Dmitri with a sigh. 'I liked him. He was very good with children. He was cuddly, playful. He could make a mouse out of a handkerchief and make it move for me ... Then his immense presumption – that he knew Russian!' Or, on the grudging assessment of a recent biographer: Nabokov was 'a good man, oh, in a peculiar way perhaps, and with certain lapses, but a good man none the less'. Dmitri threw his head back, eyes to ceiling, in a gesture of exasperation which I gather was also very typical of his father: 'Astonishing. The *presumption* ...'

Véra, whom we had by now rejoined in the ballroom-sized lounge, proved to be just as adamant on her husband's behalf and in the championship of his memory. 'The editor of the Russian *Pale Fire* – he did a lot of mischief, and I have refused to accept any of his corrections ... I have vetoed Professor Karlinsky's introduction to the second volume of *Lectures on Literature*. I wrote to the publishers and said that I im*plore* them to cancel it. And they did.' A few moments later Mrs Nabokov misheard a remark I made about the *first* volume of the *Lectures*, mistaking praise for dispraise. '*What?*' she said. And, until I had made myself clear, every atom in her body seemed to tremble with indignation.

Now Dmitri took his leave; he would catch the train back to the hospital at Lausanne. Before saying goodbye he handed his mother a scroll of clippings. 'A review of the *Tribute*, from South Carolina ... Father is mentioned here ...' This kind of talk, like the Nabokovian indignation, is all of a piece with the nature of the family commitment. It bespeaks great self-belief, but there is no self-importance in it. It is selfless, indeed almost impersonal, in the same way that art is impersonal. It is also, I imagine, very Russian in its timbre.

*

Dmitri was gone. Now the sun bore through the tall windows on to Mrs Nabokov's chair and she raised a hand to shield her cheek from its rays. She showed me the copy of the *Vladimir Nabokov Research Letter* which had been nestling on her lap, pointing to the illustrations of the imaginary butterflies drawn by her husband (reproduced from her personal copies of his books). The cod-Latin names contain various diminutives of her name – *verae*, *verinia*, *verochka* . . .

They met in 1923, in Berlin. It was surprising that they had not met before. After all, even in St Petersburg the boys of the Tenishev School often fraternised with the girls of the Obolensky. They had worked as extras on the same German films. Véra had innocently attended the readings given by Vladimir on the émigré intellectual circuit in Berlin. 'He talked with great charm,' says Véra. 'He was as a young man extremely beautiful.' In old Russia Véra had had the same kind of multilingual upbringing as Nabokov himself; she was in fact one of his few serious rivals as an English teacher in Berlin. 'But V.N. taught many subjects,' she concedes. 'Languages, tennis, boxing. And prosody, prosody.'

Véra's father had just co-founded a small publishing firm, Orbis. The young Nabokov was to translate Dostoevsky into English. Véra was working in the office to earn extra money for horseback riding in the Tiergarten. They glimpsed each other, but did not meet properly until later in the year, at a Charity Ball. Nabokov started playing a lot of chess with Véra's father. In a letter to his mother he spoke of his need to settle down. He later said of his father-in-law: 'He understands so well that for me the main thing in life and the sole thing which I am capable of doing is to write.' Véra herself must have understood this pretty well too. They were married in April 1925, and there, really, the visible story ends.

She has been described as an intensely private person –

more private, even, than her husband. She has formidable self-possession, certainly, and would, you feel, be hard on any folly or impertinence on the part of an outsider. As our conversation went on, and remained pretty cautious and general, I felt a mild unease growing in Mrs Nabokov – as if she would inevitably have to repulse some grossly personal query ('Mrs Nabokov, did you ever meet the *real* Lolita?'). Eventually, she said, 'These *questions* you will ask. Where are these *questions*?'

'Well, there were one or two things,' I said. 'Your husband dedicated all his books to you, every one. That's very unusual, isn't it?'

'Is it? . . . What should I answer? We had a very unusual relationship. But that you knew before you asked. Anything else?'

'Was he – was he great fun?' I asked helplessly. 'Were there lots of jokes? Did you laugh a lot?'

'Oh, yes. His humour was delightful. He was delightful,' said Mrs Nabokov. 'But that you knew too.'

Observer, 1981

Postscript: Véra Nabokov died in 1991, ten years after the visit recorded here. As Dmitri Nabokov said in his address at her funeral: 'Even in her eighties she helped with the preparation of many editions of her husband's works, wrote an introduction for a Russian edition of his poems, assisted in the compilation of a collection of his letters, [and] dedicated immense effort to the Russian translation of *Pale Fire* . . .' Every now and then, during that last decade, I exchanged brief letters with her; I sent her photographs of my children, when they came; there was occasionally some bibliographical news to report. I thought of her often. She remained extraordinarily vivid to me. Partly, I suppose, I valued the memory of my visit because it provided a living link with her husband, whom I have always idolised; in her, it seemed, he lived on. But this doesn't quite account for the inordinate desolation I felt when I was confronted by her obituary.

From Dmitri Nabokov's eulogy (11 April 1991):

On the eve of a risky hip operation two years ago, my brave and considerate mother asked that I bring her her favourite blue dress, because she might be receiving someone. I had the eerie feeling she wanted that dress for a very different reason. She survived on *that* occasion. Now, for her last earthly encounter, she was clad in that very dress.

It was Mother's wish that her ashes be united with those of Father's in the urn at the Clarens cemetery. In a curiously Nabokovian twist of things, there was some difficulty in locating that urn. My instinct was to call Mother, and ask her what to do about it. But there was no Mother to ask.

V.S. NAIPAUL'S INDIA*

Indian motorists are not required to use their lights after dark, though they may flash while swerving if they wish; they are obliged, however (or so it seems), to sound their horns whenever they see anything at all, mobile or stationary, animate or inanimate. English whisky costs £30-odd a bottle in India: a diplomat could support a large servant family with a quarterly gift – which would cost him £1 a time. Indians compose most of their commercial signs in English, and get one vowel wrong in every word (HOUSEBOOT was the most typically self-defeating). Indian trade-names, in addition, shyly proclaim the modesty of their wares, as if pre-empting any suspicion of excellence: STANDARD, GENERAL, RATHER, DECENT, boast the shopfronts – you half-expect to see MEDIOCRE or NOT THAT BAD. In the city streets tourists are approached for money three or four times every minute, by the beggar-women and their shrieking babies (they pinch them throughout the interview, to make them cry but also to acknowledge the child's sins in previous lives), by the stranded American hippies in their sawn-off jeans ('Hi. We're trying to do something for the people in jail over here right now. Anything you have – clothes, blankets, medicine . . . Nothing? Okay, great. Bye!'), and by the distracted, semi-

---

*India: A Wounded Civilisation, V.S. Naipaul, André Deutsch, 1977

Westernised touts (who are not currency-dealing, who have no realistic transaction in mind, who just keep muttering potent phrases like 'twenty rupees . . . nine English pounds . . . one hundred dollars! . . . *three* rupees . . .'). In the lavatory of New Delhi International Airport you might see two untouchable sweepers fleetingly embrace among the slops. At the other end of the caste scale, brahmin type 1132 (there are over 1,500 kinds of brahmin) might well refuse to speak to brahmin type 1129, let alone touch him. Dogs, chickens and old men sleep on the roads through provincial towns; Indian cows eat what they want and go where they please (Indian cows look as though they think it's a bit of luck, all this about them being sacred). Nearly everything seems to be filthy, mad, ridiculous, or all three. Nearly everyone seems to be in terrible trouble, and not to mind about it that much.

Responses to India tend towards two extremes. The first response, promoting lack of imagination to intrepidity, takes a heartily sentimental pleasure in the dirt and distress – this is the response, in different ways, of the hippy and of the colonist. The second response involves immediate recognition of one's alarm and neurotic withdrawal: initially, one sees India through the mist of one's utter rejection of it. In *An Area of Darkness*, published in 1964, V.S. Naipaul passed on the story of the Sikh who, returning to India after several years abroad, sat down among his suitcases on the Bombay docks and wept; he had forgotten what Indian poverty was like. 'It is an Indian story,' Naipaul went on,

in its arrangement of figure and properties, its melodrama, its pathos. It is Indian above all in its attitude to poverty as something which, thought about from time to time in the midst of other preoccupations, releases the sweetest of emotions . . . Poverty not as an urge to anger or improving action, but poverty as an inexhaustible source of tears . . . India is the poorest country in the world. Therefore, to see its poverty is to make an observation of no value . . .

In India, the easiest and most necessary thing is to ignore the obvious.

But to begin with, as Naipaul said, 'the obvious was overwhelming', and *An Area of Darkness* is a record not so much of Naipaul's attempts to see beyond the obvious (he would do that anyway) but of his efforts not to be overwhelmed by it. In the best and most admirable sense, the book is a labour of dramatic intellectual strain. Suppressed hysteria never leaves the narrative for long, and panic makes faces from its margins; for all the brilliance and humour, the voice of that book is skittish, febrile, wayward ('I was longing for greater and greater decay, more rags and filth, more bones'). Compared to *An Area of Darkness*, the new memoir is sharply focused, analytical and remote. But it is also angrier and less forgiving, written with a resolute coldness; and in the end it is an intransigently bitter book.

Inevitably so, Naipaul would claim, for only out of 'an eroded human concern' can any understanding start to come. *India: A Wounded Civilisation* is the result of a third visit to the country, from August 1975 to October 1976, the time of Mrs Gandhi's Emergency, the time when Indians were first asked to confront the startling fact of their own Independence. With the dismantling of its inherited institutions – and with no foreign conqueror for the first time in a thousand years – India 'is left alone with the blankness of its decayed civilisation'. Naipaul's ancestors migrated from the Gangetic plain 100 years ago, and 100 years 'had been enough to wash me clean of many Indian religious attitudes: without those attitudes the distress of India was – and is – insupportable'. Now, however, those attitudes are under threat for every Indian. The 'futility and limitless pain' of India has not changed, but attitudes to it have. India has begun to see the obvious, and is being duly overwhelmed.

As in the earlier book, Naipaul identifies the caste system as the main form of insulation . . . The bathrooms of a Bombay hotel are ankle-deep in excrement; but the hotel employs four sweepers; the bathrooms are therefore spotless. The fingers of a food-server are grimy and rank; but the food-server is of the designated food-serving caste; nothing served by the fingers of his right hand could therefore be unclean. Caste is a necessary blinker: it also secures the people in their self-defining roles. A street sweeper uses his fingers alone to lift dust from the road into his cart; a woman cleans a giant causeway with a tiny rag, achieving in a day what a child could do with a single push on a broom; but this is their function – it is what they are born to be. Such absurdities were, until recently, a source of reassurance rather than concern; like poverty itself, they were to be 'relished as religious theatre', in Naipaul's worrying phrase. 'Wanted a Telugu Brahmin Vellanadu non-Kausiga Gotram bride below 22 years', specifies a small-ad. Naipaul tells the story of the foreign businessman who educated his untouchable servant and secured him a better job. Before long the man was a latrine-cleaner again. He had been ostracised by his own caste, and no one else would have him.

During the Emergency, an opposition pamphlet was circulated giving details of alarming tortures suffered by political prisoners. A man had had his moustache shaved off! People were forced to walk the streets with shoes on their heads! A university professor 'was pushed from side to side with smearing remarks'! These of course are caste pollutions, 'more permanently wounding, and a greater cause for hysteria, than any beating up' (and not surprisingly, when you reflect that an untouchable can be killed for having a moustache of the wrong shape). The opposition pamphlet, though, as Naipaul says, serenely confuses its aims: a plea for humanitarianism becomes a cry of reactionary caste outrage. With every step forward, India always turns in on its own past.

India gets everything wrong. India never learns: its mimicry cannot rise above travesty. Naipaul has a devastating chapter on the new and expensively equipped National Institute of

Design at Ahmedabad in Gujarat. Here, important projects include a portable spraying machine with an innovatory – and very heavy – internal motor, enough to cripple any labourer who strapped it on; another team is working on a pair of bladed reaping shoes, requiring a kind of bucolic gambol from the hale and happy peasant. 'Do you know', someone said to Naipaul in Delhi, 'that the investment in bullock carts is equivalent to the total investment in the railways?' Naipaul was about to comment on this melancholy proposition when his interlocutor went on wistfully: 'Now. If we could improve the performance of the bullock cart by 10 per cent . . .' And, sure enough, high science is now seeking to improve the bullock cart. At some open-air laboratory in the south, in an attempt to analyse the animal's stresses and pressures, there is a bullock as thoroughly 'wired up as any astronaut'. At the same time, on any Indian road, you can see the peasant improving the performance of *his* bullock

in the immemorial way, by pushing a stick up its anus. It is an unregarded but necessary part of the idyll, one of the obscene sights of the Indian road: the hideous cruelty of pre-industrial life, cruelty constant and casual, and easily extended from beast to man.

In some Indian villages children are preferred to men for the few available jobs, because they are cheaper; children become a source of wealth; suicidal overpopulation is guaranteed. Needy villagers still sell their wives to the 'cages' (the brothels) of the major cities to repay small debts to employers. Bonded labour, slavery as punishment, campaigns of terror against landless untouchables, deliberate starvation: 'none of this was new,' says Naipaul, 'but suddenly in India it was news.' Accordingly, the big cities have meanwhile begun to feel themselves 'under siege'. Every day, it is said, 1,500 people arrive in Bombay to live. They gather in packed, cloacal settlements, where the huts are so crowded that families often sleep in shifts. Now the urban poor have been disinherited even of their alms: 'by becoming too numerous they have lost their place in the Hindu system and have no claim on anyone.' A politician has predicted that the cities would soon 'be barricaded against the poor and guarded by machine-guns'. And, in Delhi, the expulsion of the poor has already begun.

Naipaul sees in India now the complete and graphic failure of Mahatma Gandhi, and of the Gandhianism cheapened by the likes of Vinoba Bhave and Mr Desai. In seeking to awaken India with the example of his courage and asceticism, Gandhi turned India back on itself, on its own atavistic self-absorption. He awakened the old India.

> With or without Mrs Gandhi, independent India ... would have arrived at a state of emergency ... However it is resolved, India will at the end be face to face with its own emptiness, the inadequacy of an old civilisation which is cherished because it is all men have but which no longer answers their needs.

It is a sombre valediction to a sombre book. Although always measured and elegant, there is nothing writerly in these pages; there is no relish. In *An Area of Darkness*, Naipaul could play the country off against his own perverse anxieties and misplaced expectations; he could capture the almost definitive poignancy of the Indian people, with their teeming, incomprehensible dreams and hurts; he could 'ignore the obvious'. He cannot any longer. The early memoir was humbling because of its sheer quality, because it seemed chasteningly good. *India: A Wounded Civilisation* attempts something less congenial: it is a long and angry stare at the obvious; it is humbling in a different way, because it seems chasteningly right.

New Statesman, 1977

'FRANKFURT'

Publishers always talk of the Frankfurt Book Fair – or, more simply, 'Frankfurt' – with mystical awe and longing. If anthropologists were ever to make a study of publishers (and perhaps the subject *is* worth a paper or two), then 'Frankfurt' would have to be accorded totemic status, connected with race history and the birth of the universal mind, when the first publishers swung down from the trees. In one of the old myths, it is said that the Gutenberg Bible, on completion, was taken straight to Frankfurt, where they immediately had a book fair about it. Eden, Byzantium, Elysium, Oz, Frankfurt: to hear publishers talk, you'd think that Frankfurt was a place where only the best and bravest publishers go when they die.

The Frankfurt fable has three main components. First, the Book Fair is made to seem an event of scarcely conceivable glamour. The week-long jamboree is evidently a round of sumptuous hedonism: ensconced in ten-star hotels, the publishers gorge themselves on expensive food and drink, and have the kind of sexual encounters with each other that used to be characterised in novels by phrases like, 'Towards morning, he took her again.' You hear stories of . . . well, of what, exactly? You hear stories that, once decoded, sound like the usual fallout from the annual office party: heavy drinking, tearful passes made at secretaries, and so on. But how could the outsider understand? In the magical air of 'Frankfurt', these things must seem very, very different.

Frankfurt is also, apparently, a clearing-house for ideas, for creativity, for the exchange of geopolitical truths. In the tea houses and coffee shops of this spangled garden city, the thinkers and seekers of the publishing world can really get together and thrash out such topics as the meaning of life and the destiny of the planet. Liberated from the usual chores of the office, the great men can let their minds dance free upon the spume of things; for a week Frankfurt becomes a kind of Mensaberg, and the whole city thrums with high IQs.

Third – and here the publisher will feign a weary, regretful air – Frankfurt is the arena of super-deals, of mega-business, of transactions so high-powered that entire currencies are but pawns in the publishers' vast dream. Then, too, there are betrayals, twists, scams, stings. All day the stalls groan with egregious gullings, unimaginable skankings. Million-pound contracts, zillion-dollar auctions – these are commonplace. Wall Street looks to Frankfurt in terror as denominations boom and bust. Seen as a triple vertex of high commerce, high culture and high living – clearly, in mid-October, the Frankfurt Book Fair is the place to be.

Listening between the lines, of course, the outsider had always suspected that the whole thing was a goons' rodeo. And so it proved. Driving in from the airport, I brought to mind the descriptions I had heard of the main exhibition hall where the Fair is staged – the biggest exhibition hall in the world, the largest building in the world, the most enormous edifice in the history of mankind. Well actually the whole of outer Frankfurt resembles an exhibition hall. Corporation office blocks, like upended matchboxes in layered glass and steel, form the only extrusions on the flat land. Nestlé, Olivetti, Eurohaus, ICI, IBM. These outbuildings of capitalist HQ are no more interesting than the architects' models they were based on; they look like lots for sale. The taxi pulls up at one of the international, interchangeable four-star doghouses. I have seen the future (you can't help reflecting), and it stinks.

I didn't get to see Frankfurt proper until the next day, thanks partly to the wanderlust of the cabbie who drove me to the Fair. Expressively bannered as the Frankfurter Buch-messe, the exhibition area resembles an airport in dire need of renovation, and Halle 5 (the scene of all the international action) a windy hangar where half-a-dozen Hindenbergs might have slept. It was Tuesday, the eve of the official opening. Inside, the publishers hastily assembled their stalls. These were low-echelon men, naturally (the bosses tending to fly out later in the week); dressed in berets and chunky sweaters, they looked van-sick and liverish after two days of Belgian roads and Belgian meals. But they were cheerful, and very expectant.

You can say this for the Book Fair: it reminds you, with great force, of the extremes of human variety. With 80-odd countries represented, and God knows how many hundred thousand books on display or stowed in boxes or as yet only twinkling in publishers' eyes, there is no gainsaying the superabundance of Earthling enthusiasms. Even before the opening it was a world tour in miniature to stroll through the half-completed stalls.

The Cuban stand was a shambles, featuring countless unopened boxes and two swarthy figures slumped over a bottle of Havana Club. The Kenya stand consisted of a dapper young black, a framed photograph of the latest tyrant, and nothing else. Décor varied: the Portuguese section was all bare brown wood softened by sashes and curtains; the Unesco stall, with its piping of light blue bars, typically combined the feel of a bamboo hut with that of a Habitat kitchen. One of the main Italian stands was completely des-erted. The Nigerian stand had yet to be built.

But such glimpses of human multiplicity seemed as noth-ing the following day, when the actual *books* adorned the shelves in all their vulgar and radiant diversity. Every year there is an informal competition for the Most Unlikely Title (I spoke to one book-packager who talked fondly of an old favourite, *Industrial Sealants and Adhesives*). My search for a contender took me first to the stands sponsored by the emergent nations. In the Zimbabwean section there was a wide selection of books by and about Robert Mugabe, the odd novel (*Under a Raging Sky*, etc.), and monographs on Shona customs from the Mambo Press. More parochial still was the stand of neighbouring Uganda: *The Crisis of Secondary School Education in Uganda, 1960–70*, Abudu Kayizzi's *Revision Primary Mathematics*. Of course, these men weren't selling but buying, and hoping for distribution rights from other countries, the Third World presence at Frankfurt often being no more than a tentacle of international relations.

The titles in the European stands at first seem a little more adventurous, but after a while some of the books look as familiar as the *A to Z* sported by the AA stall. *Yo, Claudius*, for instance, rings a bell, as does *Princesca Daisy*; and you don't have to puzzle long over *El 'shock' del Futuro* by Alvin Toffler. Mills and Boon, the pap heartache people, clearly qualify as a country of their own, or even a planet: A World of Romance. The titles shimmer by – *Untamed Witch, Dark Enigma, Dangerous Rapture*. These too are cravenly duplicated across Europe: *Il Tempio della Luna, Si Beau et Si Etrange*. No doubt some frazzled translator is scratching his head over the latest run of hot paperbacks from Beeline Books in New York: *To Sir, With Lust, How Do I Lust Thee, Lust Me or Leave Me, To Know Her Is To Lust Her*.

For it is to the New World that one must go for the prize lemons, for horrendous superfluity, for that mix of the frivolous and morbidly perverse. I have never seen so many books geared to the anxieties of sexual performance. What is going on over there? *The New Couple: Women and Gay Men* provides a clue. Ditto with *Finding Hope Again: A Pastor's Guide to Counseling Depressed Persons*. With sound counselling you'll soon be back to *How to Renovate*

Yourself from Head to Toe and *Good Lovemaking*. Why not forget the whole thing and curl up with *The Second Quilter's Companion* or *Fifty New Creative Poodle Grooming Styles*?

In the hubbub of this endless hypemarket the publishers hedge and bob. They wield their special Frankfurt Diaries – all appointment-crammed. The hall is loud with false laughter and willed camaraderie. What is this year's 'Pope book' (i.e. the high-priced dud)? What will happen at the Harper and Row auction (for Thomas Thompson's bosomy novel of Fame, Passion, and Vengeance, *Celebrity*)? They cruise and hunker, closing those deals. George! Fran! Bud! Yukio, Sven, Fetnab! Simone, Gunther, Rashid! Bernardo! Ogbogbo! Piotr!

The big business is done at night, in the big hotels – the teaky Schlösser, the shadowy Gasthäuser. This would seem to be the trend: in fact the coolest of the cool don't take stands any more but simply wallow in their suites, receiving visitors and torturing room-service. In the bars of what remains of old Frankfurt, and in the dives and supermarkets and cash-and-carry outlets of the red-light district, you will find the atmosphere of the affordable resort: block your ears, and it could be Biarritz, or Blackpool, on a rainy night. 'Is this your first Frankfurt?' everyone asked me. 'Yes,' I said, 'this is my first time' (be gentle with me, Frankfurt). 'Oh *well* then,' they all said. 'You'll like it better the second time.' But there may not be a second time. Actually that's a pretty good definition of frivolity: going to Frankfurt, as a non-publisher, for the second time. Enough of this carping, and these whimpers of exclusion. You never feel at your best, perhaps, when you crash the works outing of another firm.

Observer, 1981

MORE DIE OF HEARTBREAK

This piece is a book review – with a couple of differences. It was read out loud by me in Haifa, Israel, and in the presence of the book's author. The occasion was a Saul Bellow Conference organised, or spearheaded, by the distinguished Israeli novelist A.B. ('Bully') Yehoshua. At this convocation of Bellovians most of the papers were delivered by American academics. Jolted awake on my first morning by a call from the foyer telling me that 'the Conference miniboose' was revving in the forecourt, about to begin its journey to the Conference Centre, I then sat breakfastless through two or three lectures called things like 'The Caged Cash-Register: Tensions between Existentialism and Materialism in Dangling Man'. During the first session Bellow was overheard to say: 'If I have to listen to another word of this I think I'm going to die.' Thereafter he was not often to be found at the Conference Centre. He was in stalwart attendance, however, on the day I gave my paper alongside Amos Oz and Alan Lelchuk.

The 'wallet' referred to in the first sentence was a leatherette lecture-pouch presented to each delegate on arrival with the compliments of Bank Hapoalim. My assignment was the novel More Die of Heartbreak, *published later the same year (1987).*

I am delighted to be here, for all sorts of reasons: the sun, the sea breezes, this new wallet, the convulsive coughing fits that will punctuate my discourse. And I have further grounds for self-satisfaction. We are all familiar with our Herzogs and Humboldts and Hendersons, we all know our Augies and our Arturs; but nobody here has read the new one. Perhaps you have heard tell of it, you are acquainted with its lovely title: *More Die of Heartbreak.* But only I have read it. That is to say I have reread it; and I become more and more convinced that you cannot read writers like Saul Bellow; you can only reread them. I have read the new one – and you haven't. Not even Saul Bellow has read it. Oh, he has peered at the typescript, he has agonised over the proofs. He has written it. But he has not *read* it, as I have.

Once the first days of creation are over (once life has been assigned to various hunches and inklings), writing is decision-making. After the big decisions, the medium-sized decisions; then the little decisions, lots of little decisions, two or three hundred a page. When Bellow reads *More Die of Heartbreak* he isn't reading; he is squirming and smarting, feeling the pulls and shoves and aftershocks of a million decisions. For him the book is a million clues to a million skirmishes – scars, craters, bullet-holes. For me, it is a seamless *fait accompli*. And I am here to tell you – I am literally here to tell you – that it is as dense, as funny, as thought-crammed, as richly associational and as cruelly contemporary as anything he has written. He's over seventy. What's the matter with him?

Here are further grounds for extreme complacence on my part: Bellow has been reading Philip Larkin. Now the narrator of *More Die of Heartbreak* grew up in Paris at the feet of heavy thinkers like Boris Souvarine and Alexandre Kojève who talked about geopolitics and Hegel and Man at the End of History and wrote books called things like *Existenz* (note the powerful *z* on the end, rather than the more modest *ce*). I grew up in Swansea, Wales, and Philip Larkin was a good deal around. He didn't talk about posthistorical man. He talked about the psychodrama of early baldness. Bellow quotes Larkin as follows: 'In everyone there sleeps a sense of life according to love.' 'He also says that people dream "of all they might have done had they been loved. Nothing cures that".' And nothing – i.e. death – did cure that. Love was not a possibility for Larkin. Because to him death overarched love and rendered it derisory. He died in 1985; by Bellow's age, incidentally, he had been dead for years. For him, death crowded love out. With Bellow, it seems to be the other way around. More die of heartbreak, says the title. Well, Larkin never had any heartbreak, not in that sense.* Perhaps one of the many, many things the new novel has to say is that you *need* heartbreak, to keep you human. You need it to keep America off your back. (The book is sometimes like a rumour of war against America.) The right kind of heartbreak, mind you. Anyway, whether you need it or not, you are certainly going to get it.

I have a third and, I think, final reason for impregnable self-satisfaction – though more may yet occur to me. Whereas other speakers at this conference are addressing themselves to themes and structures, to literary correspondences and genealogies, existentialism, authenticity, percussive nouns and whatnot, all I've got to do is tell a story.

---

*In *Philip Larkin: A Writer's Life* Andrew Motion says of the title of Larkin's first mature collection, *The Less Deceived*: 'The phrase stands on its head Ophelia's remark in *Hamlet* that she is "more deceived" than the Prince.' I think this is wrong. Ophelia doesn't mean that she is more deceived than Hamlet ('I was the more deceived'). She means that she is more deceived than she was formerly – or more deceived than she thought she was. The poem in which the title phrase occurs, 'Deceptions', makes a comparison ('you were less deceived ... Than he was'), but the title itself refers to comparison *and* degree ('very much undeceived' as well as 'less deceived than most'). In any case it suggests a turning away from Ophelia's world of love and risk – and rawness, raggedness, insanity, dissolution. Larkin wasn't going to have any of that.

It is a love story, but a modern one. 'Modern': what has Bellow *done* to that word? In Bellow, *modern* now comes with its own special static, its own humiliating help-lessness, its own unbearable agitation ... We begin with a conversation between the book's two main actors, Kenneth Trachtenberg, the narrator, an Assistant Professor of Russian Literature, and his colleague and uncle, Benno, Benn Crader, the distinguished botanist, who specialises in the anatomy and morphology of plants (a plant 'clairvoyant', 'mystic' and 'telepathic', as he is variously styled). The two men love two women but they also love each other: it is a 'devouring' friendship; they are central to each other's lives. As the novel opens Benn is in crisis. We see how things are going to be on the first page, when Benn draws Kenneth's attention to a Charles Addams cartoon which has come to obsess him:

A pair of lovers was its subject – the usual depraved-desolate couple in a typical setting of tombstones and yews. The man was brutal-looking and the long-haired woman (I think the fans call her Morticia) wore a witch's gown. The two sat on a cemetery bench holding hands. The caption was simple:
  'Are you unhappy, darling?'
  'Oh yes, *yes*! Completely.'

Kenneth is the younger by a couple of decades but he is by far the more worldly, with his Parisian, UNESCO, Euroculture background. On the other hand, *everyone* is more worldly than Benn. Kenneth has long hair, a 'Jesusy' look, like 'a figure in a sketch, somewhere between Cruik-shank and Rembrandt – skinny, long-faced, sallow and greenish (reflections from a Dutch canal). Modern life, if you take it to heart, wears you out ...' Benn, for his part, has 'cobalt-blue' eyes and 'a face like the moon before we landed on it'. For Kenneth, Benn has 'the magics', a char-ismatic soul, purity, innocence; and it is these qualities that

Kenneth has come to America to protect, 'to preserve Benn in his valuable oddity'. He has also come to America because America is 'where the action is', the real modern action; it is where modernity is.

This is Benn's trouble. After fifteen years as a widower-bachelor he has remarried. The second wife is 'more beautiful, more difficult, more of a torment'. What was he after? 'Two human beings bound together in love and kindness' – a universal human aim, as Kenneth concedes: 'In the West, anyway, people are still trying to do it, rounding off the multitude of benefits they enjoy.' Benn's attitude is of course not so brisk. He is, or was, *infatuated*, 'carried away by unreasoning passion' (that is the second dictionary definition of infatuation, the first being 'made foolish'). Kenneth is doubly sceptical. Benn got married on the sly, while Kenneth was away; he hadn't cleared it with Kenneth, and he damn well should have done. Benn 'had the magics, but as a mainstream manager he was nowhere'. Kenneth has always aspired to be Benn's mainstream manager, his modernity intermediary. And he has always felt that Benn had the love potential, 'he actually could fall in love', he was a strong candidate for love in 'a classic form'. To put it at its lowest (which is still pretty high these days), 'he was a man who really did have something to do – other than trouble others, which seems to be what so many of us are here for, exclusively.'

As the veteran Bellow-reader would by now expect, the full picture takes some time to emerge; it is a case of one step forward two steps back, with each sortie into the present demanding elaborate legitimisation from the past. While omens gather, we first review Benn's erotic career, and the usual modern spectacle: 'the best people are always knee-deep in the garbage of "personal life", to the gratification of the vulgar'. Or again: 'the private life is almost always a bouquet of sores with a garnish of trivialities or downright trash.' And here is Ben, 'dredged in floury relationships by ladies who could fry him like a fish if they had a mind to'. There was Caroline Bunge, the department-store heiress, the Valium queen, who, when Benn rushes to meet her at the airport, walks straight past him without blinking: 'Being on mood pills was 100 per cent contemporary. If you aren't up-to-the-moment you aren't altogether real. But crazies are always contemporary, as sandpipers always run ahead of the foam line on the beaches.' There was Della Bedell, another contemporary personage. Having learnt from TV and the magazines that it's okay for the lady to take the initiative, she comes down from the apartment above and submits Benn to a matter-of-fact seduction. She practically debags him. Thereafter she haunts his front door crying, 'What am I supposed to do with my sexuality?' Benn slides into these things out of politeness (and 'politeness gets funnier the more the rules of order disintegrate'). He gets out of them less decorously: he does a runner, or a flyer, jetting off to Brazil, Japan, Antarctica, anywhere. 'He flies around, but his thought lag is such – I refer to the gap between his personal interests and the passions of contemporary life – that he might as well be circling the Dead Sea on a donkey.' Benn is not an old-fashioned figure, he is an eternal figure; he has innocence, and we all know what modernity will do with that. Innocence is a claim to immunity, and there is no immunity any more; modernity makes no exceptions. 'Towards the end of your life,' says Benn (and this is a very Bellovian strophe),

> you have something like a pain schedule to fill out – a long schedule like a federal document, only it's your pain schedule. Endless categories. First, physical causes – like arthritis, gallstones, menstrual cramps. Next category, injured vanity, betrayal, swindle, injustice. But the hardest items of all have to do with love. The question then is: So why does everybody persist? If love cuts them up so much, and you see the ravages everywhere, why not be sensible and sign off early?

'Because of immortal longings,' says Kenneth. 'Or just hoping for a lucky break.' Meanwhile, a Miss Matilda Layamon, modernity's erotic nemesis, patiently looms.

Kenneth is immersed, or rather stalled, in his own parallel difficulties: unrequited love for a girl called Treckie, the mother of his infant daughter. Early on Kenneth remarks that the nature of his own preoccupations marks him out as 'a genuinely modern individual. (Can you say worse of anybody?)' Compared to Treckie, though, Kenneth isn't modern at all. Compared to Treckie, Kenneth is positively Hanoverian, or Pushkinian. There is a lovely phrase later on in the book, when Benn is being extravagantly lunched by his appalling, his unforgivable, his inadmissible father-in-law; Benn is trying to be cheerful, but he can't 'get the note of TV brightness into his responses'. TV brightness: Treckie has plenty of that. I have a name for girls like Treckie; I call them *Jackanory*-artists, *Blue Peter*-merchants. Radiant with non-specific vivacity, they come on like kiddie-show hostesses ('And right after the break we'll be doing it again with me on top'). 'What kind of a name is Treckie?' asks Dita Schwartz, the other contestant for Kenneth's affections. A good question: what kind of a name *is* Treckie? Here, I think, we have a bit of subliminal inspiration on Bellow's part. In TV parlance a 'Trekkie' is a devotee of the space-opera TV series *Star Trek*. Trekkies model themselves on the cast of the show, would-be Captain Kirks and Lieutenant Uhuras who boldly go out into the universe, to pester alien life forms with the American Constitution . . .

Treckie is a person with goals, a 'life-plan'. She is 'either very clever or playing by clever rules': the latter, definitely the latter. Treckie believes in growth, in change, in full self-realisation. 'The way to change for the better,' summarises Kenneth,

is to begin by telling everybody about it. You make an announcement. You repeat your intentions until others begin to repeat them to you. When you hear them from others you can say, 'Yes, that's what I think too.' The more often your intention is repeated, the truer it becomes. The key is fluency. It's fluency of formulation that matters most.

This is no kind of fluency, no kind of conversation, no kind of girlfriend for a Bellow hero. How can you discuss life with somebody who lives a 'life-style' according to a 'life-plan'? When Kenneth talks to Benn about Treckie he uses 'skinny Gallic gestures to enlarge the horizon'. The horizon needs all the enlarging it can get.

I have no clue to what Treckie is waiting for. We don't talk about me. These last few days we talked mostly about her. She wanted to tell me about her progress in self-realization, the mistakes she's correcting, her new insights into her former insights and the decisions she's taken as a result.

And yet Kenneth is crazy for Treckie, crazy about Treckie: she has the franchise on his libido, whereas he can't begin to get a line on hers. Diminutive Treckie's sexual life-choice is masochism. She's a masochist and a pushy one, too: '. . . her legs were disfigured by bruises. Her shins were all black and blue. No, blue and green circles like the markings of peacock feathers . . . When she saw me staring at her she shrugged her bare shoulders, she laid her head to one side, and her underlip swelled softly towards me. There being a challenge in this, a "What are you going to do about it?" She seemed to take pride in these injuries.' Treckie likes rough men; Kenneth is a kind man, a delicate man. And that would appear to be that. There is nothing much that Kenneth, or indeed the novel, can do about Treckie. She must, she says, have her 'multiple acculturation', her 'multiple choices': i.e., she must have her multiple boyfriends. With Treckie, says Kenneth, 'it was just me versus contemporary circumstances, and against those I never had a chance'.

Kenneth's 'private life' is a mess but a static one. With Benn, contemporary circumstances assume more dynamic form. Matilda Layamon has been ominously hovering over the first third of the book (bad news, but what kind of bad news?); now she descends. She is rich, clever, beautiful, high-gloss, 'glittering, nervous': what does she see in Benn (and *seeing* is a good deal of what this novel is about: you are what you see, not what you eat, 'as that literalist German maniac Feuerbach insisted')? Look at the men Matilda might have had in Benn's stead! 'A national network anchorman, then a fellow who was now on the federal appeals bench, plus a tax genius consulted by Richard Nixon.' Why, her father plays golf with the likes of Bob Hope and President Ford. Yet she alights on Benn, with his awkward figure, the Russian 'bulge of his back like a wing-case', the infinity-symbol figure-eight spectacles, and his paltry sixty grand a year. This isn't going to be good. And why can't Benn see it? What, in fact, does Benn *see* in her?

When we read, we read with pencils in our hands. When we read something particularly significant or apposite, we draw a vertical line in the margin. The fit reader of the perfect book could thus run his pencil down the length of every last page. And in a way he is still none the wiser – it gets him no further forward. *More Die of Heartbreak* is a bit like that: read it twice, and all you've got is parallel tracks, right the way through. In its allusiveness, its density, its vigour, the novel comes at you like the snowstorm that Kenneth sees: a storm, but with each snowflake doing everything that is acrobatically possible. Yet these allusions, while sending their specific messages, also acquire an emotional aspect. Plants, Eden, a Tree of Life with which botanist Benn cannot commune, a reclining nude, tigers of desire, 'impulses from the fallen world surrounding this green seclusion' – 'twentieth-century instability'. And against this a different setting, the

Antarctic, the setting of Benn's rambles and of Admiral Byrd's memoirs entitled *Alone*: out there, on the border of borders, the time quickly comes 'when one has nothing to reveal to the other, when even his unformed thoughts can be anticipated, his pet ideas become a meaningless drool', when 'people find each other *out*'. Hand in hand, modernity and Matilda have something in mind for Uncle Benn. It won't be anything obvious. It won't be secret drinking, infidelity, slobby habits – none of that old stuff. The takeover will have a contemporary subtlety. And it will require Benn's collusion.

As we said earlier, Benn is a strong candidate for love in 'a classic form'. Well, classic form is what Matilda seems at first to embody. Benn speaks of his bride as if she were a 'beloved' in a poem by Edgar Allan Poe: 'thy beauty is to me/Like those Nicean barks of yore . . .' 'Even a four-star general,' Kenneth reasons indulgently, 'will sing a Bing Crosby "Boobooboooo" refrain in a moment of softening or weakness about love.' But Benn? 'Thy hyacinth hair, thy classic face', 'those Nicean barks of yore' – whatever *they* might have looked like. Seeing Benn and hearing the terrible poem, Kenneth decides, 'I would as lief have had Bing Crosby.' Still, when a *botanist* starts talking about hyacinth hair, maybe he is on to something. As another observer puts it later on, when Benn married Matilda 'he followed the esthetics of botany on to the human plane'. This is a risky enterprise, for obvious and numerous reasons. Plants, for instance, don't mind living in caves, or wasting their sweetness on the desert air. Plants are innocently beautiful: they don't know that they *have* an esthetic. Plants don't have plans of their own. Plants don't bite back.

Matilda is the only child of rich parents. As a goodwill gesture (this is rich-people etiquette), Benn moves into the family's penthouse duplex:

. . . and there was Uncle in this fantasia of opulence,

every morning wandering in the long rooms of Persian rugs and decorator drapes, lighted cabinets of Baccarat and Wedgwood, and schlock paintings from the 18th century of unidentified (and I'd say uncircumcised) personages from Austria or Italy. Were *they* ever out of place! And Uncle perhaps was even more of a misfit than the portrait subjects, acquired by purchase.

Benn's awkward figure is itself soon draped in an $800 tweed suit. The plant observatory of his head is similarly encased in a costly haircut. Benn's transplantation has begun.

Matilda's mother Jo is deliberately pale and shadowy but Matilda's father, Dr Layamon, is one of the most memorable characters in all Bellow. He is, in fact, a boiling nightmare of sly candour, frank cunning, corruption, complacence and 'TV brightness'. A modern entrepreneur, picking up 1 per cent of everything from his patients and pals, not so much a doctor as a health concessionaire, Layamon is locally known as Motormouth. What Sammler called 'the mad agility of compound deceit' is here elevated to 'conspiratorial inspiration'. When he sits next to Benn his face is so close that it 'is hard to tell whose breath was whose'. Horrible in itself, this TV intimacy has its ulterior aspect.

He was very physical with people. He dropped a hand on your knee, he caught you by the cheek, he worked your shoulder. He played every emotional instrument in the band. You couldn't, however, depend on the music. Suddenly a wild bray would break up the tune. He complimented Benn on his eminence in botany. Then he'd say, 'too bad those overlapping front teeth weren't corrected'; or else: 'Either you're wearing a tight shirt or your *pectoralis major* is overdeveloped – big tits, in other words.' At dinner, when Doctor passed behind Benn's chair, taking his time about it, Uncle couldn't doubt that his bald spot was being inspected. And when they were using old-fashioned urinals at the club, Doctor set his chin on the high partition and looked down through crooked goggles to see how Uncle was hung. His comment was: 'Fire-fighting equipment seems adequate, anyway.'

Matilda is not only Layamon's daughter: she is one of his prime investments. And what does a modern person do with an investment? He protects it, as best he can. 'Don't be annoyed,' he tells Benn, 'but we ran a little check on you, purely private and absolutely discreet. You can't blame us. These are kinky times ... If there was anything bad we wouldn't be sitting here together. Also, if there was serious stuff in the fellow's report, he would have gone to you and tried to sell it to you first. That's the customary blackmail. One expects it.'

Meanwhile the Matilda omens build. Very ominously indeed, Layamon has said of his daughter; 'She didn't have to futz around in Paris with all that postwar sleaze. This girl had brains enough to be chief executive of a blue-chip corporation. With her mentality [mentality!] you could manage NASA ... She's always watching from her satellite. She's never been too absorbed in the French junk to lose track of economics.' The French junk that failed to keep Matilda's mind off economics is sufficiently sinister in itself. She was researching cultural activities under the Nazi occupation: Ernst Junger, Céline.

> ... she won the confidence of the hysterical persons she interviewed, crooks, most of them, whose strange idea was to reconcile the atrocities of the war period with the highest goals of France as a civilization. For instance, to get information for the Resistance you slept with a collaborator, or after a double-dealer was shot you might discover that you truly loved him after all – that way you could have it all: pornography, heartfelt *douleur*, corrupt

love, patriotism, and a fine literary style, so that the purity
of French culture was preserved.

'Rotten through and through,' Kenneth decides. 'No reasonable person would pursue such a subject.'

Here is another early sign that there is something seriously
wrong with Matilda: she sleeps late in the morning. Now, in
most auditoria around the world that sentence might cause
some puzzlement. Not here, though. Oh yes, we all know
that this means something pretty major is up. Remember
Henderson and 'the spirit's sleep'. Remember Citrine, 'out
cold' for most of his manhood and his prime. History is a
nightmare from which we are trying to awake. For Charlie,
history is a nightmare during which he is trying to get
a good night's sleep. Remember Corde, in deep spiritual
trouble in Bucharest – going to bed straight after breakfast!
'As he did this, he sometimes felt how long he had lived
and how many, many times the naked creature had crept
into its bedding.' I trust that my fellow delegates, here in
Haifa, are doing the right thing by their shut-eye. No lie-ins
or siestas or prudent early nights. Sometimes I imagine the
Nobel Laureate checking on the lights-out schedules here at
the university, or grilling the early-call telephone operators
at the hotels, or even prowling the corridors at night, examining the breakfast dockets on the doorhandles. Sleep: my wife
and I, as the fugitive parents of two infant boys, came to Israel
with thoughts of little else. But we haven't had a wink. Saul
wouldn't like it. Perhaps this explains a good deal. If I were
the envious or competitive type, given to brooding about the
superior energies of certain rivals, I might simply conclude
that the enemy never sleeps. All I've got to do is give it up
entirely: then I'll write *The Adventures of Augie March*.

Is Matilda the enemy? 'She hated waking – *hated* it',
'silently warring against bright day and full consciousness'.
As Kenneth observes, 'The lesson she taught was that you
don't often have beauty which doesn't carry some affliction

for the observer.' Her plans for Benn – the uses she will find for him – start to edge into visibility when she takes him to view their prospective home, a place of macabre size and grandeur in an old apartment block called the Roanoke. 'The chairman of the Physics Department is overhead, and the woman whose father invented artificial sweeteners is underneath us.' More American eclecticism. What are they to do in this palazzo? Cower in the pantry? Benn is given to understand that a certain amount of entertaining will be done here. Is this what Matilda sees in him? 'An absentminded professor isn't so bad,' says another appraiser of the match, 'if he has the prestige and isn't *too* absentminded, so you don't actually have to check his fly before letting him out of the house.' Whom will they entertain? People like Pavarotti, Kissinger, people like Bob Hope, the great Shwarzenegger, the woman whose father invented artificial sweeteners? Who cares? Matilda shows Benn the nice view of the sycamores that line the building. It is a marvellous passage:

The thick sycamores he gazed into were pale and brown. The root systems, like hairy mammoths, spread under pavements, around the sewer system and other installations, working underground and drawn towards the core of the earth ... As he stared at them he thought he heard a moan coming from behind, from the pasture-sized room at his back. What would it be moaning about? (It was not a human sound.) The only responsible interpretation was that it was a projection, pure and simple, inspired by the bare sycamores ... He himself would have made such a sound if he hadn't been on his best behaviour ... This vast place put up in 1910 by dry-goods merchant princes – its rooms, he said, made him think of cisterns of self-love that had dried out ...

And who will pay for all this? Will Benn, on his salary of $60,000 ('just about what it costs to keep two convicts down in Stateville')? How can he? Yet Benn will pay, in more senses than one. Benn will pay.

Each morning, in the penthouse duplex, while Matilda scowls, swears at the maid, and drinks her pints of *caffe espresso*, Benn sits in the breakfast nook, obscurely waiting.

> ... all he could do was look out at the city, which fills so many miles. All those abandoned industries awaiting electronic resurrection, the colossal body of the Rustbelt, the stems of the tall chimneys nowadays bearing no blossoms of smoke. One of your privileges if you were very rich was to command a vast view of this devastation.

About now, one realises that the city, 'the great Rustbelt metropolis', is unnamed. I read *More Die of Heartbreak* in two slightly different versions, in British galleys and in an American bound proof (for when the books of great men go forth into the world they spawn and mutate, geometrically multiplying like a beneficent virus). In the earlier version it was possible to suppose that the city was an unnamed Chicago, nudged a little towards the north-east. In the later version Bellow has headed off this supposition. It is not an unnamed Chicago; it is not an unnamed city; it is a nameless city, and the more resonant for that, like a nameless dread.

From the window, 'dominating those miles of rubble', Benn sees the Ecliptic Circle Electronic Tower, a high-tech, 'Jap-built' colossus. Bellow's spectral city is structured round that Tower. And so is his novel. Like all Bellow's most powerful symbols (though it is a symbol made concrete – massively concretised), the Tower steals up on you with meaning, looming into significance, casting a lengthening shadow. 'My old life is lying under it,' says Benn (and he is not speaking metaphorically), ' – my mother's kitchen, my father's bookshelves, the mulberry trees.' Matilda dislikes reminiscence about the humble past (she thinks it betrays a 'steerage mentality'), but Benn Crader's musings about the Electronic Tower are quietly indulged. For the Tower is built on the site of the Crader Home for Invalids. The usual nervous dinner at the Layamons':

'We used to live on that spot. We moved there from Jefferson Street when I was about twelve . . . It came with a nice yard. There were two big mulberry trees and they attracted lots of grackles in June.' Little notice was taken of this natural history. 'Very fine trees, the kind with the white fruit. The purple mulberries have a better flavor.' Expressive looks passed among the Layamons. Uncle was aware of these but interpreted them as signs of boredom. There he was definitely wrong, as we shall see.

Benn and his parents once 'owned' the Electronic Tower, or its foundations. Thereby hangs a tale i.e. a deal, i.e. a swindle.

It is time now to gather Harold Vilitzer into the story: Vilitzer, *Uncle*'s uncle. Here would seem to be a vastly contemporary phenomenon, a man formidably equipped with goals, a life-plan, a dream: 'His main objective was to pile up a huge personal fortune, and the hell with everything else.' Enter into a disagreement with Harold and he will put your head in a vice; either you change your mind or he will change your head. In the early days,

. . . he went on the street, right here in town, taking bets, paying off the police. As a bookie, he was such a success out in the fresh air that when he had a big loss the cops collected 50,000 bucks among themselves to keep him in business. It was worth it to them. Next thing we knew, he was in politics.

Where else? Political office, in this novel, is seen as a knife-edge between farcical elevation and federal indictment. In the Electronic Tower deal, Vilitzer routinely screwed his family out of several million dollars. Benn, always intoxicated by consanguinity (and Jewish consanguinity is a special phenomenon, we remember, an anachronism of which the Jews were about to divest themselves, until the present century intervened), Benn still loves his uncle and bears no grudge about the fraud. Vilitzer, over eighty and not well, has no regrets either, naturally: Benn is only a 'collateral relative', and the money rule, besides, is *mercilessness*. Kenneth understands: 'Death is merciless, and therefore the ground rules of conduct have to include an equal and opposite hardness. From this it follows that kinship is bullshit.' All very modern, and, compared to Benn, Vilitzer looks unpierceably contemporary. Compared to the Layamons, though, Vilitzer is a dinosaur.

Benn had come 'haunting around the edges of the Layamon world, drawn by his longings'. And they received him, for much simpler – or much clearer – reasons of their own. As these become clear to him (and he will not quite face their clarity, clinging to that semi-spurious absentmindedness, the immunity claim, simultaneous innocence and guilt) something goes wrong with Matilda's beauty. As beauty, as polish, as gloss, it remains the same, but Benn's 'prophetic soul' (My prophetic soul! My uncle!) has been sending him messages from the other side. These are dreadful pages, full of high and harrowing comedy: an onslaught of mutinous impulses, 'associational anarchy', thought murders, sexual goblins that nip giggling past the bedroom door. Surveying the Electronic Tower one night, Mrs Layamon, with full TV suavity, dubs it 'an important piece of modern beauty'. Benn has to resist the temptation to reply: 'That's what your *daughter* is.' A thing of beauty is a joy for ever, sang the poet. A thing, or a piece, of *modern* beauty is a joy for about ten minutes, if that. It is more like an eternal torment. This is Kenneth:

Why shouldn't a man want a beautiful wife? If he's going to renounce all others, he might as well get a beauty. Only the present happens to be an all-time world climax, a peak of genius for external perfection and high finish . . . Heartless beauty has never been so wonderful. But with men and women, human warmth is poured into the invention. When there's light and heat in the eyes and cheeks of a woman, you can't possibly tell if it's genuine. Does your beauty yearn for love, for a husband, or is she after a front man, a suitable cover for her beauty operations?

These beauty operations Benn cannot penetrate. 'The higher the range of vision, the more your control is weakened': the only clues he gets are images of fear and repulsion. And by now, at night, 'the Electronic Tower floats close till it's right on top of him, every single window lighted and on a dead course for the penthouse'.

Just as reason 'doesn't seem to have the social base it once had', so 'the natures that could love have become too unstable to do it'. Looking at his uncle's face Kenneth decides that 'a head as round as that was born to roll'. Self-betrayed (the vision failed him), Benn falls in with what Dr Layamon calls 'the overall game-plan' ('You're entitled to live in style, a rich scientist and not just a research rat'). He agrees to confront Vilitzer; and this act involves him in a further sexual ordeal, itself a savage contrivance in this vigorously intricate novel. On the edge of indictment, only a few feet from the slammer, Vilitzer wheels himself up from Florida, from the sunbelt to the rustbelt, to attend a parole-board hearing – not as defendant but as supervisor. A rape case, a forensic spectacular, lab analysis, spermatazoa experts, a man with a ten-foot pointer identifying two images on a lit screen: a blow-up of the girl's underpants ('all those spatter marks, and ragged circles like spacecraft photographs of the moons of Uranus'), and one of her belly, on which the letters LOV have been scrawled with a broken Budweiser bottle. What makes this such a shrill image of modern sexuality? Not the rape, not the violence and the (thematically resonant) possibility of self-injury, not even the three gory letters, illiterate or merely forgetful. No, it is the display, the slides, the glare, the patient television cameras that comprise the gladiatorial blood-sport of contemporary Eros.

The meeting with Vilitzer, like so many significant meetings in this book, takes place in the middle air, fifty floors up, in a tinted cloudscape presided over by the Electronic Tower.

> The scattering light of the morning spectrum all over the glassy conference room surrounded this conversation with a contemporary equivalent of church illumination. The sun itself, without the usual obstruction of nature prevailing at ground level, transmitted directly a message about our human origins. Signals from our earth's star circled us in radiant threads. It was our option to take note of them or not. Nobody is forced to, of course.

And what a conversation ensues, equally eloquent about our human origins and our human destinations. Enraged, 'proud of having dedicated himself to the high service of money', Vilitzer asks Benn: 'What do you need two million dollars for?' The answer is, of course: to make atonement to the Layamons – to pay for their wasted time. 'You see!' says Vilitzer in triumph. 'He doesn't understand even the first basic principle.' And this is how it goes, just before Vilitzer attempts to strike:

> 'You won't answer this, Uncle Harold,' said Benn. 'But what did you make on the sale of that property?'
> 'You think I'm going to go into that with a man like *you*?'
> 'Why not with me?'
> 'Because you don't *know* anything!'

I shall foreclose the narrative here, on this great epiphany: the illiterate half-dead hoodlum rejects, excludes, dismisses the world-famous pure scientist – because he doesn't *know* anything. And Vilitzer is right, he is dead right. Benn's world is entirely other; he has no business here. It is the Layamons, the new villains or the new utensils of villainy, the truly modern, who proclaim that there *is* no other, who bring everything in and use whatever is there to be used, including innocence, including beauty, including love.

I said that *More Die of Heartbreak* is like a rumour of war against America. Here in three widely separated quotes is how it is going, and how it will continue to go: America, and the war against her.

Doctor Layamon then said to him, ... 'Glad to see you stand up for yourself'.
Down from the sublime regions, where you had no access to him. Now, owing to self-interest, you could get a grip on Uncle. The Layamons had set themselves to bring Benn in, that is, to bring him back to the one great thing that America has, which is the *American*. You can't have a son-in-law by your American hearth who has another habitat – extraterrestrial or some such goddam thing.

People like ourselves weren't part of the main enterprise. The main enterprise was America itself, and the increase of its powers.

I could feel the perturbation widening and widening as I lay there and became aware that I had come to depend on his spirit. Without its support, the buoyancy went out of me, the city itself became a drag. The USA, too, that terrific posthistorical enterprise carrying our destinies, lost momentum, sagged, softened. There threaded itself through me the dreadful suspicion that the costs of its dynamism were bigger than I had reckoned ... The price was infinitely greater than the easy suppositions

⌐f the open society led you to expect ... There seems
to be a huge force that advances, propels, and this pro-
pellant increases its power by drawing value away from
the personal life and fitting us for its colossal purpose. It
demands the abolition of such things as love and art ...
of gifts like Uncle's, which it can tolerate intermittently if
they don't get in its way.

In *To Jerusalem and Back* Bellow wrote: 'for the first
time in history, the human species as a whole has gone into
politics. What is going on will not leave us alone. Neither
the facts nor the deformations.' Not only politics. Also economics. Also the military, since we are all in the army now,
we are all on the front line. And, countervailingly, we have
all entered the love race, the 'sexual marathon', whether we
have the talent for it or not. Thus everyone seeks the sexual
remedy, or as Kenneth more gently puts it: 'they do the act
by which love would be transmitted if there *were* any'.
Interviewed on TV about Chernobyl, Benn says that, bad
as radiation is, he is sure that more die of heartbreak. 'And
isn't that a crazy remark?' Kenneth is asked. 'Maybe not. If
people were clear about it, more aware of their feelings, then
you'd see a real march on Washington. The capital could
never hold all that sorrow.'

I know that *More Die of Heartbreak* is a work of inspiration, another great efflorescence. How? Because it changes
the way you see everything. It harrows and it enhances.
In the age of science, in the modern age, the arts might
become 'the nursery games of humankind, which had to be
left behind when the age of science began. The humanities
would be called upon to choose a wallpaper for the crypt,
as the end drew near.' If I were feeling despondent, rather
than exalted, I would tell Mr Bellow that he could pick my
wallpaper any time he liked. But I will go the other way,
with Kenneth, who demands that we make a turning point,
that we make *ourselves* a turning point – I, we, you. 'No

use for existing unless your life is a turning point. No use joining the general march . . .' It sounds like a tall order. It is a tall order. But *he's* done it. Thank you. And thank you, Mr Bellow.

SNOOKER WITH JULIAN BARNES

Julian Barnes and I agreed to dispute the best of five frames of snooker and then write about it for Esquire *magazine. This is my version.*

By analogy with Whirlwind White and Hurricane Higgins, I am known, in the snooker world, as Earthquake Amis. A *flair* player, one who relies on *natural ability*, his only academy the pool halls and borstal rec-rooms of a *misspent youth*: inconsistent, foul-tempered, over-ambitious, graceless alike in victory and defeat, and capable of missing *anything*. On the other hand, I do hit the ball tremendously hard and with various violent spins. A while ago I considered changing my snookering nickname (which I am at complete liberty to do, because I'm the only one who ever uses it), to take account of the New Weather: global warming, and so on. I briefly became known as Ozone Amis. But the past summer saw a reversion to the Old Weather (cloud and warm rain: England in July, where the cricketer casts no shadow), and somehow Earthquake has stuck.

I have thought long and hard and often over the years about a suitable nickname for my opponent. Let's see. Snooker frames with Julian last about twice as long as they do with anybody else. His play is marked by exaggerated, even psychotic caution, as if, after the slightest lapse on his part, I will coolly rise from my chair and assemble a century clearance – rather than a single miscued jump-shot double-kiss *in-off*. Otherwise he is persistent, deliberate, gentlemanly, and unpitying. He is at his strongest (and I am at my weakest) when only six or seven balls remain, when wariness is all. Oh, how he loves to thwart and hamper . . . Blizzard Barnes, then, I quickly rejected: the temperature's right, but the agitation is way off target. The way he wears you down, the way he bleeds you white – if his name were Julian Garnes, he would have long been known as the Glacier. The appealing aptness of slow-moving natural processes led me to flirt with Geology Jules. Finally, though, because his style resembles not a force of nature so much as a medium of measurement or response (response to pressure, atmospheric pressure), I settled on something less personal: Barometer Barnes.

We used to play for money, he and I, twenty years ago. Pounds sterling changed hands, in note form – and they really mattered. A win or a loss could affect how well you lived for a day or two. I nearly always won, as I remember; and as we left the club or the hall I would make quite a show of hailing a taxi, offering to drop Julian off at the nearest tube. When, years later, he bought his own table (and a house big enough to put it in), and we started playing regularly, almost weekly, we wondered whether we should go on playing for money. Because the money didn't matter now, and our games were more evenly and bitterly fought, and we agreed that the rivalry shouldn't – and indeed couldn't – get any tenser. It's all a nightmare anyway.

Unlike the Barometer, who is largely faithful and wholly site-tenacious, the Earthquake puts out all over town. My casual opponents include a biographer, an entrepreneur, a political analyst, a tennis pro, a handyman, a philosopher and a hustler (who casually obliterates the fifty-point leads he gives me in a torrent of pinks and blacks). All these players can make me flinch and squirm: but it's nothing compared to the torment meted out by the Barometer. With him, even when I'm an inch away from clear victory, I sometimes wonder if I have *ever* suffered so. Why is this? Because we have 'contrasting styles', and go back a long way, and are both novelists? No. It's because there's nothing in it. We're equal. Each frame is decided by the tiniest psychological edge, by sniggering fate – by the sneer of the snooker gods who determine the rub of the green.

I prepared for the match with an early night, a breakfast rich in carbohydrates, and, later that morning, a secret visit to a local club, where, with a pensive pint of low-alc lager, I practised alone: to get the spasms out of my cueing arm, to neutralise the excitement (i.e. panic) of one's induction into the verdant six-bagged oblong. With epic nonchalance I motored north. We've each had our hot streaks, I won't deny: the whammy has changed hands many times. For a while, as Julian once accurately and hauntingly said to me, 'You now come here with fear in your heart.' But in recent weeks the whammy has been mine: just. Barometer Barnes received me calmly. He was pretending to take an interest in the Edberg-McEnroe fourth-rounder at Wimbledon, further claiming to see an encouraging paradigm in Edberg, the expressionless icicle, versus McEnroe, the scowling has-been. Of course, we hardly needed to say, as we made our way upstairs, that we were both nervous wrecks.

Our cues bespeak us – both, coincidentally, presents from our wives (pious admirers, naturally, of their husbands' baizecraft). The Barometer's cue is a one-piece broadsword, the Earthquake's a two-piece rapier, which, moreover, comes in a yob-heaven black leatherette case with twin combination locks. His tip is ponderously large, half the size of the cue-ball; mine is as slender as a sting – excellent for spins and miscues. The blinds were lowered. The gentlemen ruminatively chalked. I felt confident and self-possessed, and recovered quickly from the catastrophe of losing the toss.

The pattern of our recent frames has been as follows. I go into the end-game (the colours) with a lead of about 30 –

and then win on the black. The equivalent in tennis would be a 6–0 lead in the tie-break, and eventual victory at 19–17. This was, at least, an improvement on an earlier pattern, where I went into the end-game with a lead of about 30 – and then *lost* on the black. That's the Barometer for you: never more dangerous than when in the portals of the slaughterhouse. The man's an animal. My brain is encrusted with scar tissue from all the frames he has pinched and nicked. I can so easily fall apart . . . In frame one I went into the colours, feeling completely hysterical, with a lead of about 30 – and won on the brown! 61–32. No sweat. Rack 'em.

Frame two, I say with tears of pride in my eyes, was a near duplicate, 51–14, my opponent disgustedly resigning with blue, pink and black still on the table. I was impressed. I was astounded. I hadn't relaxed or over-reached or crumbled or collapsed. I saved all that for frame three. All wobble and tremor, the Quake just wasn't making it on to the Richter Scale. His eyes now lit by a weak leer of hope, Barometer Barnes closed me out on the pink: 35–43.

Here's a little confession. Julian and I are not terribly good at snooker. But we *can* be terribly bad at it. The longest, if not the highest, break of the day was my five-baller, which scored 8 (green, yellow, three reds). There was also a 15 (me), a 13 (him) and a 12 (me). My opponent secured his third-frame win, for example, by rifling in breaks of 4, 7, 6, 5 and 3. The fourth frame, though, was an all-howler affair, a series of abject calamities. The builders on the scaffolding outside must have thought that the house contained a pack of feral beasts, groaning at their captivity, their ill-treatment, their lousy food. At one point the score stood at 13–18, without a colour potted. The only ball that seemed to find the pocket was the white, in a bad dream of *in-offs* and *in-withs* – plus, from Julian, a world-class *in-instead*, the cue-ball struck with such a prodigious unintentional side-spin that after a deadened impact it ambled on grimly into the corner bag. Altogether appropriately and ingloriously, the frame ended with the Barometer's *in-off* the black, the ball lasering in on the middle pocket at a preposterous angle. 58–46. The taste of victory is sweet.

Actually I felt strangely subdued as I drove home. Gutted for the Barometer, no doubt. He took it like a man, which is better than I would have taken it. I would have taken it like a boy. Later, though, I felt tremendously happy and high-souled. I felt as if I had singlehandedly wrecked San Francisco. It occurred to me that all the pleasure of snooker comes either in anticipation or retrospect. On the table, everything is a falling-short, hamfisted, cross-purposed – a mortified groping. Come to think of it, the same goes for tennis, chess, poker, darts and pinball. Asked about his writing, the great Jimmy White once admitted that he wasn't much good at it, adding: 'Not much good at the reading neither. Either.' I *can* read and write, and to a high standard. As for the snooker, well, to approach the televisual ideal, by which we all measure ourselves, I'd have to do nothing else for the rest of my life. Then snooker might work out and measure up, with everything going where you want it to go, at the right weight and angle. Then snooker might feel like writing.

1991

ROBOCOP II

ROBOCOP: PRIME DIRECTIVES
1 Serve the Public Trust
2 Protect the Innocent
3 Uphold the Law

RoboCop II – and I mean the robot, not the movie – looks like a wasp-waisted three-ton Swiss Army penknife with all its blades outturned: cutters, skewers, pincers, gougers. Called 'The Monster' in the script and on the set, this sizzling cyborg is not RoboCop's successor but his adversary. 'The concept of two robots duking it out', says one of his creators, 'was a given.' Part Man, Part Machine, All Psychopath, RoboCop II is also, for good measure, a drug-addict, a vigorous abuser of a substance called *Nuke*. He is programmed to Break the Law, Protect the Guilty, and Trash the Public Trust. 'We're very pleased with him,' says his chief designer. 'The face is great. Those twin panels shoot back revealing a digitalised screen, with receding lines giving a weird to-infinity effect.' For now, the curved diagonal panels remain closed, impeccably hostile and severe, like the sharp prow – the leading edge – of the future.

Last fall, downtown Houston was also giving a good imitation of the henceforward. The main precincts are deserted after 6 pm – for this is a modern city, and no one is seriously expected to live in it. You *work* in it. Elegantly alienated youths rollerskate through the empty malls. They aren't sullen or simmering or smashed; they are just not interested. Later, the night sky will contain the faint reports of gunfire: the crack wars of the crack gangs. Driving through the more depressed areas the next day, you will find the streets littered with beercans, hookers ('Hey, white boy!'), undergarments, human wigs – and the nomadic poor, clustered in the steel and concrete crevices of the city; soon, the police will come and briskly pressure-hose them out of there, and they will be obliged to regroup somewhere else. But not downtown, where the future is contentedly going about its business. Look into the magenta glass of the looming skyscraper, and what do you see? The reflection of another skyscraper – and then another, and then another.

This month there is street theatre in Houston: the making of *RoboCop II*. Onlookers gather early behind the police lines. The crowd (mostly black) has come to see what the imported natives (mostly white) will get up to this evening, what explosions and firestorms they will stage, what miracles of wreckage they will achieve: what strafings, what stompings, what splatterings. The *ah*s and *ow*s of this first preview audience are strictly calibrated to the size of the bang, the height of the flamespout. All week the night action takes place amid the fortress architecture of Houston's cultural centre: between the theatre and the opera house. The filmmakers are obliged by the city to get through their most thunderous scenes before 8 pm, when the curtain goes up on the other performance (tonight, a rock opera of *Measure for Measure*). But they never make it.

'HOLD THE SMOKE!' says the Assistant Director into his bullhorn. 'I'LL NEED SOME BEEF.' Beef means muscle, means sceneshifters – for the upended cars, the shattered stanchions. 'I SAID HOLD THE SMOKE . . . *MORE* BEEF!'

A mist of stardom shrouds the trailer of Peter Weller,

who has yet to appear. Everyone waits. A rejuvenated, reglamorised Nancy Allen sits chatting on a director's chair (her handsome new boyfriend is near by, the silent custodian of her second blooming). Nancy plays Lewis, RoboCop's sidekick. It is a pivotal role, and she understands its centrality. She is the only 'real' presence in both movies: everyone else is either a hood, a corporation ogre, a scientist, or a robot. Nancy is happy to kill time; indeed, she is an expert time-killer, like all movie stars, for there is much time to kill. Everyone waits. Weapons expert Randy Moore trundles on to the set to deal with 'a blanks problem'. Randy's outrageous handguns and bazookas look at home in Houston: they wouldn't seem out of place, you feel, in the average Texan kitchen. At length, Randy resolves the blanks problem, and everyone goes back to what they were doing before: waiting.

Unbelievably, about five hours later, two whole shots are in the can. Nancy has scaled an armed-personnel carrier and successfully back-kicked a security guard in the face. And Peter has scaled a media truck and readied himself to pounce on The Monster. But the street audience is unconvinced, and gives a collective shrug before it disperses, as if to say, 'Is that *it*?' And you sympathise. You want to explain to the Houston crowd that what they are getting is, as yet, only half-formed, only half-made. As yet, the illusion is embarrassingly – but necessarily – incomplete. Peter hasn't got his RoboCop pants on, for instance (the shot is only waist-up). And Nancy's back-kick looks dainty and innocuous. And the battleground is littered with scene-coordinators with their walkie-talkies. And the corporation HQ seems punily small-scale. And The Monster is still in the prop shop . . .

This is the thing with *RoboCop*: it all comes later – the sheen, the *finish*. What you see here in Houston is just raw material, the chaos of the merely contemporary. Only in the lab will it take on the hard edge of the future. *RoboCop* is itself a sign of things to come: the new depth of illusion, the widening gulf between set and screen. On screen, the corporation HQ will have a matte painting on it and will loom eighty storeys high. The scene-coordinators will be blacked out of shot. The Monster will be on duty. Peter will appear to have his pants on. And Nancy's back-kick will be crunchy.

The *RoboCop II* team has a boy-genius or crazy-professor feel to it. On the set the atmosphere reminds you of the exotic unsalubriousness of Washington Square Park in New York, where all the skateboarders are chess prodigies, the bums are International Grand Masters, and the lounging brothers have four-figure IQs. Director Irvin Kershner (*Never Say Never Again*, *The Empire Strikes Back*) looks like a radical Sixties academic. Producer Jon Davison (*Piranha*, *Airplane!*, *RoboCop*) has the droll, wheedling delivery of a Greenwich Village intellectual. All around there is a reassuring sense of strength-in-depth. Unit publicists are usually cyborgs themselves, but *RoboCop II*'s Paul Sammon is an omnicompetent film-maker, writer, computer ace. And here's cold proof of how hip and classy this outfit is: nearly everyone had read my stuff. Even the continuity girl turns around and quotes me, word perfect . . . And shabbily lurking by the coke-machine and the chow-trailer are Oscar-winning designers, make-up artists, stop-motion animators, stunt illusionists – tricksters, wizards, futurists.

RoboCop made money (£50 million in the US alone), and everybody hopes that *RoboCop II* will do at least as well. But they are in it for love – obsessive love. Between rehearsals they crouch down among the cables, the webbing, the gizmo wagons and gadget trolleys and gimmick barrows, the cans of engine enamel, the bottles of Havoline. They talk about the film – 'the show' – with almost parental earnestness and cautious pride, as if they were preparing an enormous machine, or an enormous robot, for smooth functioning, fully tuned and 'tweaked'. Someone is going around with a box of Noisebuster earplugs. We help ourselves. One of the redetailed Ford Taurus turbocruisers is about to blow. 'Not the "beauty car" – the one nearest camera – but the *oldest* car,' Paul Sammon tells me. 'They might not get it done in time, but if they don't they'll want to do something else noisy.' The atrocious detonation comes and goes, and the team gets ready to do it all again.

'Wetdown,' says Irvin Kershner – Kersh – to his assistant. 'WETDOWN,' says his assistant. There ensues, of all things, a long delay, as every inch of the set is hosed with water. The set is regularly wetdowned to give it a glossy, slinky, *noiry* look – also to preserve continuity, in case it rains. 'BEEF . . . MORE BEEF.' On comes the beef: unsmiling figures who all seem to be called things like Tug and Tiff and Heft. The beef on *RoboCop II*, you feel, will be better beef than usual, real thinking man's beef, the most skilled and dedicated beef you can buy.

That night's shoot spluttered on until 4 am, but Jon Davison is at his desk early the next morning. Like all on-the-job moviemen he has an air of exalted exhaustion, of priestly fatigue. 'The whole thing was *awful* the first time around,' Davison croaks. 'Robo himself just didn't work visually. You know: his ass moved in a funny way, he looked smaller than the women. But now . . . it's all going along.' Nobody knows exactly how much the first movie's *frisson* owed to its director, Paul Verhoeven, and his 'neurotic elan', in the phrase of one team-member (here are some other phrases: 'He's a wildman.' 'A sick genius.' 'A real extremist.' 'Bananas.' 'Nuts'). 'Kersh', says Davison, with some concern, 'is, of course, *much* less violent than Paul . . .' Kersh is also sixty-seven; and at present he is too busy to sleep, let alone be interviewed. There is a feeling that Kersh will have to be kept an eye on. He may have a weakness for the *light*. Others, then (the deep talent), will have to make sure it's *heavy*.

The floors of the production offices are heaped with Fed Ex envelopes and copies of *Variety*, but the walls are papered with fanatically exact 'storyboards' of the scenes to come, frame by frame. The drawings remind you of RoboCop's imaginative origins: comic books. Comic books, given flesh, and metal – given hard life. 'What made you choose Peter Weller?' I asked. I wondered if it had anything to do with his mouth (his only visible feature for much of the film) and what my wife described as the 'unerotic perfection' of its cupid's-bow lips. 'His mouth? No! Peter was chosen because no other actor would do it.' Like all surprise successes, *RoboCop* was something of a lucky accident. It gathered the right people at the right place at the right time. Davison put them there. He is the puppet-master – or rather the master of the puppeteers: Verhoeven, Weller, the designers and animators, right the way down to all the unsung eggheads at Dream Quest, Praxis, Intervideo, Screaming Lizard and Visual Concept Engineering.

RoboCop was a genuine original. All its admirers know this, and even its detractors partly sense it. *RoboCop* was *doubly* futuristic. As a movie, and as a vision, it wasn't just state-of-the-art. It was also state-of-the-science: when you see its twirling rivets and burnished heat-exchangers, when you hear its venomous shunts and succulent fizzes, you suspect that the future really might feel like this – that it will act this way on your very nerve-ends. Technology is god in *RoboCop*, but it is also the villain, with its triumphant humourlessness, its puerile ingenuity, its dumb glamour. And that ambivalence explains why *RoboCop*'s special effects had a special effect.

Also a special *affect*. To define: *affect* means 'feeling tone'; and *affectlessness* means 'no feeling tone' – no heart. And the heartlessness of our response to the *RoboCop* future is most noticeable, of course, when we confront the movie's extreme violence. American children laugh at *Rambo* because they don't yet know what violence means, because they shouldn't be watching *Rambo* (what, you wonder, will *their* children be laughing at?). The hoods in *RoboCop* — and in most American thrillers of the past twenty years — laugh as they kill and rape and devastate because this is the expression of their anti-ethics, their sociopathology. But *we* laugh at the violence in *RoboCop*, even though we really should know better. We laugh because we have no response to it. We laugh to fill the silence, to fill the vacuum, like embarrassed Japanese.

Take the celebrated and show-stealing scene in the corporation boardroom, when the grinning VP introduces the executives to his latest concept in 'urban pacification', Enforcement Droid 209. An android is supposedly 'a robot with human form', but there is nothing humanoid, or even organic-looking, about ED 209, whose otherness is in fact emphasised by its weird borrowings from the animal kingdom: the shape of the 'face' (killer whale), its warning growl (angry black leopard), its squeal of distress (dying pig). By way of demonstration, the VP asks a young executive to raise a gun at ED 209 'in a threatening manner'. The robot jerks into its attack mode, and says, in its warped baritone (the voice is actually Jon Davison's, slowed and distorted), *Please put down your weapon. You have twenty seconds to comply.* The executive complies, but the machine advances, citing the appropriate penal violation before announcing, with robotic probity, *I am now authorised to use physical force.*

There instantly follows a scene of startling butchery, partly cut by the censors, in which ED 209 applies physical force — with twin machine-guns. 'We always knew that sequence was going to be excessive,' Jon Davison has said. 'I sent somebody down to the local 7-11 to get the biggest ziplock baggies they had; and then we filled them with blood.' In the footage submitted to the MPAA, the executive's corpse received an additional 200 rounds. 'I thought it was funny and the preview audience thought it was funny. The censors didn't think it was funny. The result was that they took something that was basically funny and turned it into something horrifying.' Actually, the comic element survives. Where there is no affect, there is no horror. And we laugh because there's nothing else to do.

But our laughter isn't entirely wanton. I finally met up with ED 209, in one of the unit's prop shops. It looks smaller than it does on screen, and slightly bedraggled: one of its gun-arms was ripped off while it was making a PR appearance at a Los Angeles theatre. But it still inspires real menace and amusement, because of the integral brilliance of its design. This is ED's creator, Craig Davies:

> I did include things that were my own digs at what I see as a really lame current corporate design policy. For instance, there are four huge hydraulic rams on the legs, even though a creature like ED wouldn't need nearly that many. So it's like complete redundancy – a true corporate product.

The violence of *RoboCop* isn't the 'poetic' violence of, say, Peckinpah. It is 'sweet' violence: violence as technological fix. When we laugh at ED 209, we laugh at corporate overkill, corporate literalism. Here is a death-dealer with a heart made by Yamaha: thoroughly sophisticated, thoroughly murderous, and thoroughly moronic. When we laugh at ED 209, we laugh at something that already exists in the present and eagerly awaits us in the future. The future won't just happen: it will be our creation, our machine.

The time had come to do the star interview – a nervous interlude. Peter Weller was chosen for *RoboCop* because he was the only actor who would do it. For the sequel, naturally, he is the only actor who would do. This is a period of what Hollywood calls 'dignity' for Peter. Already, the night before, Paul Sammon and I had tiptoed to the star trailer. Covertly we watched Peter limbering up in his cycling shorts, his face already 'gone' in Robo's numb glaze. We tiptoed away again. For RoboCop, also, must come close to affectlessness incarnate. Not quite incarnate, because he is part machine. And not quite affectless, because he is still a man.

There are three distinct phases in the evolution of a movie star. Stage 1 represents the swirling, gaseous years of ambition, fever, hard work. In Stage 2 (the briefest stage: you might call it 'Denial'), the star solidifies and heats up, all the time pretending that nothing irreversible is happening to him. Stage 3 brings the nuclear burning of full deity; hereafter, no mortal can ever really look his way. Peter Weller is halfway through Stage 2, still struggling somehow to *combine* stardom with his original identity. It can't be done. Such laws are universal. The old Peter will be lost for ever in the cosmic fire. And then the star awaits its final destiny: white dwarf, red giant, black hole.

Wonderfully opaque and stylised on the screen as RoboCop, Peter Weller, in real life, is *all* affect: it's like being in a room, or a trailer, with about fifty different people. Simon Schama's new study of the French Revolution is cracked open on the table; so is *Teach Yourself French*; so is *Teach Yourself Italian*. He puts down his trumpet, looks up from the stack of inspirational videos (*Ivan the Terrible*) and shouts out of the window for more classical CDs. His feeling-tone is intense; but so is his muscle-tone. He hums with vigour. I would too, I suppose, if I got up at three and ran 16 miles every morning, which Peter does, before settling down to his two-hour make-up session. What with one thing and another, he's neglecting his yoga and karate and aido – or was it his ashinto, or akimbo? 'He's a maniac,' says Moni, Peter's mime coach, admiringly. '*Very* systematic.'

'The patience factor on number one was nuts,' says Weller, in his hybrid style. 'It took *ten hours* just to get into the suit. Then five. Then four. Now it's one-and-a-half. *Robo II* is easier because we're over the hump of making this shit *work*. There's a Harvard professor who teaches *RoboCop* in a course on the Hellenistic hero. But I tell you, it's heroic just to be in that suit. The real preparation went much deeper. Moni and I worked our ass off, man.'

I believed it. There is nothing accidental about the strange beauty of RoboCop in motion; the effect is fully thought out, and fully achieved. Like many others on the team, Weller is more than a perfectionist. He is an absolutist. For him, it is a kind of liberation, and not a hindrance, to do all his acting with his neck. 'Did you have any doubts about doing the sequel?' I routinely asked. 'Now that you're a major – '

'Now that I'm a major shit, you mean?' He smiled brightly. 'No. I didn't worry about the dangers of all that career shit. I thought: Do I want to judge up all *that* jazz?'

'What's the key to the part? For you.'

'Aside from executing the physicality of the robot – I think of him as like a guy with amnesia. That's the only plane on which I address this character.'

Later, Weller arrives on the set in a caddycart; he stands there, holding the rail – a modern Steve Reeves, on a modern chariot. An entire truck-sized cooling unit is trained on him as his dressers do the final clip-on and polish. Additional helpers attend to his itches and aches and stiffnesses. He looks charged. He is *the man*. Like the creation he plays, though, Weller is only partly human now; to some extent, inevitably, he is *product*. The lost-self theme works so powerfully on us – perhaps we all feel it. Perhaps, as we speed into the future, we all feel that something has been left behind.

RoboCop II was being made by a kind of brotherhood – a brotherhood of know-how and can-do – and on the set there was an attempt at a kind of moose secrecy. One of Paul Sammon's duties was to thwart paparazzi ('They want shots of The Monster. Or Peter without his suit on'). Similar interdictions apply to the script. I'm not allowed to quote from it. But presumably I'm allowed to praise it.

The author is another boy-genius, Frank Miller, who wrote the cult comic book *Batman: The Dark Knight Returns*. He is perfectly placed to expand and deepen the RoboCop idea; he understands how 'this unique creation' vibrates with myth, everything from Frankenstein to Captain Marvel. *RoboCop II* will feature the same underlit corporate boardrooms, the 'mediated' reality of ads and newscasts, the same reflexive corruption and passionless violence. The script also offers us a more pained and plangent hero, and two resonant new villains: a murderous twelve-year-old drug baron, and RoboCop II itself – the heir, not of RoboCop, but of ED 209, the latest concept in machine literalism, machine justice. Frank Miller has seen the future. And it sucks.

On the last night I patrolled the set with Paul Sammon. We quizzed and banished a lady 'onlooker' with a four-foot lens on her camera. The street audience had already gathered for the night's viewing ('They're going to blow *that* one'). All around, monitoring the set, was the city's superstructure and its real personnel: real firemen, real cops.

And beyond them, meanwhile, on the higher ramps, the young rollerskaters loop and glide, remote and self-possessed. Ironically, these incurious youths are themselves much talked about and widely celebrated; magazine articles have been written about them. They exude calm and indifference and silent *esprit de corps*: immaculately affectless. They are the audience of the future. They will watch the *RoboCop* double bill with no response at all – without a tremor, without a smile, without a flinch of recognition.

Premiere, 1990

SALMAN RUSHDIE

Salman Rushdie, the author of a much-discussed novel called *The Satanic Verses*, is still with us. One feels the need to emphasise this fact: that he is still around. He is caught up in a trap or a travesty; he is condemned to enact his own fictional themes of exile, ostracism, disjuncture, personal reinvention; he occupies a kind of shadowland; but he is formidably alive. The Rushdie Debate has reached a chokepoint where no one seems to be able to speak naturally. In that sense the forces of humourlessness have already triumphed. Rushdie's life has been permanently distorted. I hereby assert, then, that his humanity is unimpaired and entire.

Direct encounters with the man remain infrequent, and tortuous. If you want to meet up with the Minotaur, you have to enter the labyrinth of his security arrangements. Yet various glimpses and sightings are always current among his friends: Rushdie, at midnight, proposing to recite the Complete Works of Bob Dylan; or watching the World Cup on television last summer (with his remorseless parodies of the sportscasters); or falling over while demonstrating an ambitiously low-slung version of the Twist; or eating pizza and listening to Jimi Hendrix. Rushdie's situation is truly Manichaean, but he is neither a god nor a devil; he is just *a writer* – comical and protean, ironical and ardent. To bear this out, Rushdie has now produced a defiantly high-spirited and chivalrous novel, a children's book for adults called *Haroun and the Sea of Stories*. There are times when Rushdie's predicament feels like a meaningless divagation, a chaotic accident; there are other times when it feels rivetingly central and exemplary. Rushdie's friends, I imagine, think about him every day. But his writer friends, I suspect, think about him every half hour. He is still with us. And we are with him.

'When I first heard the news, I thought: I'm a dead man. You know: that's it. One day. Two days.' This interview took place in September, at a Mystery Location. We had joined up via something that *Haroun* would call a P2C2E: a Process Too Complicated To Explain. 'At such moments you think all the corny things. You think about not being able to watch your children growing up. Not being able to do the work you want to do. Oddly it's those things that hurt more than the physical idea of being dead. In a way you can't grasp that reality.'

Reality seemed to be generally elusive on that day, 14 February 1989 – the day of Khomeini's *fatwa*. Even the sky, I remember, was preternaturally radiant. Rushdie first heard the news when a radio station rang him up – to ask for his response. 'How do you feel about being sentenced to death by the Ayatollah? What about a quote?' He managed the quote ('God knows what I said'), and then ran around the house drawing the curtains and shutting the shutters. Next, he sleepwalked through an interview for the CBS morning show, and proceeded to what would be his last public appearance: the church service for his close friend Bruce Chatwin.

The church was Greek Orthodox, sombre, dusty, big-domed, and full of writers. Rushdie entered promptly with his then wife, the American novelist Marianne Wiggins. 'I was in shock,' he now says. He looked excitable. We were all excitable. Saul Bellow calls it 'event glamor'. 'Salman,' I said, as we hugged (he likes to hug his friends, and never routinely, always meaningly), 'we're *worried* about you.' And he said, '*I'm* worried about me.' The Rushdies sat down beside me and my wife. I had a shameful impulse to recommend all those nice empty pews at the far end of the church. Rushdie kept glancing over his shoulder: representatives of the press were being kept at bay by his agent, Gillon Aitken. 'Salman!' called out Paul Theroux, boyishly. 'Next week we'll be back here for you!'

Appropriately, the service was a torment, a torment in its own right, with much incomprehensible yodelling and entreating. I found that my thoughts were all mildly but stubbornly blasphemous. The robed clerics waved their fuming caskets in the air, like Greek waiters removing incendiary ashtrays. This, I concluded, was Bruce Chatwin's last joke on his friends and loved ones: his heterodox theism had finally homed in on a religion that no one he knew could understand or respond to. We sat down and stood up, stood up and sat down, trying not to subvert with sigh or yawn the dull theatre of an alien faith. When it was over, Salman and Marianne ducked past the waiting journalists and were driven off in a friend's limousine. Rushdie would spend the day searching for his son Zafar – searching too, I suppose, for a way to say goodbye to him, as he prepared to take up his new life.

I briefly attended the post-service reception. In normal circumstances we would have taken the chance to air our preoccupation with the mourned friend. But no one was thinking and talking about Bruce. Everyone was thinking and talking about Salman: his danger, his drastic elevation. As I went home I did about half-a-dozen things that Salman Rushdie was no longer free to do. I visited a bookshop, a toyshop, a snack bar; I went home. On the way I bought an evening paper. Its banner headline read: EXECUTE RUSHDIE ORDERS THE AYATOLLAH. Salman had disappeared into the world of block caps. He had vanished into the front page.

*

His case is of course unique. It is an embarrassment of uniquenesses. The terms of the *fatwa* (it is, at once, a death sentence and a life sentence); the size of the bounty (three times the reputed fee for the Lockerbie crash); the nature of the exile, which removes the novelist both from his subject (society) and from his object (sober literary consideration): in his own phrase, Rushdie is firmly 'handcuffed to history'. His uniqueness is the measure of his isolation. Perhaps, too, it is the measure of his stoicism. Because no one else – certainly no other writer – could have survived so well.

I often tell him this. I often tell him that if the Rushdie Affair were, for instance, the Amis Affair, then I would, by now, be a tearful and tranquillised 300-pounder, with no eyelashes or nostril hairs, and covered in blotches and burns from various misadventures with the syringe and the crackpipe. He has gained a little weight ('no exercise') and has resumed a very moderate cigarette habit; for a while he developed a kind of stress asthma. But Rushdie is unchanged: the rosy complexion, the lateral crinkle in his upper lip when he smiles (which gives an impression of babyishly short incisors), the eyes so exotically hooded that he has long foreseen minor surgery to prevent the lids from engulfing the irises. His urgently humorous presence is undiminished, undiluted. Sometimes, when you call him, his 'Oh I'm fine' lacks total conviction. Otherwise, he is a miracle of equanimity.

How is this? Unquestionably Rushdie has a great deal of natural ballast. He knows about exile, its deracinations, its surprising opportunities for expansion, how it can make you feel both naked and invisible, as in a dream. There has always been something Olympian about Salman Rushdie. His belief in his own powers, however (unlike other kinds of belief), is not monolithic and therefore precarious. It is agile, capricious and droll. The first time I met him, seven years ago, he mentioned to me that he had recently played football for a Writers' Eleven in a historic fixture in Finland.

'Really?' I said. 'How did you do?' I expected the usual kind of comedy (sprained ankle, heart attack, incompetence, disgrace). But I was given another kind of comedy, out of left field.

He said, 'I, uh, scored a hat-trick, actually.'

'You're kidding. I suppose you just stuck your leg out. You scrambled them home.'

'Goal number one was a first-time hip-high volley from twenty yards out. For the second, I beat two men at the edge of the box and curled the ball into the top corner with the outside of my left foot.'

'And the third goal, Salman? A tap-in. A fluke.'

'No. The third goal was a *power header*.'

Even if you don't know the game, you'll probably get the idea. This is Rushdie's style. He is always daring you to decide whether or not to take him literally.

Well, certain contemporary forces have made *their* decision, and they have duly arrived at a literalist's verdict: eternal remainderdom. Rushdie can take the weight of the anathema, and the vastly generalised animus, I think, because he has long been in training for it. He has skirmished with world leaders before, after all: in *Shame* with General Zia (the book was of course banned in Pakistan), and in *Midnight's Children* with Mrs Gandhi (who sued him for libel). But then came the intensive training, which began on 26 September 1988, the day *The Satanic Verses* was published. Bannings and burnings, petitions and demonstrations, rioting in Islamabad (six killed), rioting in Kashmir (one killed, 100 injured). Rushdie maintained at the time that these deaths were 'not on [his] conscience'; but by this stage he was feeling, he says, 'completely horrible. It was the most shocking thing – until the *other* most shocking thing.' The riots took place on consecutive days. On the third day the *fatwa* was announced. Rushdie knew by then that his book had raised mortal questions. He had no choice; he was obliged to become world-historical.

*

'At first, I found it more or less impossible to switch off, to turn away. Before the Ayatollah made his move, I saw myself as being part of a debate. Now the debate went on, but I was excluded from it.'

Another dreamlike state: Rushdie was a ghostly spectator at his own trial. And he found it was a full-time job keeping abreast of developments. His day began with *Breakfast News* at 6.30 and ended with *Newsnight* at 10.45. At that point the Rushdie story was at least three pages deep in every national newspaper; and for odd moments in between there was always the *Bradford Telegraph and Argus*, the South African *Weekly Mail*, the *Osservatore Romano*, the *Salzburg Kronen Zeitung*, *Al Ahram*, *Al-Noor*, the *Muslim Voice* and *India Today*. Everywhere he looked he saw torched hardbacks and writhing moustaches.

Question: What's got long blonde hair, big tits, and lives in an igloo in Iceland? Answer: Salman Rushdie . . . Such jokes, current in every pub and at every bus-stop, were relayed to Rushdie by his Special Branch bodyguards; he also became a staple for TV comedians, as a type for the hunted, the marked, the evanescent. Rushdie found some Rushdie jokes funnier than others. But what disturbed him was the sudden promiscuity of his fame. 'I kept thinking, What the hell am I *doing* here? What the hell am I doing in a TV sitcom? What the hell am I doing in the Jasper Carrot show?' In a sense, though, the *fatwa* itself is a Rushdie joke. The blasphemy issue is at least debatable (and Rushdie wants to continue that debate); but what can you make of Khomeini's ravings, which portrayed Rushdie as a literary dog of war, hired by world Jewry to soften up Islam for a neocolonialist blitzkrieg? Now that really *is* funny. When you write, when you try to instruct and entertain, you want the world to sit up and take notice. But not literally. And here on the evening news are the pulsing flashpoints on the colour-coded worldmap, Bombay, Los Angeles, Brussels, riot, fire and murder. What's the story?

You are the story; your book is the story. And now another chapter of crossed lines, ungot ironies, atrocious misunderstandings.

To scrutinise him is to jeopardise him, but a little can be said about the way he lives now. He lives like a secret agent; he is both nomad and recluse. 'An average day? I don't have average days, because there's always the possibility of having to move. I read a lot. I talk on the telephone a lot – two or three hours a day. I play computer games. Chess. Supermario. I am a *master* of Supermarios I *and* II. Otherwise I do what I'd do anyway. I start work at 10.30, I never eat lunch, and I knock off around four.' A writer is, on the whole, most alive when alone. You can then get on with the business of imagining other people. But there is normally a gregarious murmur behind the solitude – a murmur which Rushdie no longer hears. 'The strange part is not being able to go out in the evening. Or indeed in the afternoon. Or in the morning. To clear your head out.'

It comes as no surprise to learn that a death sentence *doesn't* concentrate the mind wonderfully. *Haroun and the Sea of Stories* is the result of unprecedented struggle. 'The distractions were internal rather than external. When I write, I sink into the bit of myself where the novel comes from. But I had to fight my way past all this other stuff: the crisis. And by the time I got there I'd be wrecked.' *Haroun* began as a series of bedtime stories which Rushdie told to his son Zafar – 'or bathtime stories. He would lie in the bath and listen, or sit wrapped in towels.' When Rushdie was close to finishing *The Satanic Verses*, Zafar made his father promise to forget about grown-ups for a while and write a book for children. 'I *couldn't* have written a grown-up novel. I didn't have the distance, the calm. I had to keep this promise to Zafar because it was the only thing I *could* keep to him. That was the whip I used to beat myself. It gave me the energy to do something as weird as write a fairy story in the middle of a nightmare. There's no more absolute thing than a promise to your child. You can't break it.'

The new book can and will be read as a fantastical commentary on the author's situation. Such a reading is no doubt naive, but purity of literary response is another privilege that Rushdie must resign himself to losing – for now. *All* his books suddenly seem to predict and explore his present situation, and parts of *The Satanic Verses* are almost vulgarly prescient ('Your blasphemy, Salman, can't be forgiven . . . To set your words against the Words of God . . .'). In any case *Haroun* is a minor classic of passionate invention. The change in genre is after all quite seamless: what is 'magical realism' but the wishful laxity of a child's imagination? Here are the stories that Rushdie wanted to tell his child. More than that, though, you also see the child in Rushdie – his delight, his mischief, his innocence, his eager heart.

Asked if he has a plan for the future, Rushdie says, 'A *plan*. Well, "plan" would be a rather glorified word for it.' His survival, like his capacity for hope, will continue to be a matter of daily improvisation. From time to time one hears a statement from Tehran along the following lines: that if Rushdie (a) admits he was wrong (b) renounces the paperback (c) recalls and pulps the hardback (d) makes extensive reparations and (e) becomes a devout muslim, it *still* won't be enough. What will be enough? The tone of the challenge makes one think of the lovelorn, the wounded adolescent. It could almost be a less benign and forgiving Haroun. Fill the ocean with your tears. Cry me a river.

Once Rushdie got going on his fairy story all the difficulties fell away. He wrote the first draft in two and a half months; he wrote the second in two weeks – 'at enormous speed. A chapter a day.' The breakthrough was unrelated to any change in circumstance. It had to do with the framing of the first sentence, 'which seemed to contain a lot of energy. It was like a tuning-fork.' And Rushdie quotes it:

There was once, in the country of Alifbay, a sad city, the saddest of cities, a city so ruinously sad that it had forgotten its name.

But the reader is already sad, already moved and haunted, by the book's dedication (an acrostic) which refers to enforced distance, to a sense of thwarted homing, and to a lost time that no Happy Ending can redress:

> Z embla, Zenda, Xanadu:
> A ll our dream-worlds may come true.
> F airy lands are fearsome too.
> A s I wander far from view,
> R ead, and bring me home to you.

Vanity Fair, 1990

POKER NIGHT

GQ *magazine asked me and four other writers (A. Alvarez, John Graham, Anthony Holden and David Mamet) to spend an evening playing poker and then report on the experience for its pages. The fee was paid in advance and in the form of poker chips: £500. The game was to be Texas Hold 'em: two cards each, face down (bet); three shared cards, face up, known as 'the flop' (bet); a fourth shared card, face up, known as 'Fourth Street' (bet); a fifth shared card, face up, known as 'Fifth Street' (bet).*

A man can find out a lot about himself, playing poker. Is he brave? Is he cool? Does he have any money left? I am obliged to say that I felt pretty hip and well-hung for much of the evening, in that little paradise of the private room, with its pro dealer, its full bar, its pleasant company, its complimentary poker chips – and the oncoming cards, from which hope unceasingly springs. By the end of the evening, I confess, I was feeling much less formidable: much less butch, and much less rich. But what an enthralling process. When can I go through it again?

From the start I sensed that I was the *rabbit* (the easy mark). This suspicion, along with all the free money, had a liberating effect on me. Unlike the scarred sharpers I faced, I wasn't bringing any rep to the table. I hadn't *sat down* for a decade, and had never played hold 'em. Originally, the fashionable poker variant was draw; then stud; then, during my brief heyday (in my late teens I played every night for three years), it was seven-card high-low. Now it's hold 'em, the purists' game, with its austere and subtle variations on the theme of the shared five cards.

When you sit down, you confront the force fields of opposed personalities. You shouldn't do this (it's a callow distraction), but you do. You look around for someone to bully, someone to be scared of. I found John Graham, the noted bridge player, to be easily the most emotional presence at the table: his operatic profile, tranced pauses, flustered raises. He is all joker, all wild card: he seems regularly astonished by his own unpredictability. As it happened, he lost; and was soon eagerly into a thousand pounds of his own money. But on another night you could imagine him cleaning you out with a jack high.

Al Alvarez I took to be an expert percentage man, interspersing his play with the occasional and prohibitive bluffs that his accuracy earns him. Al's style is as metronomic as the wheezing of his pipe. He won't come in often; when he does, you can't wait to get out of the way. But it was Anthony Holden who appeared to me to possess the most dangerous mixture of froth and flair. Tony is toney; he has his Vegas mannerisms: the exaggerated slouch, the languidly scornful flickaway of the dead cards. When the pot gets high, the hour late, and you need to see what he has in the hole, then the lounge lizard melds into a loanshark. Like his mentor Al Alvarez, Holden writes whole books about hold 'em. He is the Imam of hold 'em. He is practically *called* Holdem.

David Mamet was the only stranger. The others were familiar presences (I have known Tony for twenty years, Al for thirty) but Mamet I had only glimpsed electronically – on the small screen. There, he struck me as someone who had been put together by an Atlantic City biochemist: a human construction called POKER I. The opacity, the staring stillness, the transcendental inscrutablity. In addition, Mamet is American, and what's more he wrote *House of Games*, that tour de force of manic hazardry and compound deceit. On top of all this he was only drinking *tea*. Son of a bitch ... Men with a sheen of silence easily intimidate their fellows (these helpless prattlers); we imbue that silence with an unblinking censoriousness – or with our own self-doubt. Anyway, it's perfect for poker. Humanly, David Mamet opened up over the course of the evening. But his style remained impeccably closed. I felt very potent and twinkly when I called an early bluff of his, and was then reduced to a pale onlooker as he slowly bled me white.

Oh, we all talk tough at the table ('it's not about reality', 'it's all ifs and buts', 'you gotta speculate to accumulate') and then go home and sob in our wives' arms: tears of loss, tears of gorgeous relief. As you play, unfamiliar chemicals flood the body – money chemicals. In the colour-coded diagram, you could portray them as poker chips, helixed and value-stamped. Money is the language of poker. A defeat at chess leaves you flattened, chastened, but not visibly poorer. In poker, defeat means a submission to a more worldly power. It's tough out there. And it's tough in here. The winner's silence says to you: *That's* why I'm rock-hard. *That's* why I'm ice-cold. If I weren't, do you think I could get through this either?

1990

Postscript: Anthony Holden was the big winner (well over a thousand pounds); David Mamet doubled his money; Al Alvarez lost, and John Graham lost heavily, as they say; I came out with £200 of the magazine's money. But then I had to write the piece. Holden, in effect, was paid £2 a word for his contribution; I was paid 25p.

JOHN LENNON

In my teens I had a friend called Barry who resembled John Lennon to a disconcerting degree: the fluted nose, the beaked mouth, the eyelids thin and insolent. Barry's method of accumulating girlfriends was laborious but original. All day he studied the 'Pen Pals' section of *Beatles Monthly*. He selected the girls who lived preferably no more than a few hundred yards from where he lived, and wrote to them, enclosing a photograph of himself (complete with peaked Lennon cap; later with rimless spectacles), and the signature 'Barry Lennon' – or 'Buddy Lennon', depending on his mood.

In crew-necked Beatles jacket and chelsea boots with cuban heels, I often made up the foursomes that Barry would subsequently arrange. He would present himself now as Lennon's kid brother, now as his cousin, now as some more exotic relation (co-foundling, for instance) – sometimes, I think, as Lennon himself.

We were well up on Beatle lore. We knew that John was five feet eleven (as were Paul and George: mascot Ringo, of course, was five feet eight), that his taste in clothes encompassed 'anything casual', the sort of jellybabies he liked, the characteristics of his wife and his child – who was Barry's little nephew, after all. Considering his other plentiful demerits, Barry's success with his pen pals was very consistent. As I went along with it all, as Barry Lennon's sidekick and gofer, I sensed that the girls – though unquenchably gullible – really saw through Barry's imposture. But they didn't want to break the illusion of proximity, and neither did I.

John Lennon was born in 1940. Barry and I were born in 1949, and so were well placed to have our teenage years utterly dominated by the Beatles and their music. As a thirteen-year-old I witnessed their first-ever TV appearance – on some innocuous news-and-views show that I usually watched on my return from school. They sang 'Love Me Do'. I knew at once that they would become a part of my life. Shortly afterwards I made a five-shilling bet with my father, who claimed that the Beatles would be more or less forgotten within a year. When the time came for him to pay up, he confessed to a liking for one or two of their songs. My mother was a devoted fan. Everyone was.

Initially regarded as wanton and subversive figures – after all, they reinvented long hair – the Beatles quickly established their family appeal, an appeal nurtured by their manager Brian Epstein. The lovable moptops, the Fab Four, turned out to be nice lads really – to nationwide sighs of parental relief ... But John Lennon remained a wayward and unpredictable element, thwarting the homogenisation that Epstein clearly had in mind. Musically and personally, Lennon gave the Beatles their edge.

He mugged to camera and taunted compères. He coined or at any rate popularised the phrase 'Little girls should be obscene and not heard.' In interviews he could be very funny or, alternatively, very unfunny. He published two books of prattling word-play, *In His Own Write* and *A Spaniard in the Works*. He got drunk and caused scuffles in restaurants and clubs.

As song-writers and lead singers, Lennon and McCartney captured and divided the fans, while George and Ringo were mere innocent bystanders. There was something over-cute and chirpy about Paul: he wanted to be loved not only by your mother but by your grandmother too. Preferring Paul to John was like preferring Cliff Richard to Elvis Presley, or Donovan to Dylan. John was the leader; he was his own man. After their musical summit in the late Sixties, with *Rubber Soul*, *Sergeant Pepper* and *The White Album*, it became clear to me and a million other anxious readers of the rock press that the Beatles' days were numbered. And we all knew that it was John who was breaking away.

In the old days, Barry reminded me of Lennon. Later on, Lennon reminded me of Barry – trend-crazed Barry, a fantasist, a chameleon. Barry was now having a terrible time trying to stay abreast of Lennon's startling changes in appearance and philosophy. Having created the Swinging Sixties, Lennon became a hold-all for the thronging credulities of the next decade, a decade whose demise coincided with his own.

Lennon's career in the early Seventies reads like a telex of banal headlines and captions. Lennon returns his MBE; meets with Pierre Trudeau; John and Yoko take out advertisements praising peace; they consort with the Maharishi, Timothy Leary, assorted minor gurus; LSD, cocaine, heroine; beard, shades, crew-cut, scalplock; bed-ins, bag-ins, be-ins, in-ins ... Then Lennon 'got tired of waking up in the papers'. He succumbed to depression and hermitism. He became a 'househusband', rearing his son and baking bread at home while Yoko went out acquiring real estate. Their dream was to buy up the whole of the Dakota, the *Rosemary's Baby* mansion block on Central Park West. When questioned about this, Yoko once said, 'The thing is, John never had a house of his own.'

Separated from the melodic balance of the Beatles, Lennon's music became harsh and spikey, occasionally memorable and moving but more often strident and sloganising. He died just as his lyric talent seemed to be resurfacing. What took him to America was a desire not just for (comparative) anonymity but also for the teeming classlessness of New York. His murder was very typical of the city – flukey and meaningless. Deaths of this kind are what happens when the Warhol catchphrase – Everyone a Star – teams up with psychopathology. In New York that night, Lennon met up with the wrong kind of Barry.

Like countless others I played the Beatles' records into the turntable. They measured out my teens. Any Beatles track instantly transfers me to a specific segment of my past. When I heard of Lennon's death I felt a sense of shock well beyond what I felt at the deaths of the Kennedys and Luther King. I suffered this shock as it were helplessly. I thought of Barry – dreaming Barry, who bought two copies of 'Strawberry Fields' in case he broke one on the way home. I can only guess at his present sufferings. For both of us the past will never be the same again.

Observer, 1980

EXPELLED

It wasn't easy to get expelled from the school I got expelled from. Boys had fist-fights with masters and did not get expelled. Boys played hookey for weeks, terms, entire academic years and did not get expelled. Boys robbed banks in the lunch hour and did not get expelled. But I got expelled. It wasn't easy.

The school was a rugged grammar in Battersea, South London. My family was in disarray: I was the child of a breaking home, thirteen years old, and a sudden resident of Knightsbridge, just across the river. From the first day of term, when I alighted from a taxi to join the boiling, grimacing mob at the school gates, my notoriety was ensured. (I had arranged for the taxi to stop round the corner; but it was the wrong corner, I was lost and late, and had to hail another.) Although my hair and my accent were dutifully tousled, there was no disguising the furtive glow of my middle-class origins.

As a result, and understandably enough, I was beaten up on a pretty regular basis. My only two defences against the playground bruisers were the many stolen cigarettes I dispensed and my growing reputation as a palmist. I would tiptoe into the playground, half hat-check girl, half Madame Sosostris. When the first raised fist jerked towards me I would either thrust a few Marlboro into it or carefully unflex it into a palm. 'Very long life-line,' I would murmur. 'Whew, that's some love-life *you've* got coming. Now let's see . . . Although you're big and tough and good at beating people up, deep down you're really a gentle, thoughtful, artistic kind of guy.' 'That's true what he says,' they would remark as I lit their cigarettes. 'Deep down, that's really true.'

If I'd known how to get kicked out of this dump, then I would have lost no time in doing the necessary. But the place was practically Broadmoor as it was. It seemed that you could burn the school to the ground or kill the headmaster without getting much more than a terrified caution. And although I was unaffectionately known as 'the Demagogue' (owing to my ability to define this word in an English class), I was no firebrand or rabble-rouser. For two terms, along with everyone else, I just smoked cigarettes, cheated in exams, stole things, bunked off, stared out the masters, did no work at all, and generally kept my nose clean.

This was the third grammar school in my peripatetic school career. I had flirted far more successfully with expulsion at the other two, while always avoiding the final disgrace. On balance, I suppose the worst thing I ever did was to steal the diary of a fat, speechless classmate and fill it with a year's worth of bestial, obscene and quite imaginary antics. The only reprintable entries, I remember, were as follows: 'June 8: Got my new supply of Durex from the Chemist' and 'June 9: Stole £5 from Mum.' The father of this unhappy boy found the diary, brought it to school and confronted the headmaster with its contents. The headmaster, as he flexed his cane, told me that he would not permit 'the sewer vocabulary' to gain currency at his school. I got six of the best, and they hurt a lot; but I was allowed to stick around.

So how did I contrive my expulsion from the Battersea rough-house? Through good behaviour, or conspicuous achievement? In a loose sense, that is what happened. Quite fortuitously and out of the blue, I was offered a part in a film, which involved four months' work, two of them in the

West Indies. There was some kind of semi-illegality involved in taking children abroad for work, and 20th Century Fox thought it prudent to wait until we were out of the country before notifying the school. Accordingly, my mother and I composed a letter and duly dispatched it from Runaway Bay.

The headmaster's reply never reached us. This was unfortunate. Four months later I returned to school, becomingly tanned, sporting a brand-new blazer, and readying myself for a fresh round of playground chastisements after my exotic long vac. The form master seemed surprised to see me. I was sent to the headmaster's study. He seemed surprised to see me, too. His letter to Runaway Bay had been a letter of expulsion. He summarised its drift, pointing out that in any case I had been an 'unusually unpromising' pupil. The head was an intelligent, scathing character; he enjoyed this interview, and I now suspect that he too might have been doing his bit in the class war.

'Sacked', 'sent down', 'slung out' — these are public-school phrases. There are no euphemisms for state-school expulsion: it is a disgrace, a disaster, the beginning of the end of everything. I walked towards the school gates, stunned, bitter, intensely embarrassed about my new blazer. I had been 'expelled', and felt all the heaviness of this rejection. My playmates formed their usual gauntlet; I expected to be helped on my way with a taunt and a kick, but now the boys looked my way with respectful sympathy. Halfway across Chelsea Bridge I cheered up dramatically. I took off my cap and skimmed it into the Thames, comforting myself with the obvious thought that I had far less to fear than those who remained.

Observer, 1981

NICHOLSON BAKER

Writers' lives are all anxiety and ambition. No one begrudges them the anxiety, but the ambition is something they are supposed to shut up about. The two strains are, of course, inseparable, and symbiotic. Early on in his autobiographical meditation on John Updike, *U and I*, Nicholson Baker considers some likely responses from the great man:

> Updike could react, feel affronted, demolish me, ignore me, litigate. A flashy literary trial had some fantasy appeal, except that I knew that I would burst into tears if cross-examined by any moderately skillful attorney. But it probably wouldn't come to that.

No, it probably wouldn't come to that. A few pages later, Baker attends a literary party in Boston, hoping Updike will be there. His 'foolish beaming pleading' gaze eventually seizes on an acquaintance, the novelist Tim O'Brien, who quickly reveals that he 'goes golfing' with Updike. 'I was of course very hurt that ... Updike had chosen Tim O'Brien as his golfing partner,' writes Baker, although he doesn't know Updike and can't play golf. Perhaps the golfing friendship will solidify at some later date? (Out on the fairway, as he masters the game, Baker's bookchat will soon have Updike thinking, 'Hm, I guess that Nick Baker is not to be underestimated.')

But that's not good enough: 'I want to be Updike's friend now!' All writers will recognise the truth of these childish desires. It took Nicholson Baker to own up to them, and to realise their comedy. Writers want to disdain everything, yet they also want to have everything; and they want to have it now.

Well, everything – in the form of a capitalised Success – is suddenly on offer. I arrived for our meeting in New York, and there it all was: the Hiltonic hotel room, the dilatory and much-encumbered photographer, the appalling schedule, the tuxed waiter bearing the club sandwich on his burnished tray, the soothing prospect of a public reading (that night) and a transcontinental plane ride (the next morning), and, finally, *another* interviewer coming through the door, with all his dreams and dreads and character flaws ... The cult author of *The Mezzanine* and *Room Temperature* has now come cruising into the commercial mainstream. Baker's third novel, *Vox*, is the season's hot book, sexually explicit, much promoted, ambivalently received; for the moment it seems to stand there, stark naked, in the primitive fever of scrutiny and demand.

Although I was of course very hurt that *Vox* was doing quite so well, it should be said – to get the B-and-Me stuff at least partly out of the way – that I entered Baker's domain with an air of some knowingness. I myself had granted many an interview, if not in this very hotel room (it was a non-smoking room on a non-smoking floor: Baker doesn't drink, either), then in this very hotel; and I was a stupefied veteran of the writer's tour that Baker now contemplated with such disquiet. He was, on the other hand, inadmissably young (thirty-six), and never before had I interviewed a literary junior. This imagined hurdle turned out to be a liberation and a pleasure, but I somehow found it necessary to pre-devastate Baker with the news that one of *Vox*'s supposed coinages (a synonym for masturbation) had been casually tossed out by me two novels ago. Baker was duly devastated, and the interview began.

Those who know and therefore love his books might expect Baker to prove barely capable of sequential thought, let alone rational speech. The novels suggest a helpless egghead and meandering pedant whose mind is all tangents and parentheses. His radical concentration on the mechanics of everyday life – the escalator, the shoelace – prepares one for a crazy professor, even an *idiot savant*. One is also steeled, by his own self-mockery, for Baker's physical appearance: a balding, four-eyed, pin-headed drink of water. He is, to be sure, fabulously and pointlessly tall, tall beyond utility, and waveringly plinthed on his size 14 shoes. But these impressions soon fall away, just as the cold surface of his prose is warmed by the movement of its inner ironies, as they ceaselessly search for intricate delight. Baker, it turned out, was both droll and personable. I might even have glimpsed a quiet charisma behind his barbered beard, his mesmeric spectacles. Or was that just Manhattan and the dawn glow of celebrity?

'There are a lot of *numbers* now,' said Baker when I asked him about his current ascendancy. 'The fact that success is quantified is very exciting.' *Vox* has entered the bestseller list at number eight. We already know that it will move on to number six, and then to number three. 'But that's not good enough. Only number one will do.' But then – how *long* will it be number one (there is, after all, the very worrisome example of Stephen Hawking)? Perhaps two years. But why not three? Why not for ever? 'Actually I thought *The Mezzanine* was going to be a bestseller,' said Baker. 'The writer's mind is always leaping forward.' So in that sense he is fully prepared, as all writers are – even the most obscure, even the unpublishable. In their minds they have all been bestsellers, and golfed with John Updike, and lost sleep (as Baker has) over acceptance speeches for prizes they haven't been entered for, let alone won.

'I felt as famous as I ever wanted to be with *U and I*. And I thought that when you wrote a bestseller you were ... rich. It isn't the case. But there *are* prices for ideas, for certain bits of information. Like a subtle piece of software. You can design a good Argyle sock or a bad Argyle sock.' So perhaps *Vox* can be viewed as a 'needed' or gap-filling product. *The Mezzanine*, in particular, reveals a sober respect for market forces, as one commercial process succeeds another; and Baker admits to being less interested in fashion and accident than in the firmness of the merit-value equation. 'You can get very fired up about these things. It's what drew me to the stock market.'

Baker was drawn to the stock market. But he didn't stay there very long. Nor, as we see, did he go on to write portly financio-sexual thrillers about junk-bond dealing and highroller love affairs. His background forms the kind of directionless hotch-potch which, in retrospect, seems to have been exactly what was needed: quietly classy university (Haverford), musical training (bassoon), Wall Street (research reports), writing workshop (Berkeley), then temping, then technical writing (network-management software manuals). His spell as a stockbroker came about halfway through: a fortnight of dramatic but salutary disintegration. 'It's called "smile and dial". You call up complete strangers and try to be their investment analyst. The first day I was *very* intrusive. The second day I was increasingly damaged and tentative. The third was marked by hysteria and weeping. After two weeks I was engulfed by psychosomatic illness. Then I decided to be a writer.'

There now follows a digression or a 'clog' in which I shall pounce on the fact that Baker, at university and on Wall Street, flirted with philosophy.

Philosophers are said to be condemned to one of two strange relationships with the world of objects: either indifference or near-crippling obsession. Twenty years ago I drove the late A.J. Ayer to White Hart Lane, to support Tottenham Hotspur. On the way Ayer smoked three cigarettes. For his first butt he disdained, or did not see, the obvious – and butt-infested – ashtray, favouring the naked tape-deck with the fiery remains of his Player. (The tape-recorder itself had been stolen, true, but the empty console had the word PHILIPS clearly stamped on it.) His second butt he squeezed into the base of the handbrake, his third he ground out on the speedometer. The high point came with his third spent match, which, with incredible skill, he balanced on the bare ignition key, where it wobbled for at least three seconds before dropping inexorably to the floor.

When I recall this now I imagine the bespectacled Nicholson Baker, at fifteen, doubled up on the Mini's back seat, already as tall as Ayer and me put together, staring in anguish at these forgetful violences, and fully immersed in the car's flange housings, its quarter-window release nodules, its galvannealed dash frame flute slopings . . .

Baker is the poet of all the things we call thingies and thingamajigs, all the things we don't know the name for: nubs and tines, spigots and sprockets, roller-cookers and tone-arms and pull-tabs and slosh-caps. The French call it *choseisme* – but Baker is very far from the po-faced stock-taking of, say, a J.M.G. le Clézio. The 'corporate setting' of *The Mezzanine* gives way, in *Room Temperature* (oh, the soaring dullness of that title!), to the domestic landscape and the sacraments of marriage and parenthood, in a prose full of cadences and free of false quantities, beneath which the engine-room of English Literature confidently thrums. Baker's perceptual style is both gleefully perverse and wantonly sunny: throughout his corpus there is barely an ordinary sentence or an ungenerous thought.

So now we move on to *Vox*, a single-issue novel (sex), also a single-mode novel (dialogue), and further disembodied by the fact that the two protagonists never touch or meet, communicating only by party line. The object, the thing, in this case, is the telephone – that friction-less technology. *Vox* is frictionless too, and thus meets a contemporary demand: it asks nothing of you. Modern tendencies – safe sex, pornography, human dwindling – are present as accepted guests, not as intruders. Sunniness and perversity are smoothly joined in the monotonous vacuum of long-distance.

'Don't let Nick fool you,' Baker's editor has said. 'He wants to be rich and famous.' Perhaps Baker should be grateful that this remark came from his editor rather than from someone really central, like his publicist. In any event, I sat in the audience at the Manhattan Theater Club, where Baker was to read that night, trying not to let Nick fool me. As he loped up on to the stage his neck and knees were bent in what might have been ordeal readiness, or simple height-effacement. And of course he *didn't* read aloud from *Vox* (which would have tested anybody); he read aloud a piece *about* reading aloud.

After handing *Vox* in, Baker explained, he told his publishers that he would not do 'any public performances of any kind'. There was evidently some discussion at Random House, though, because when the proofs arrived Baker saw on the back the following italicised promise: National Author Reading Tour. His stance at the lectern was impressively rigid and spavined, but the performance felt assured and effective. In conclusion Baker offered to field comments on *Vox*, and a tentative Q-and-A session began. Performing writers can usually count on at least one strongminded hold-out in any audience, and finally an elderly lady (a stranger to this author's habitual indirection) came up with: 'How can you ask for questions on it when you haven't read from it? What are we supposed to do? *Guess*?' Baker hesitated. 'This book is in its fifth printing,' he said. '*Someone* is reading it.'

When I breakfasted with him the next morning, before he flew out to Los Angeles, Baker confessed that this unguarded remark had supplied the grist for the previous night's insomnia. He suffers from insomnia, also arthritis, also psoriasis (a link with Updike, who 'had one unfortunate fictional representative *vacuuming out* the bed every morning'). Baker was, in addition, percolating anxiety about his trip to England. 'They're going to be disappointed by *Vox*. Why should I be there *while* they're being disappointed? Why should I *fly into* disappointment?' And then there were the worries about the presentational style of the British publishers, Granta Books. The subtitle: 'A Novel about Telephone Sex'. The blurb: 'a classic of bedside reading'. The bookshop dump-bin: 'Great Art Or Just A Good Dirty Read?'

Sometimes I think I am not cut out for literature. A true writer would have been much more pleased that a novel as successful as *Vox* was indeed an artistic disappointment. I found I was genuinely sorry as opposed to hypocritically sorry, that the book wasn't better (but its slightness is inbuilt. It has no room to manoeuvre. It has *no prose*). And I certainly didn't care how humble/ambitious/ascetic/greedy Baker 'really' was, because I know that writers are all these things at once; and have to be. The writer may scheme and dream; but the words on the page are always free of calculation. Lingering to chat, and to defend his book, ('I meant it to be human and touching'; 'I like it more than any of the others – I . . . *love* it'), Baker left for the airport sophisticatedly and daringly late – and even managed to telephone before embarking, to moderate his mild grumblings about Granta.

This is from *U and I*:

> When the excessively shy force themselves to be forward, they are frequently surprisingly unsubtle and overdirect and even rude: they have entered an extreme region beyond their normal personality, an area of social crime where gradations don't count . . . The same goes for constitutionally ungross people who push themselves to chime in with something off-color – in choosing to go along they step into a world so saturated with revulsions that its esthetic structure is impossible for them to discern . . .

One would like to apply the above, not so much to *Vox* (where a sortie of this kind is attempted; and nothing much actually happens), but to the standard Baker prose paragraph, where scarily delicate senses are exposed to the Brobdingnag of workaday life. So placed, Baker stares with the clean eyes of a child, and speaks with a child's undesigning but often terrible honesty.

Independent on Sunday, 1992

SHORT STORIES, FROM SCRATCH

In 1985 I judged the Whitbread Prize for the best short story by a writer aged between sixteen and twenty-five. My co-judge, Christopher Sinclair-Stevenson, then edited a selection of the entries (twelve out of 150), The Whitbread Stories.

> The heat was stiffling. Moodly he looked out of his bedroom window. Yes, the day was far too hot to be sleepy. He *had* to chose. To win, to suceed would be incredulous. But to fail, to loose, would be contemptuous!

This string of illiterate clichés is of my own making; but it fairly reflects the style of the least promising entries. Whenever the writing hit this level, I assumed that the story had been submitted in a serendipitous or lucky-dip spirit, like a bingo card. Send the thing in: you might pay that gas bill with the winnings, or settle the rent. Anxiety about the future – the stories' great common theme – had here found its most basic form.

Before one got to the good stuff, of which there was plenty, one had time to be amply scandalised by the lawlessness of the prose. The apostrophe and the hyphen proved to be especially confounding. Many stories featured a *had'nt* or a *ca'nt* in the first sentence; turning with some wariness to the last page, one saw that the writer was still contentedly tapping out his *would'nts* and *wo'nts*. There were similar difficulties with *its* and *it's*, as in *cut it's losses* and *its raining*: and many hybrids along the lines of *no-body, how ever* and *anymore* ('*noway,*' he growled). Idiosyncrasies of spelling one tended to overlook (any publisher's reader will tell you that most of our leading writers are afflicted by near-dyslexia). But the aura of an otherwise well-worked paragraph can be instantly frittered away by some callow phoneticism like *pitty* (*for pitty's sake!*), *hatered* or *dezire*.

It is hard to say whether standards of literacy have actually declined. Certainly a morbid fear of dictionaries would seem to be abroad. What has changed, perhaps, is the attitude to linguistic law. Thirty years ago the would-be writer might at least concede that correctness was something worth aiming at. Now the edifice of syntax is regarded with impatience, almost with aggression. Of course, no new freedom will ever be found by this route. One writer, however, did contrive to create something out of chaos, developing a post-punk anti-style ('a cup of t', and so on) which none the less struck me as distinctly literary. Perhaps the effectiveness of this piece owed a little to chance and will not be repeatable; but it had plenty of sullen power.

The response to language is, as always, an ingredient of something larger. Mrs Thatcher and Mr Tebbit, when they mull over their achievements, can now congratulate themselves on the final destruction of the work ethic which they claim to admire and embody. One would expect, in the closeted thoughts of young people on the brink of adulthood, a good deal of misgiving about the adult dance of work, money, preferment, acquisition. A twinge of alienation in this area seems to me a sign of health. When you are twenty years old, society has a conspiratorial look, as if planned and put together without fair consultation; it feels indifferent, settled, impervious. Then, usually, the money-value takes over and the young person gets on with the job. Judging these stories, and judging by them, I would guess that this process is being quietly yet radically undermined.

Not surprisingly, there were dozens of stories about dossers, tramps, the dole, living on at home (with petulant or depressive parents), stories about looking for jobs and not finding them (there *aren't* any, seems to be the consensus). Not surprisingly, again, there were many ingenuous attempts to celebrate some notion of 'the good life', usually period pieces, with the emphasis on fine clothes, drawing-rooms, sumptuous meals. (One thinks of *Brideshead Revisited*, written in wartime and later denounced by Waugh when he re-read the book 'on a full stomach'). But considered *en masse* the stories give a more pervasive presentiment of disaffection, of wear and tear in the social contract. The idea of work, getting on, becoming adult looks not only distant and improbable; it also looks inane, hostile and accusatory.

There is another anxiety, more insidious and inclusive, and palpable even when it remains unspoken. This is the nuclear anxiety – the unclear anxiety – and it was perhaps expressed least eloquently in the stories that directly addressed it: Oval Office melodramas, superpower countdowns, sagas of life in the post-cataclysmic tundra, and so on. What stays with the reader is not a general uncertainty about future survival so much as a contingency about the present, about time itself. The real singularity or uniqueness of the post-Einsteinian age is the sudden vulnerability of the past as well as the future. Intimations of meaninglessness are consequently that much harder to ignore.

If you ask people what they feel about the Bomb they will often say that they never think about it. I believe them, but there is a sense in which the answer fails to satisfy the question. If you don't think about it, what *do* you do about it? The fact that the planet has a cocked gun in its mouth will inevitably be absorbed in some way – psychologically, physiologically. When we do think about the end of the world, we tell ourselves that at least it hasn't happened yet, that it is not yet a reality. But the threat is a reality; and people react to threats. Clearly there is plenty of reason to start running the damage checks, as these stories hauntingly demonstrate. Second-generation post-nuclear, they are habituated to fear; and the present they evoke and describe looks thin, isolated, mysteriously sapped of its essences.

Not that this foreboding was an enemy of good – and vigorous – writing. From the workmanlike to the highly competent, from the merely amiable to the charming, from the glib to the indisputably talented – nearly all the contestants had an experience to transmit and some notion of how it might be turned into art. Obvious literary influences were few, but there were glimpses of an intelligent and humorous post-modernism, a playful awareness of form. Every genre was represented, with the lone exception of the Western. If the stories were rather less literary than some notional bygone equivalent, then this says something apposite about the observed life. It doesn't look very literary out there, not just now.

For me the biggest surprise was how seldom I was bored by these fragments, how little I disliked the work, and how fixedly I followed (practically) every story to the end. Sometimes, of course, one read on out of sheer disbelief at the concerted talentlessness nestling on one's lap. And often, certainly, it was human interest, not literary relish, that compelled one. I was reminded how astonishingly intimate the business of fiction is, more intimate than anything that issues from the psychiatrist's couch or even the lovers' bed. You see the soul, pinned and wriggling on the wall.

Observer, 1985

PHILIP LARKIN 1922–1985

Philip Larkin was not an inescapable presence in America, as he was in England; and to some extent you can see America's point. His Englishness was so desolate and inhospitable that even the English were scandalised by it. Certainly, you won't find his work on the Personal Growth or Self-Improvement shelves in your local bookstore. 'Get out as early as you can,' as he once put it. 'And don't have any kids yourself.'

All his values and attitudes were utterly, even fanatically 'negative'. He really was 'anti-life' – a condition that many are accused of but few achieve. To put it at its harshest, you could say that there is in his ethos a vein of spiritual poverty, almost of spiritual squalor. Along with John Betjeman, he was England's best-loved postwar poet; but he didn't love postwar England, or anything else. He didn't love – end of story – because love seemed derisory when set against death. 'The past is past and the future neuter'; 'Life is first boredom, then fear' . . . That these elements should have produced a corpus full of truth, beauty, instruction, delight – and much wincing humour – is one of the many great retrievals wrought by irony. Everything about Larkin rests on irony, that English speciality and vice.

Anti-intellectual, incurious and reactionary ('Oh, I adore Mrs Thatcher'), Larkin was himself an anti-poet. He never wanted to go anywhere or do anything. 'I've never been to

America, nor to anywhere else, for that matter.' Asked by an interviewer whether he would like to visit, say, China, he replied, 'I wouldn't mind seeing China if I could come back the same day.' He never read his poems in public, never lectured on poetry, and 'never taught anyone how to write it'. He lived in Hull, which is like living in Akron, Ohio, with the further advantage that it is more or less impossible to get to.

His meanness was legendary, and closely connected to the solitude he built around himself. It is said that he never owned more than one kitchen chair, to make sure that no one could stop by for lunch – or, worse, come to stay. Christmas shopping was, for him, 'that annual conversion of one's indifference to others into active hatred'. Sometimes, though, he weakened:

> Finding Stevie Smith's *Not Waving but Drowning* in a bookshop one Christmas some years ago, I was sufficiently impressed by it to buy a number of copies for random distribution among friends. The surprise this caused them was partly, no doubt, due to the reaction that before the war led us to amend the celebrated cigarette advertisement 'If So-and-So, usually a well-known theatrical personality, offered you a cigarette it would be a Kensitas' by substituting for the brand name the words 'bloody miracle'.

His feelings about money were complicated and pleasureless. He pronounced the word *bills* as if it were a violent obscenity. (He brooded deeply about his bills.) He always had enough money and, anyway, there was nothing he wanted to spend it on.

> Quarterly, is it, money reproaches me:
> 'Why do you let me lie here wastefully?
> I am all you never had of goods and sex.
> You could get them still by writing a few cheques' ...

... I listen to money singing. It's like looking down
From long french windows at a provincial town,
The slums, the canal, the churches ornate and mad
In the evening sun. It is intensely sad.

Money meant work, and there was a priestly stoicism
in Larkin's devotion, or submission, to his job as University
Librarian at Hull. He supervised a staff of over a hundred;
typically he was a brilliant administrator, with a great talent
for drudgery. Work was the 'toad' that he let 'squat on my
life'. In the last decade he didn't need the job any longer, but
he thought (with maximum lack of glamour), 'Well, I might
as well get my pension, since I've gone so far.'

> What else can I answer,
>
> When the lights come on at four
> At the end of another year?
> Give me your arm, old toad,
> Help me down Cemetery Road.

He never married, naturally, and made a boast of his
aversion to children. 'Children are very horrible, aren't they?
Selfish, noisy, cruel, vulgar little brutes.' As a child himself, he
has said, he thought he hated everybody: 'but when I grew up
I realized it was just children I didn't like.' His own childhood
he repeatedly dismissed as 'a forgotten boredom' ('Nothing,
like something, happens anywhere'). You feel that the very
notion of childhood, with all its agitation and enchantment,
was simply too sexy for Larkin. He regarded married life as a
terrible mystery, something that other people did (and 'Other
People are Hell'), a matter for appalled – and double-edged
– ridicule:

> He married a woman to stop her getting away
> Now she's there all day,

And the money he gets for wasting his life on work
She takes as her perk
To pay for the kiddies' clobber and the drier
And the electric fire . . .

And so on, until the inexorable revenge:

> So he and I are the same,
>
> Only I'm a better hand
> At knowing what I can stand
> Without them sending a van –
> Or I suppose I can.

The clinching paradox may be, however, that Larkin will survive as a romantic poet, an exponent of the ironic romance of exclusion, or inversion. One review of *High Windows* (his last book of poems, and his best by some distance) was headed 'Don Juan in Hull'; and this says a great deal, I think, about the currents of thwarted eroticism in his work. Of the shopping-centre, the motorway cafe, the old people's home, the madman-haunted park, the ambulance, the hospital, Larkin sang. Even his own inner ugliness ('monkey-brown, fish-grey') he made beautiful:

> For something sufficiently toad-like
> Squats in me, too;
> Its hunkers are heavy as hard luck,
> And cold as snow . . .

'Do you feel you could have had a much happier life?' an interviewer once asked. 'Not without being someone else.' What we are left with is the lyricism that Larkin seemed to be shedding or throwing away as he moved towards death. From 'The Trees':

Philip Larkin 1922–1985

> Yet still the unresting castles thresh
> In fullgrown thickness every May.
> · Last year is dead, they seem to say,
> Begin afresh, afresh, afresh.

It was in my capacity as a cruel and vulgar little brute that I first met Larkin – at the age of four or five. He was my elder brother's godfather and namesake, and, to my brother and me (true to type: indeed, it might have been us who put him off), visits from godfathers meant money. *My* godfather was rich, generous and seldom sober when he came to stay: half-crowns and ten-shilling notes dropped from his hand into ours. But it was always a solemn moment when it came for Larkin to 'tip the boys' – almost a religious experience, as I remember it. At first it was sixpence for Philip against threepence for Martin; years later it was tenpence against sixpence; later still it was a shilling against ninepence: always index-linked and carefully graded. Other poets I came across during that time – notably Robert Graves – tended to be ebullient, excitable, candidly bardic. Larkin was simply a melancholy man, prematurely bald and with the remains of a stutter. In my later dealings with him, he was always quietly amusing, doggedly honest and (in the widest sense) exceptionally well-mannered. Larkin may have written poetry, but he spent no time 'being a poet'.

The death was as comfortless as the life. And it had its element of ironic heroism. There was no real family, of course, and visits from friends were not encouraged. All his life he had girded himself for extinction; but when it came (and this is appropriate and consistent) he was quite unprepared, resolutely helpless, having closed no deal with death. He instructed his doctors to tell him nothing – to tell him lies. It is said that Evelyn Waugh died of snobbery. Philip Larkin died of shame: mortal, corporeal shame.

He made no effort to prolong matters. In the last year of his life he used to start the day with three glasses of supermarket port ('Well,' he explained to my father, 'you've got to have some fucking reason for getting up in the morning'). In the last week he was subsisting on 'gin, Complan and cheap red wine'. 'Couldn't you at least get some *expensive* red wine?' my mother suggested on the telephone, three days before his death. But no. Live out the comfortlessness, in fear and bafflement – that was the strategy. Although he was Larkin's best friend, my father saw him infrequently and now wonders if he ever really knew him.

Postscript: This piece was written as an obituary. The (usually hostile) revaluation that attends a poet's death was postponed, in Larkin's case, until the recent publication of the *Letters* and the Life. A couple of years ago Larkin was still our best-loved postwar poet; now, for the time being, he is the most reviled. That revaluation has been unprecedentedly thorough. The Life and the *Letters* stand ready on my desk: I will be writing at length about them, and about him. Already I can trumpet the assurance that the present controversy will soon evaporate; nothing of importance will have been affected by it.

Vanity Fair, 1985

CANNES

This piece was written sixteen years ago and is included here as a curiosity. It is certainly a curiosity to me. I still can't understand how I was quite so thrown by the spectacle of topless sunbathing. On the other hand I have never known a woman who liked or approved of it. So the question is still vivid for me. Who are they all?

My first glimpse of the sea featured the middle-distant prospect of a girl sauntering topless along the water-line. She wore the smallest bikini-pants I had ever seriously seen on anyone, about the size of a dab of tissue with which one might staunch a shaving-cut. The girl mounted a small pier, at whose far end a fat motor-launch wallowed. No doubt some huge young filmstar stood waiting for her there on the deck (his shirt open to the last button, his restless legs planted well apart). My gaze returned to the sea, which dappled weakly in the midday sun.

When I looked again, the girl was naked. Either she had removed her bikini-pants, or they had simply been blown away in the salty wind. A man was jumping about taking photographs of her; accordingly, the girl swivelled and preened, raising her arms to flatter her breasts. I turned in alarm towards the three tyrannous gendarmes standing near by. I thought that they would at least kill her, like they do if you cross the road at the wrong moment, but they consulted one another with zestless shrugs.

I looked again. The pier now sagged with gesticulating journalists, kneeling, leaping lensmen (rolling on to their backs like puppies for the angle-shots) and random perverts and voyeurs, among whom the naked girl continued gamely to pirouette. Ten minutes later she forged her way back to shore – by this time about two hundred viewers lined the promenade – emerging from the crowd bashfully clothed in her triangular sequin.

Within seconds, the posse of photographers, tom-peepers, etc, had encircled another, hidden figure down on the beach. Must be a new superstarlet, I decided, moving down the steps to join them. This one wore bikini-pants – the lion's share of which, admittedly, seemed lost for good between her buttocks – and was moreover reclining primly on her stomach. But she *was* kissing a dirty pet terrier, and French-kissing it apparently, much to the guttural delight of the assembled newshounds. Every few seconds the newshounds urged the superstarlet to turn on to her back. Every few seconds the superstarlet took her tongue out of the dog's mouth and politely refused. Tickled, the newshounds snapped and gawped.

Why the bother? – I thought suddenly, scanning the beach with a blush. I had never seen so many breasts in my life, and all nonchalantly bared to the breeze – there were those two over there, and that pair there, and that row of them over there, and look at that lot over there, and ... Compared to the other females on the beach, the harried superstarlet was an example of painful inhibition. Perhaps this was what had roused the hacks: Hold the front page – we've found a girl on the beach in Cannes who *isn't* showing everyone what her breasts look like.

I have never been to Cannes before, nor to any other Cote d'Azur resort, and I have never seen any girl over the age of ten half-naked on the sands. I was of course aware

– first alerted, I suspect, by the vigilance of *Daily Mirror* cameramen – that there were topless beaches at Cannes. What I didn't know is that *every* beach is a topless beach at Cannes. They say it all began in the early Sixties, became a bore in the early Seventies, and has now been re-embraced quite unselfconsciously, the only way for women to dress for the shore, half-naked as nature intended.

Oh well, I said to myself, wringing my pinball-calloused hands – I'll just have to spend the entire week here racing up and down the strand. After all, the girls don't seem to mind you staring at them, and with as much puerile awe as you care to muster. Conscientious, album-minded perverts, indeed, wander along unhindered with their Brownies, pausing to snap at leisure while the girls stretch and yawn. Once, when I was seated comfortably on the shore, with my back to the water, a thoroughly topless girl abruptly addressed me in harsh French from her sun-couch. Now this is an *arrest*, I assumed – and high time too. But no: holding up her own camera, she asked if Monsieur would be kind enough to take a topless snap of her and her topless friend, so that, in the years to come, they could re-evoke the memory of this lost summer.

And up on La Croisette itself, the esplanade along which the jet-setters swank, aggressive pulchritude reigns. Here is Le Palais du Festival, the flat-topped, marble-foyered complex where, on the ground floor, all the principal entries are screened, where, on the first floor, the assorted movie-hawkers set up their lurid stalls, and where, on the second, the Press office swelters in a mess of fanned bulletins and discarded handouts.

In this warren the etiolated cineasts grope and blink about their business. Some of these men and women are seeing ten films a day, here and elsewhere. They look it. They are seeing films of the calibre of *Women Behind Bars*, *Dynamite Girls*, *Kiss Me Killer* and *Kidnapped Coed*, of

Savage in the City, *Axe*, *Viol* and *Rattlers*, of *The Crater Lake Monster* and *Legend of the Dinosaurs* and *Monster Birds*, of *Fun Truckin*, *Symphony of Love* and *La Principessa Nuda*, of *Le lunghe notti della Gestapo*, *L'ultima orgia del III Reich* and *Elsa Fraulein − SS* (all postered in the first-floor booths). The cineasts' skin is numb and luminous. Their eyes are angry red holes. When they stumble late into the crowded Grande Salle, it takes them about twenty minutes to find a seat. The cinema isn't *that* crowded. It's just that their eyes can no longer acclimatise from the outside dazzle. Halfway through the film they are still tousling your hair and trying to sit on your lap.

Flanking the Palais, in festive contrast, are the two main see-and-be-seen cafés, the Bar Festival and, more fashionable still, the Blue Bar. It takes colossal stamina to fritter away your money in these places. Only occasionally, nowadays, do the harassed and contemptuous waiters simply promise to attend to you and then go away again. Seldom, even, do they claim that your table is the preserve of some mythical colleague. What they do now is pretend you're not there. When you rugby-tackle them, bring them crashing, tray and all, to the pavement, and yell Monsieur, *Monsieur*, MONSIEUR! in their ears, they pretend you're not there. An intelligent procedure. During Festival fortnight these places are going to be clotted with the rich anyway, no matter how negligent the waiters contrive to be. So why do we come?

We come to watch. The routine, quotidian viewing, while varied enough in itself, sticks to a predictable schedule. All day the lovelies and hugies thread past to the sands, as stooped cineasts trudge up the Palais steps. By late afternoon, spidery transvestites − who look remarkably like the Platonic ideal of a British tart − flit among the tables, chatting to the Japanese nabobs and bejeaned Swedish pornographers who slump grumbling there. Minor thespians sometimes join us. A pretty French actress sat down next to me one evening. I wasn't very excited. I had already seen what her breasts looked like the day before, in *La Dentellière*.

By seven o'clock, in preparation for the far grander evening showings, the dour procession of Moguls' Wives forms along the parade. Sweating in their crinolines and farthingales, in their flounced gowns of flame-coloured taffeta, like so many Queens of Hearts, the Moguls' Wives seem to comprise a suspended, forgotten enclave in this teeming town. The result (one imagines) of alliances formed long before their husbands' success, they tend to approach in girlish pairs, joined at the last moment by their errant, tuxedoed consorts. Only the Moguls' Wives – and they only at evening – dress in a manner remotely appropriate to their years. Everyone else in Cannes divides their age by three and dresses accordingly. 'How far did you have to go,' I used to wonder, watching the clownishly spruced menfolk convene on the Palais steps, 'how many helicopters and jungle-beaters and water-diviners did you have to hire, before you found a dinner jacket as comical as *that*?'

From eleven until three, after the moguls have dispersed with the Moguls' Wives, ritzy yahooism simmers along the strip – and suddenly Cannes is very much like anywhere else where people come to exchange high-spirits for cash. Sounds of brutish revelry that you would be startled to hear in, say, Yates's Wine Lodge in Blackpool mingle with the familiar clatter of dropped glasses and upended chairs. At one of Cannes' premier venues, the Night Bar at the Carlton, I sat at a table smothered in 1,000-franc notes and untouched champagne; I watched a fat little millionaire climb a graph of drunkenness so unswerving that it would have offended the sensibilities of a Glaswegian publican. The millionaire shouted, sang, danced, fought, sobbed – at one point managing to do all five at once. 'Why are they here so late?' I asked a regular visitor to the port – 'Have they been to late films or are they just nightowls?' 'No,' said my American friend. 'They just didn't get laid yet.'

*

Promotional gimmicks of one kind or another supply the main distractions. These gimmicks are often endearingly low-budget – a kid giving away oranges in the interests of some indeterminate forthcoming attraction, a little bouncing badge called a 'gizmo', designed to whet your appetite for a film called *Gizmo*. The presence in Cannes of a mauve taxi made you all the keener to see *Un Taxi Mauve*. A line of cars with girls in them went past beeping their horns (you couldn't tell why). A very competent brassy jazz-band struck up on La Croisette, and momentarily one's spirits lifted; but within seconds the band had been asphyxiated by photographers, and gaiety lapsed once more into staged frivolity.

Yum Yum Shaw, the oriental pornographess, drew attention to herself at the Martinez Hotel, thus doubling speculation about her *Concubine* film. Bigger breasts by far (the biggest I ever saw in Cannes) were being tensed down on the beach; they belonged to Arnold Schwarzenegger. Surrounded by starlets, Arnold showed photographers the appalling shape he had let his body get into. A pair of aeroplanes tirelessly circled the shore, day after day, bearing streamers saying SUPERMAN NOW SHOOTING and BRANDO HACKMAN AND SUPERMAN. By their thirtieth circuit or so, I felt I had made myself master of this information. 'Nah,' I heard a nearby mogul moan, 'the *Superman* hype has been building for years.'

Dunaway was there. People arched in their chairs when people mentioned Dunaway's name. Heston out-hyped Montand (was it he?) in Cartier. Bronson was there, with Ireland, his wife. Loren was there, at a Lord Lew lunch thrown in the Eden Roc: 'All my films are great,' cracked Lord Lew. 'They're not all good, but they're all great.' Savalas was there. They threw a party at the Carlton, to welcome Telly to Cannes. Telly won a bomb that evening at the Cannes Casino (a repulsive gin-palace from whose Doric portals I was jeered away two nights later: it costs a fortune to join for *huit jours*, and a star's ransom to join for *la saison*). Ustinov was there. Finney was there ... On La Croisette, closely ringed by personal bodyguards, secretaries, agents, shoe-polishers, tie-straighteners and about a dozen municipal policemen, an unseen star moved down the strip, raising heads, blocking traffic. This must be big. Nicholson? Streisand? Redford? *Brando*?

'Quinn,' someone muttered appreciatively – 'Quinn.'

Now it was only after mature thought that I decided *not* to let Quinn know I was in Cannes. Many years previously, when the present writer was no more than a boy, I had co-starred with Quinn in a Fox production based on the Richard Hughes novel *A High Wind in Jamaica* (Price, Ventura, Frobe, Kerdrova and Coburn had all co-starred along with Quinn and me). It was my only experience of motion pictures – and one so traumatically embarrassing that it can still make me gasp with shame. I had got the part at the last minute, by pure chance. I was a plump and bewildered pubescent, with no theatrical talent whatever. My RADA-spawned kid co-stars could weep or giggle to camera at the drop of a hat; I said such things as 'hello' and 'yes' as if I had been heavily bribed to do so. (I once fainted with self-consciousness. During my death-scene, the distracted director, McKendrick, asked me to vivify matters with a death-scene death scream. 'Try one now,' he said, between Take Twenty-three and Take Twenty-four. 'What, now?' I asked, 'Now.' 'What, now?' '*Now.*' I released a barely audible moan, and blacked out.) Luckily my part was a small one, and most of it was cut.

To complete my humiliation, adolescence went and broke my voice during the course of shooting. In a series of great lurches and leaps, it descended from a piping soprano to its present didactic baritone. As you probably know, films aren't shot chronologically; as you probably don't know, when kids' voices collapse in this fashion they employ *old ladies* to dub you over. I never dared actually see the film, and only a couple of years ago, when it was shown on the small screen, did I catch a glimpse of the nauseous eunuch they had made of me.

Anyway, Tony and I had tangled over a game of chess. I had beaten the star – or at least the star was clinging on to a hopelessly compromised board, knowing full well that he would soon be rescued by a summons to the set. Quinn was ludicrously vain about his chess-playing prowess (he used to like playing simultaneous chess, so that he could get beaten by two or more people simultaneously). 'Will Mr Quinn please come to the set?' a megaphone inquired. Quinn cracked shut his pocket board. 'I think you lost,' I said, in a variety of octaves. But the great man, Fischer-like, had stalked off. In the four months of shooting it was the one recognisably human gesture I saw him make. For the rest, like virtually every other movie high-up, he was distinguished only by his celebrity from the hypocrites, hysterics and hangers-on that people his world.

The British contingent over here is depressed – with some show of reason, it would seem. An obsessive British cineast told me that the entire British budget for the Festival was a lousy £2,000, as compared to the Canadians' £50,000 and God knows what for the Australians (DOWN UNDER DELIVERS, says their poster). I could not establish whether this £2,000 defrayed the courtesy visit of HMS Apollo, the frigate in the bay whose ketchup-nosed, centime-less crew miserably walks the streets. The £2,000 *does* defray Britain's incompetently run booth up on the despised third floor of the Palais. The facilities for doing deals are apparently quite inadequate. The British Film Producers Association, the obsessive cineast told me, is not doing its stuff; obsessively he went through a list of British representatives in Cannes and explained how second-rate most of them were. The obsessive cineast was named Rex, by the way – so obsessive that he is even *called* a cinema.

Rex is not as depressed as some of the people here. The beggars are more depressed than Rex is. I grew fond of the beggars — they cheered me up. Apart from the itinerant hippies and the odd knapsacked desperado, everyone here looks so healthy, happy and rich that the heart soars like a hawk to see this little lunatic fringe, to see these people so spectacularly down on their luck.

Or are they? There's a pair of self-mutilators, a toothless cowboy in a fringed jacket and his swarthy, Tonto-like side-kick, who work the strip thrice daily. They munch on lit cigarettes, eat entire kitchen-boxfuls of flaring matches, and gobble up razor-blades while the café crowds snicker and wince. I contributed to their purse, on the understanding that they would both need to be fed intravenously by the time *la saison* was over. One night I saw them flouncing up La Croisette, as sumptuously dressed as any of the butterflies.

There's a trio of fire-eaters, moustachioed lads in denim, who drunkenly ask you for money ('Un franc? *Un* franc? Non, deux francs, *deux* francs') whether they're eating fire for you or not. They approached me three times in half an hour, but were very apologetic when I said I had already coughed up. Then they coughed up — for my delight. They filled their mouths with paraffin, placed a taper to their mouths, and hawked out great zeppelins of flame. I contributed again, and handsomely, in lieu of their imminent deaths from internal combustion. The leader juggled a bottle of wine with his cask of paraffin; he confused the two quite frequently, taking a refreshing swig of high-octane hemlock to wash away the taste of that nasty *vin ordinaire*.

There are, of course, real beggars in Cannes, people who don't just beg for the hell of it. They haven't the effrontery to disfigure La Croisette (perhaps the gendarmes restrain them), and tend to drop back to rue d'Antibes, which runs parallel some way inland. There's an old hooked woman who holds out a bent hand, saying Monsieur, Monsieur, Monsieur in the pitiful tone which I use on waiters.

There's a little girl who crouches all day on the pavement; making a bowl of her skirt, she counts centimes with rapid fingers. *These* beggars don't seem to be doing very well. The appearance of suffering may be good for a laugh, but the evidence of poverty amuses no one, least of all the golden denizens of Cannes. We don't like thinking of these people. We wish they weren't here. We wish they wouldn't hang about the place like this, trying to spoil our holiday.

Sunday Times, 1977

ISAAC ASIMOV

Professor Isaac Asimov sat in the opulent lobby of his New York apartment block, counting on his fingers. 'It took me nine months to write my autobiography.'

'Really?' I said. Isaac Asimov's autobiography is considerably longer than *War and Peace*.

'Sure. It took me so long, I only published seven books the next year.'

'And that's well below average?'

'Yeah! People thought I was *dead*!'

This week Gollancz publish Asimov's *Casebook of the Black Widowers*, a collection of waggish mystery stories. It is his 212th book. For the last decade he has averaged a dozen books a year. 'The Monthly Asimov' is no longer a joke: it is a statement of fact.

Asimov has been called 'the world's foremost science writer'. The description is inadequate. A random selection from the eight-page catalogue which ends his autobiography gives a more telling glimpse of Asimov's extraordinary energy and range: *Quick-and Easy Math*; *What Makes the Sun Shine?*; *Mars*; *How Did We Find Out About Antarctica?*; *The World of Carbon*; *The Roman Republic*; *Understanding Physics*; *Animals in the Bible*; *Quasar, Quasar, Burning Bright*; *Constantinople*; *ABC's of Ecology*; *Asimov's Annotated 'Paradise Lost'*; *Ginn Science Program – Advanced*

Level B; *The Sensuous Dirty Old Man*; *Still More Lecherous Limericks*. When I spoke to Asimov last spring, he was up to Opus 216. But that was several books ago now.

Asimov is probably best known in the UK as a pioneer of 'hard' science fiction – one of the old school, along with Robert Heinlein, Fred Pohl, Arthur Clarke, Poul Anderson and Clifford Simak, the men who filled the pages of magazines like *Astounding Science Fiction*, *Amazing Stories*, *Fantastic Universe*, *Super Science Fiction*, *Satellite* and *If* in the 1940s. Like his peers, he wrote mock-technical conundrums about robots and computers (*I, Robot*), ecological jeremiads (*Earth is Room Enough*), schmaltzy space opera (*Lucky Starr and the Pirates of the Asteroids*) and mediaevalised colonial fantasies (the *Foundation* trilogy). But Asimov started to diversify very early on and, by his mid-thirties, SF was for him no more than a sideline.

'My interest in science-*fiction* ended on 4 October 1957' – when the USSR sent up Sputnik I. After *Lucky Starr and the Rings of Saturn* in 1958, Asimov produced no full-length work of original fiction until 1972, when he managed to complete his worthy, wordy epic, *The Gods Themselves*. Nearly a hundred non-fiction books separate the two titles; and, since 1972, Asimov has published a hundred more. Nowadays, he is not an SF writer so much as a writing phenomenon.

Before going off to meet the great man, I took the trouble to absorb – or, at any rate, to buy and stare at – the hulking twin volumes of his autobiography, *In Memory Yet Green* and *In Joy Still Felt* (1979 and 1980). Asimov says that the books took about nine months to write. Well, they take about eight months to read. 'I had forty years of diaries to use,' Asimov would later tell me – and it shows.

Structurally, the autobiography makes an average collection of showbiz memoirs look like Nabokov's *Speak, Memory*. Furthermore, and on Asimov's own admission, nothing ever happened to him. I toiled through the first volume in a mood of scandalised admiration. How could anyone *dare* to record a life with such fidelity to the trivial? The book reads like an outsize experiment in tedium by Andy Warhol or Yoko Ono. After a while the effect is hypnotic and remorseless: you read on in tortured fascination.

The heroic tale begins in 1920. Born 250 miles southwest of Moscow, Asimov sailed to New York with his parents and younger sister at the age of three. The family ran a candy store in Brooklyn. In the best pages of the book, Asimov describes how he taught himself to read English at the age of five. (If you ask Asimov whether he was a child prodigy, he will reliably answer: 'Yes, I was – and still am.')

Punctuating his narrative with phrases like 'Another memory is this one' and 'Oh well. I apologise for the interruption', Asimov tells us how his interest in science fiction took shape. Through his father's shop little Isaac had access to the SF magazines that had started proliferating in the 1920s. By the age of nine, he was an addict; by eleven, he was a scribbler. In 1938 he sold his first story.

Asimov contentedly explains that he was 'a major figure' in the genre at the age of twenty-one. The claim is probably justified: the awkward, friendless, pimply boy, still shackled to the candy-store counter, was also being hailed as a seminal figure. Asimov devotes the odd hundred pages here and there to his vicissitudes in academe (the Columbia University Graduate School) and in military service during the war (the US Navy Yard at Philadelphia); but his writing schedule provides the main thread of the book. At one point Asimov recalls a short story that he never managed to place anywhere. Startlingly, he then reprints it, in full. It is terrible. Such failures were rare, however, and the Asimov writing robot soon came stalking off the assembly line.

Two books a year, five books a year, ten books a year! A cent a word, a dime a word, a dollar a word! A $1,000 advance, a $10,000 paperback sale, a $50,000 royalty cheque! . . . All autobiographies are success stories, and we share Asimov's gratified awe as fame and money start pouring in.

After a while, the reader is in some danger of feeling like a bailiff or a tax-inspector. Fortunately, though, Asimov often puts his ledgers aside to keep us up to date on everything else: problems with the air-conditioning, buying a new car ('This time it was going to be a Ford'), his children's bouts of measles, a faulty incinerator in his flatblock. All this information is quite unreflectingly compiled, with no variation of tone or style. Asimov writes about his divorce and remarriage in the same way he writes about tussles over contracts with Doubleday or Abelard-Schuman. And the ills which afflict most middle-class lives are given their dutiful due: there are consecutive chapters entitled 'My Thyroid' and 'Janet's Breast'.

But the book's most persistent theme is Asimov's inexhaustible, all-conquering self-love. Every anecdote is subtly, or openly, gauged to bolster his charm. His reported jokes begin with the phrase 'I said at once', and end with the phrase, 'Everyone laughed'. The mock-mandarin boasts transmit a serene collusion with their own coquetry. It is all meant to be very 'disarming'.

I went along to meet Asimov having just let *In Memory Yet Green* crash to the floor, and having just winched *In Joy Still Felt* on to the lectern. I knew more about Isaac Asimov than I knew about anyone else alive. What could there be left to add?

He is a bearish, messianic figure with porkchop sideburns, cowboy boots, a 'bolo' tie (silver brooch on a neck pulley), and a lumpy, muscular, overloaded forehead. I expected cheerful volubility, but Asimov gives off an air of irritated preoccupation, as if silently completing a stint of mental arithmetic.

We met at a Broadway radio station, where Asimov was giving an interview prior to the one he had promised me. He sat hunched at the round table, nodding at me as I was shown into the control room to wait with the elderly, chain-smoking lady producer.

'No funny stuff in there,' said Asimov gloomily. 'She's a nymphomaniac, you know.'

When the interview was over, Asimov mooched out into the street. 'You want something to eat?' he asked. 'You look skinny enough.' It was a typical New York spring day – 90 degrees, the tarmac spongy beneath your feet. In the cab, Asimov frequently fell silent as his gaze followed the lightly-clad women in the lunchtime crowds. 'Look at them all', he said abstractedly, ' – all out in their summer uniforms.'

We talked about robotics, psychohistory, inflation, future shock, fear of flying, space travel, marriage, overpopulation, Jimmy Carter, biological warfare, workoholicism, auto-biography and Isaac Asimov. He is a far more reflective figure than you would have any right to expect, stoically resigned to his own eccentricity and waywardness.

'I wanted my autobiography to be unanalytical, without wisdom. I wanted to show the reader what it was like *to be me*. A genius, maybe, but also a schmuck. It's a big effort for me to behave like other people. I have to concentrate on it, otherwise I'd be impossible.'

Earlier that day, Asimov had absentmindedly jumped a coffee queue in the radio-station canteen.

'A girl turned to me and said, "Just because you're so famous doesn't mean you can go to the head of the line." I turned to her and *nearly* said, "Just because you're so damned insignificant doesn't mean . . ." I shut myself up this time. But I got to keep trying about things like that.

'You know, everyone gets the idea I'm so bright I must be dumb. My wife Janet, she doesn't like the idea of me crossing the street by myself. She knows I'm always writing books inside my head – sort of crazy professor. I live inside my head all the time. But why not? I *like* my head.'

Asimov looked at his watch, for the fourth or fifth time. I thanked him for the interview and got up to leave – for a long afternoon with *In Joy Still Felt*.

'I'd like to give you more time,' said Asimov, as he skulked off to his apartment. 'But if you'll excuse me, I've got a few books to write.'

Sunday Telegraph, 1980

DARTS: GUTTED FOR KEITH

Let us imagine the following scene. It is Men's Finals day at
Wimbledon. Ivan Lendl and Boris Becker flex themselves on
the same baseline, next to two little tables, on which stand
tankards of lager. They have cigarettes in their mouths. A
tuxed MC with a matinee mike steps forward and introduces
the players. His voice is, if not the worst voice of all time,
then certainly the worst voice yet. 'Best of order now. Game
on. Ivan tyou er, throw first.'

Lendl refreshes himself with a husky drag and a few
gulps of lager, steps forward with a deep breath, and *throws* a
tennis ball at some arbitrary point in the opposing court – the
junction of centre and service lines, perhaps. Becker follows,
in his turn. The monotony of the contest is relieved only by
the excitations, the fruity trills and graces of the scorer's
voice. 'Love-*thirty*! Fifteen-FORTY!' and so on, until the
concluding, 'Yayce. First game, Ivan. Unlucky, Boris. Second
game: Boris tyou er, throw first.'

I could have mentioned that Lendl and Becker have been
outfitted by Rent-a-Tent and tip the scales at a couple of
hundredweight each. But this would merely add to a sense
of anachronism, or nostalgia. Always endearingly sensitive,
always touchingly touchy about its image ('Let's face it . . .'),
the world of darts is yet again in the process of cleaning itself
up. With a groan of effort and many whimpers of protest

(what about tradition? what about *civil rights*?), darts is trying once more to burst into a new dawn.

There is, to begin with, a fresh emphasis on personal appearance. It is now accounted a 'victory for darts' when a thin player beats a fat one. No smoking at the oché (the throwing line), at least in the televised stages. 'They're even thinking', said Martin Fitzmaurice, the large and affable MC, 'of banning *that*.' 'What?' I asked, looking round. 'That,' he said. 'What?' I said. '*That*,' he said, indicating the pint of lager I had obediently ordered. No piercing whistles from the crowd, no hoarse screams of *poof* and *wanker*. You even hear tell that the sport's gentle giant Cliff Lazarenko (known as Big Cliff, which is one way of putting it) has whittled himself down to nineteen stone.

I sought guidance from the world number one, Bob Anderson, as he prepared for an exhibition match at a Bishopsgate pub called Underwriter. We were in Bob's 'dressing-room' at the time (a frosty wind-tunnel stacked with empties and beer crates), and Bob was trembling in his underwear. The Limestone Cowboy (explanation for nickname: lives near Swindon and likes Tex shirts) had brought along a selection of outfits in a zippered suitbag. He contemplated the scarlet tassels of what might have been an Elvis jumpsuit, and shook his head. 'No, I think this tartan job,' he said. He shivered. 'I shouldn't think many other world number ones have to put up with this kind of thing. But there we are.'

'You must be a godsend', I said, 'to the people who want to take darts up-market.' For Bob is sportsmanlike, articulate, well-spoken, above all slender.

'Thank you. That's the nicest thing a journalist's ever said to me.'

Bob's reaction surprised me, but not for long. The darters I spoke to all felt starved of 'recognition'. They were additionally gratified to attract the attention of the *Observer*, accustomed as they are to the odd smudged scurrility several pages from the back of the *Star*.

'I regard myself', Bob went on, 'as an ambassador for the sport. Darts *has* to improve its image. We're talking about television, sponsorship, endorsements.'

'Get it out of the pub?'

'You can't get it out of the pub, and I wouldn't want to get it out of the pub. But it has to find a broader appeal. It has to move from the bar-room to the ballroom.'

I had entered Underwriter to a blizzard of badinage and dirty jokes (nymphomaniacs, vibrators) and there was more fierce cajolery when me and my mate Bob emerged from behind the heavy drapes. Mr Fitzmaurice and a personage known as the Clacton Stallion were jovially assembling the darts clobber: Mimic Board, Indicator, Enumerator. One-lining regulars, fourteen of whom would soon face Bob at the oché, now cackled away with the anecdotal landlord. In this milieu, you suddenly see the urgent meaning of that phrase about everybody needing a good laugh. The Algonquin Round Table could never have been so remorselessly pawky.

In fact, an atmosphere of piss-taking one-upmanship is the natural background of darts – appropriately, too, for the game is all about *scoring*. No sport is more bound up with nerve, with nerves, with nervelessness: the sense of your own resolve, the predatory awareness of an opponent's weakness. This is what darters are praising when they talk of 'the killer instinct'. And maybe that's all it comes down to: the savagery of your desire to get that dart *to go where you throw it.*

'Man is the hunter,' Bob had told me. He competes against nature, but also against other hunters. 'If you hit the target, you bring home a haunch of venison. If you don't, it's turnips and gravy.'

That night in Bishopsgate, Bob's line sounded a bit on the grand side. Yet perhaps there's life in it. After all, in evolutionary terms, man has spent a lot more time throwing spears than he's spent in cities – or hanging around in pubs, throwing darts.

What will never change about the game is its essential simplicity. You could put it differently: what will never change about the game is its irreducible and dumbfounding starkness. Hand, projectile, target, through a medium of thin air – and that's that. Remove one umpire, both batsmen and all the fielders from a cricket pitch, and you get some idea of the dourness of darts. Even ten-pin bowling (the other great proletarian sport of the North Atlantic) has dimensions that darts could only wonder at: the spun or powered ball hits skittles, which then hit other skittles in varying ways, and the scores progress geometrically. There are things you *can* do with the darts and dartboard that involve strategy and complication. But these games are chess to the checkers, snooker to the billiards of 501, the format to which televised darts has grimly dwindled.

In 501, nine-tenths of the board is in effect never used. Of the board's wide face, the flat nose of the treble 20 (the size of an elongated postage stamp) is alone the grail of the players, the G-spot of the crowds. True, as each leg concludes, the player must 'finish' or 'check out' or 'make the pick-off', using the doubles. But this is just a different target, not a different *kind* of target (and the much-touted 'maths' of darts can be mastered over a weekend). There is no equivalent, in darts, to the wrong-footing cross-court topspin backhand half-volley. Every shot is the same shot.

Totally lacking in strategy, darts is also quite without technique. 'You got to get the basics right,' say the darters: head still, smooth arm, legs steady. But do you? Jocky Wilson hasn't got the basics right: he seems to be *riding* that dart into the cork. Alan Glazier looks as though he's throwing a harpoon. Ceri Morgan looks as though he's throwing a baseball.

'Ceri Morgan', said Bob, when I put this to him, 'looks as though he's throwing a baseball *bat*. No, everyone evolves a personal style. It's like golf.'

I didn't point out that no golfer addresses the ball sideways with one foot in the air (never mind a fag in his hand, or his mouth). We agreed, however, that in the absence of everything else darts came down to a natural ability – hand-eye – and natural resilience: i.e. bottle.

'Then what's wrong?' I said. 'Help me, Bob, help me.'

On a reasonable day a top thrower will 'average' about 30. This is my average too – but with three darts rather than one. I am what you might call a twenty-sixer: a dart in the 20, a dart in the 5, and a dart in the 1. Sometimes the magics descend on me, and I am in the darter's nirvana: I'm not throwing them in – I'm *putting* them in.

Once, for instance, while throwing away, I threw 180: three treble 20s, the maximum. No sweat, I thought. Now I'll do a John Lowe: the fabled nine-darter. Three more treble 20s, then treble 17, treble 18, double 18. No sweat. I was, as they say, in a non-pressure situation: I was alone in the kitchen. I plucked the arrows from the board and returned to the line. I took a deep breath, and threw.

I got 26. My subsequent scores were 22, 3, 26, 41, 30, 11, 26, 45, 15, 6 (a bad bounce-out), 22, 26 (featuring two treble ones), 45, 7, 22, 63 (helped by, of all things, a treble 14), and 26, which put me on a finish. 167: treble 20, treble 19, bull. I threw 26. Then 9, 30, 17, 24, 43, 0, 0, 9 . . . Twenty minutes later I tearfully skewered the double 1. So, a distinction of a kind: the 180-darter.

I motor out to North London's Enfield for lunch with Keith Deller. Shock winner of the 1983 World Championship, Keith was for a while the great white hope of darts: young and apple-cheeked, a breath of fresh air. But then Keith showed that in darts it is hard to do your ageing one year at a time. By 1984, he looked like a darts player.

It would have suited my preconceptions if I had found Keith half-drunk in some roadhouse, smothered in tattoos and darts magazines. On the contrary: Keith and his pretty wife, Kim, awaited me over their Perriers in the ante-room of a pleasant businessman's restaurant. There was talk of the gym, and countryside rambles with dog Sheba. No alcohol and no nicotine. It was I who felt like the true darter of the company, with my drink, my roll-ups, my North Circular pallor.

Keith is genial, straightforward, considerate, clear-eyed. He is also charmingly uxorious, constantly deferring to Kim, who, for her part, is fully abreast of Keith's darting hopes and fears. In a conversation that often went like this –

'143?'

'Treble 20, treble 17, double 16.'

'127?'

'Treble 20, treble 17, double 8.'

– Kim Deller was in no sense left out. 'I like double 10, don't I, love?' Keith would say. Or again: 'Treble 14 – it's one of my favourite trebles, isn't it, Kim?' Courteous, clean-living, an ambassador for his sport. The only thing that might upset Keith, you felt, was if you had forgetfully sworn in front of his wife. Tomorrow would see the start of the Winmau World Masters. For Keith this spelt an early night after a sandwich and a spot of TV. You can't live the old life now, he suggested, not in the modern game. The standards are too high.

So *that's* the thing that will eventually clean up darts: *darts*.

To Kensington's Rainbow Room, for the Winmau. A Parliament of Darts, a vast arena entirely devoted to darts, darts, darts. At the central tables, darts families – darts dynasties – have gathered for the day (darts kids in darts shirts charm tenners from darts grannies). Darts accessories are on sale, and darts literature. And darters are darting, in dozens of booths around the hall.

Here, darts cuts through the barriers of age, sex, race and creed. Big names mingle with small, and many a Lars and Sven and Costas rubs shoulders with the Eric Bristows, the Mike Gregorys, the Davie Whitcombs. The stars *do* look relatively slim, but this is partly because the fans look relatively fat. Reassuring, in a way, to see that the human butter mountain is not exclusively a British physical type. Among the cries of 'Unlucky', 'Good darts' and (the supreme accolade) 'Darts', one also hears *pintlager*, *gooddarts*, *unloeucky* and *scotchverybig* in Belgian, Dutch and a variety of Nordic tongues.

I team up with my boy Keith and hobnob with him and not-so-big Big Cliff. Keith has a bye in the first round ('he didn't turn up') but is soon tackling a black Netherlander called Ellis. I watch anxiously as Keith does the biz. We hardly have time for a lager shandy before Keith is back at the oché, up against an eighteen-year-old beanpole called Kurt. Keith throws well but Kurt (moustachioed, unsmiling) throws 'superb', smacking in the ton-forties. I stand in the little pocket of howling body-heat saying, 'Go on, Keith,' and, 'Darts, Keith.' Six minutes later Keith sits slumped on the scorer's desk, rubbing his eyes, his Winmau challenge over for another year.

Gutted for Keith, I return to the bar and hobnob with Bob. Bob is having an ambassadorial pint with his latest scalp, a nervous young lad from the North. Bob is generous in victory. After a discreet pause I go to Keith and comfort him. He is statesmanlike in defeat. We agree that the lad threw good darts.

'He was a maniac,' I said. 'But Keith — what happened? You had a dart to finish him.'

Keith shrugged. 'Bad darts,' he explained.

The next day I saw Bob go on to win it, beating Lowie in the final. The explanation for that? *Good* darts. Or, more simply, *darts*.

I had bashfully taken my darts pouch along when I went to interview Bob Anderson. We didn't play, but I made him give me some tips. I had also hoped to learn something at the feet of Keith Deller. Back in the kitchen I addressed the dartboard with a new stance and a new action. I threw five consecutive 26s. Then I threw the darts to the floor and had a smoke and a drink instead.

All sports are eventually confining, and there is no cave deeper or darker than darts. During my visit there I felt no hostility, remarkably enough, but I constantly felt the symptoms of asphyxiation. Can darts progress? Its limitations, surely, are set by the game, not by the players. What draws me and many others to the sport and the spectacle, I think, is a liking for human variety, specifically a drastically primitive activity in a drastically modern setting. I don't want to see sporting ambassadors. I want to see the usual arrow-shower. Darts is going upmarket. But where to? My suspicion is that it may have to come right back down again.

Observer, 1988

JOHN BRAINE

In 1975 the New Statesman ran a series called 'The Defectors': profiles of more or less distinguished figures who had abandoned the left and embraced the right. My father was included in the series; so were several forgotten politicians, and several half-forgotten politicians like Alun Chalfont and Woodrow Wyatt. Such pieces were unsigned and usually written by the staff. I got John Braine. In my time at the New Statesman I also got Esther Rantzen ('Household Faces') and Sir Peter Parker ('Captains of Industry'). John Braine earns inclusion here on the grounds of his eccentricity – and his pathos (see Postscript).

'They're a bit liberal, are the Monday Club – but they're basically sound.' Few defectors of recent years can have crossed the floor with quite the outrageous swagger of John Braine. One-time charter member of the Committee of 100, Labour Party proselytiser, apologist for the USSR and (so it's said) darling of the working-class *literati*, Braine is now established as the most wild-eyed and querulous champion of the literary Right, a more colourful turncoat by far than either Conquest, Osborne or Amis. Although any study of what one might call Braine's political 'thought' quickly reveals it as a shambles of folly and recklessness, a rehearsal of his views is well worth undertaking: he shows

231

us, with exuberance and candour, how to get both ideologies wrong.

Success came late and suddenly to Braine, and this may account for the thoroughness with which it changed him. The son of a sewage-works superintendent – origins which Braine these days describes as 'petit bourgeois' – he was born in Bradford in 1922 and educated there at St Bede's Grammar. He now sees himself, and some of his literary *confrères*, as flowers of the grammar school system, whose imminent passing he greatly regrets. After a period of uncertain employment the teenage Braine became in 1940 an assistant at the public library in nearby Bingley, where he worked, with a spell in the forces, until 1951. That year he came to London to try his luck as a freelance journalist. He published a few articles in papers like *Lilliput*, *Tribune* and the *New Statesman* (intriguing pieces to look back on, these, with their fierce class-hatred and almost lyrical Leftiness – 'empty shops . . . their boarded windows blind with failure', etc.); but ill-health struck again, and Braine was invalided out of London just as he had been invalided out of the navy ten years earlier. In hospital, and back at Bingley, the dream that was to become *Room at the Top* took shape. Within months of its publication in 1957, Braine was in a position to give up his job and turn to writing – and polemicising – full time.

The extraordinary impact of *Room at the Top* is getting no easier to explain. One wonders what sort of shape the late Fifties imagination must have been in to get itself captured by such a modest and unsophisticated book. Its reception, at any rate, succeeded in putting it about that John Braine's views were worth listening to, and a period of exultant self-advertisement in the media had begun. With that indifference to contradiction which was always to serve him well, Braine presented himself as an unspoilt Northerner, bluff, honest and definitively working class, while at the same time gloating impetuously about his new-found wealth. 'I always travel first-class. I always stay at a good hotel,' he told interviewers in 1958, confessing, more frankly, to Robert Pitman: 'What I want to do is drive through Bradford in a Rolls-Royce with two naked women on either side of me covered in jewels.' Braine saw the film version of *Room at the Top* several nights running, and wept every time.

Perhaps the most rollicking chapter of Braine's public career came a couple of years later, after a visit to the Soviet Union in 1960. Still based at Bingley, Braine went East in a typically two-tier capacity: to be a guest of Alexei Surkov and the society of Soviet authors, and also to blow as much of the frozen Russian royalties of *Room at the Top* as he could on a quick package tour. In March of that year he had contributed a 'peace message' to the *Daily Worker* ('My Golden Dream — To Finish With War'): 'It's absurd', he had said, 'to regard the Soviet Union as our enemy . . . I have no fear of the Soviet Union, neither am I frightened of communism' — which so impressed staff-writer Monty Meth that he urged Braine to write a best-seller which would 'rally thousands more to the cause'. Braine did what he could, anyway, with an open letter to Surkov in *Tribune* that December. It is fascinating to see here the note of painless credulity which Braine was later to revile in others: praising the USSR's cultural awareness and 'genuine idealism', Braine wrote, 'Of course, I don't know anything about the forbidden areas — rocket bases, and so on. I presume they exist in your country as they certainly do in mine.' And when John Wain, who had also paid the USSR a visit, suggested in the *Observer* that Soviet publishers were not given an entirely free hand by the state, Braine cleared the matter up. 'Rubbish,' he explained. 'Russian publishers choose books on merit.' Their only criterion, he reported, was 'whether the public will want to read them'.

Braine being Braine, though, there were many less considered disclosures in the popular press. 'Russia is the place to make money, if you're a writer,' he said; the food, too, was 'infinitely superior to ours', the shops 'full of stuff' for him to spend his Moscow roubles on. In the same piece the interviewer teased Braine about his poor film-rights deal for the money-spinning *Room at the Top* (only £5,000). 'It's just agony,' Braine admitted. 'Night after night I twist and turn in misery thinking of it.' Money was, as always, never far from Braine's thoughts at this time. The film rights of his second novel, *The Vodi*, for which he had forecast a deal of 'perhaps £100,000', were not taken up. Possibly as a result of this, Braine agreed to write a sequel to his first best-seller; the rights of *Life at the Top* were duly sold for about £45,000, implanting in the novelist a deep and enduring hatred of income tax.

Meanwhile, of course, Braine was involved in campaigning for CND, a commitment that appeared to do little for his argumentative sobriety. For a while he gamely toured the country making speeches, but disillusion soon claimed him. As early as 1961 he resigned, apparently 'convinced' that the organisation would be made illegal within a year. What Braine took to be the futility of CND membership further embattled his sense of the political realities: 'I can see little difference between Khrushchev, Kennedy, De Gaulle, Macmillan, Adenauer . . .' 'They're all mad,' he decided, later amending the verdict to 'they're all filthy homicidal maniacs'. Clearly, if you've resigned yourself to ineffectiveness, it ceases to matter what you say.

Braine's heart, at least, was still in the right place at this stage, though the about-turn wasn't far in the distance. In 1960 he had affirmed in the *Daily Worker* that the 'main hope for peace lies with the Labour and trade union movement', and four years later he was prepared to elaborate the point in an election piece for the *Sunday Citizen*. It was to be his last statement as a socialist.

Having been born and bred in the industrial North, there's never been any choice for me politically. It's always been socialism or nothing. And by nothing I mean complete political apathy, a complete and savage concentration upon my own material advancement.

Prophetic words, some might say. In retrospect, Braine adduces two main causes of his disaffection from the Left – a liking for capitalism as it was revealed to him by a tour of the US, and the 'we are all guilty' response to the Moors Murders; but only something basic to Braine's psychology could explain the helter-skelter that his political thinking subsequently became. It was heralded – or confirmed – by his removal from Bingley to the Surrey stockbroker belt, a personal defection that he had always loudly resisted. He could never leave the North, he told the *Daily Express* in 1958, because the South was dirty, expensive and people wouldn't recognise him in the streets. Smartening up his motives for the *Daily Worker*, he had said that he would regard it 'as a kind of betrayal to live cut off from the working class'.

In 1966 the move happened – as did much else. The same year he was volunteering the information that 'when pacifists go on about the wickedness of war, I feel I want to go out and kill somebody'. The following year he joined the West Byfleet and Pyrford Conservative Association, and a year later said his 'Goodbye to the Left' in no uncertain fashion with a Monday Club pamphlet, electioneering in the press meanwhile for the Tories' 1970 campaign; unless the Conservatives won, he argued with his usual prescience, it would be the last election we'd see this century. Around this time, too, he denounced the 'absolutely consistent left-wing bias' of the BBC, called Kennedy 'the worst president the US ever had' and Luther King 'a trouble-maker and a very stupid man', welcomed the Pope's encyclical on contraception, observed that African freedom fighters were 'not fit to live', agitated for the restoration of hanging (it was 'squeamish and heartless' to resist it), and championed corporal punishment – 'Oh, I think flogging is an admirable thing,' he'll now tell you. No defector could have retraced his steps more ploddingly.

Nowadays Braine's socio-political thinking is a veritable rumpus-room of prejudice and obsession. Retributive punishment, he believes, is sanctified by a reading of the Bible. (When asked about the biblical creed of forgiveness, he says: 'Let God forgive them. It's his *métier*, not mine.') Young Socialists, in Braine's view, are 'only in it for the money', trade unions wish 'to lay the country open to communist invasion', foreign aid is 'a waste of time and money', and Enoch is a 'dangerous Leftie'; 'Down with Oxfam!' is his parting salute.

Braine has a name for what has happened to him: it's called 'growing up'. As a young man, he saw himself facing a largely right-wing Establishment; now he thinks that the Establishment has defected, has gone Left, while he has remained more or less where he was, adjusting his views only to meet the improvement in his social standing. And yet the 'savage' self-advancement which, in 1964, he posited as the only alternative to socialism will not do as a description of his present concerns (anyone who regards him as a *bon vivant* should have a look at the 'office' where he writes, a tiny hovel behind Boomerang Taxis in Woking's Chertsey Road). Braine is a meritocrat, and sees his own career as a moving tribute to that system, which in some senses it is. Ultimately, Braine's political statements have always been a personal business, a rhetoric thrown out by his own needs and anxieties. His outbursts may continue to be punitive and flailing, but his nature, as all who know him confirm, has remained generous, docile and quite without malice.

And he is an innocent. The level of artistic sophistication to which he aspires is well illustrated by his absurd 'handbook', *Writing a Novel* (and, more endearingly, by his *Desert Island Discs* choice, which included *Plaisir d'Amour*, *Goodnight, Irene* and *Land of Hope and Glory*). From *Room at the Top* on he has been an able, lower-middlebrow chronicler of the workings of sex and money, with a good eye and a passable ear. But what he has never been is a realist. Lord

Soper once asked Braine about his views on America, shortly after the novelist had returned from his 1964 visit. Braine replied that, despite its many imperfections, he had found it a wonderfully free and democratic land. 'All right if you're not black,' said Soper. Braine was puzzled, indignant, and finally triumphant: 'But, you fool – I'm *not*' was his clincher. After recounting the anecdote Braine will glare at you for several seconds, nodding intently. It is futile to argue with such people, and ridiculous to be worried by them. Braine will adorn the Right just as he adorned the Left – noisy, opinionated, and not at all dangerous.

Postscript: On his last Christmas Day, Braine ate lunch at a Community Centre, in the company of indigents. All but the last months of his last years were spent in a murky bedsit: narrow cot, wobbly table, one knife, one fork. Among his last public appearances was a visit to the Newcastle Literary Festival: fortified by a hearty breakfast, many cigarettes, and much gin, he rounded off an incoherent hour-long address to a gathering of nine or ten people by reducing himself to tears as he read the closing lines of *Room at the Top* ... His later fiction devolved into a uniquely transparent form of wish-fulfilment, or self-therapy, in which the novelist hero hobnobs with celebrities, gets recognised wherever he goes, and is assured by his mistress that – on top of all this – he has the body of a young boy. It was vanity publishing in the fullest sense: he had lost his audience. Awarded a modest grant by the Writers' Benevolent Fund, Braine (it is said) behaved as if he had just won the Nobel Prize. He was not self-pitying; he persisted with delusion; he continued to care about the literary canon (Flaubert, Dostoevsky) and remained convinced of the security of his place within it.

CARNIVAL

Most Notting Hill homeowners simply leave town for the Carnival weekend. Long-sufferingly they decamp to some Home County or other (at least their cars will be safe) and return on the Tuesday, when it's all over. They expect their houses to be gutted, torn down – they expect a heap of rubble with a mumbling brother or two sorting through the wreckage. It's never like that. WII is still standing. Street life goes on.

'Carnival', as we call it, here on the Front Line, has given me good times and given me bad times. It once nearly killed me, for instance: ten minutes of authentic mortal terror (to which I shall duly return). But its scattered pleasures are not easily found elsewhere; and even its torments are memorable.

If you are a writer, then the weekend can be confidently written off. You park the car somewhere in Acton and stroll home through the surging crowds of police officers. No non-neighbour can come and see you, and you can't go and see them. At midnight the children will still be pulsing to the various street parties and roof parties and windowsill parties up and down the block. For months the rap-rhythm lingers in my head. It goes like this: *a fashy bashy cashy dashy lashy mashy pashy. Fashy wha, fashy wha. A fashy bashy cashy dashy lashy mashy pashy.* And so on. In your head. There are also unforgettable miracles of scansion. For example:

I took my problem to the EEC,
The European Economic Communitee . . .

But don't mock the rap-artist: envy him. A rap-artist is
definitely the thing to be. As well as the affection, reverence and erotic perks traditionally due to the musician, he
is also accorded the status of poet, philosopher, dissident
and redeemer. Nobody ever had it so good.

Early on Tuesday morning I will walk the mile from the
house to the flat where I work, through the sodden silence,
the eviscerated rubbish bags, the billions of lager cans like
cartridges spent in a new kind of urban war. And most of
that lager is still around: the briny tang tickles your throat.
But by Wednesday all signs of the debauch have been hosed
off the street. With relief the little manor returns to normality
– to the settled randomness and rancour of everyday life.

Where are these Carnival pleasures I mentioned? They
exist, even though they do pall as you get older – as you
get more conspicuous out there, the bourgeois raver (or street
anthropologist), bobbing along to the music with one hand
holding your beer can and the other crushed to your wallet.
Carnival is for the young, the brave, the self-destructive, the
smashed, the light-fingered, the fleet-of-foot. But its freedom
and expressiveness remain hard to duplicate. Your body
responds to it before your mind does. There is candour.
Life seems to come out of doors.

If I am going to have a carnival, though, I do want
a *carnival*, not a ten-acre tourist trap, not a venture in
free enterprise, and not an over-invigilated flea circus. This
year (1989) Carnival is apparently scheduled to succumb
to Thatcherism, or better say to Maggification, since no
ism will answer to the chaos of short change and short
measure that will always characterise the Carnival small
trade. You used to be able to buy food through people's kitchen windows. Now the five-quid hotdog will duly

give way to the punnet of strawberries and the split of Pomaine.

Already, today, the police will be showing their 'presence'. Carnival is a big item in their PR calendar – the perfect lab for the latest policing theories. A more-or-less hard-edged interaction will occur, and this is inevitable, because the West Indian spirit resists supervision *especially* when it is at play. Here, the media have only two ways to go: either it's riots and looted shops, or else it's a black lady dancing in a bobby's hat. The reality is stealthier and more inhibited: a pyjama party, overseen by uniformed step-parents.

It was in 1985 that Carnival nearly killed me. That year the attendance took an exponential leap, and all the new multitudes seemed suddenly to coalesce around me as I inched down Westbourne Park Road. The human jam was soon a gridlock, then a screaming scrum. I felt that death was coming nearer, borne by a fatal surplus of life. But it eased. The police had closed off so many streets, 'in case of emergency', that they almost choreographed another Hillsborough, right there on Portobello.

But the football comparison prompts a sure argument for Carnival's right to exist, and to be fully funded. I like football and used to go to it until I realised that such congregations are entirely dedicated to ugliness: ugly voices, ugly looks, ugly thoughts. The Carnival crowd is at least trying to be about the opposites of these. Think of the misery that descends on the environs of a football ground, not once a year but once a fortnight. Think, with due pity and terror, of the dead and the near-dead on the Sheffield terraces. This is what society will let its people go through, in their search for a good time.

Evening Standard, 1989

ANTHONY BURGESS

'NIGEL BURGESS – Agent Maritime' said the dynatroned tape on the door, halfway up the narrow rue Grimaldi, Monte Carlo. Cunning old Burgess, I thought as I pressed the button. The modest alias seemed typical of this well-known loner and maverick, adept of imposture and verbal disguise – the man who once lost a book-reviewing job for praising his own pseudonymous novel. That *Nigel* was perfect . . .

'Who?' asked the voice from the grille. 'No, we're ship-insurers, mate. You want the writer. Four doors down.'

Anthony Burgess is sixty-three, an asymmetrical, floppy-shirted figure, with a cap of greying hair swiped forward over his brow like a sub-editor's eye-shade. 'I'm in a bad way,' he had said on the telephone. 'Can't walk. Can't eat.' But he appeared to be in resilient, even combative shape when we strolled from the apartment block to his local café – and began a five-hour lunch. He was hailed by the waiters and gruffly bantered with them in his mumbled French. (Burgess is, of course, practically omnilingual: 'Yes, I read all the Romance languages,' he admits, 'plus Russian, Indonesian, Gaelic, Swedish, a few others.' When Burgess met Borges, they chatted in Anglo-Saxon.) He talked straight English to me, however, and was throughout far more approachable than the manic erudition of his prose would lead one to expect. I found him warm, entertaining and highly responsive, quite without the Great Writer's delphic glaze.

The null if sparkling principality of Monaco seemed an odd place for him to end up. It would, for instance, be hard to imagine Burgess asking Bjorn Borg or Ringo Starr round for the evening. 'No,' he says, 'there isn't much company here – though I did meet Frank Sinatra at Princess Grace's recently. A very curious man. Luckily I've quite lost my gregariousness. Never had much. Monte Carlo is over-policed but clean and safe, and it leaves you alone.'

Burgess's last two points of exile were Malta and Italy. Malta was full of bridge-playing admirals and retired squadron-leaders – and full of censors. 'They waited at the airport every morning with felt pens and scissors, ready to deface the *Daily Mirror.*' One day some books sent to Burgess for review were confiscated; the new Doris Lessing had attracted the censors' attention. 'I went along to the post office and upended a desk over two officials. I knew I had to leave.'

He misses Italy, where he had a flat in Rome and a house in Bracciano. 'For me, Italy is the only country in the world.' But then he was tipped off that his son Andreas, now sixteen, was next on the local kidnap roster. 'They thought: Burgess, he write *Naranya Mecanica*, must have lots of money. We moved straight out to the next state – Monaco.'

These days, Burgess *has* got lots of money, owing to his cross-cultural screenplays, film-scores and such things as his 'teleJesus' collaboration with Zeffirelli ('terrible, terrible man') and Lord Grade ('very ignorant, incredible the depth of it, but gets things done'). And now, too, his spectacular novel *Earthly Powers* has been sold to America for something like half a million dollars. 'Oh, I've been technically a millionaire for some time now. It doesn't make much difference to anything, after a point. One still *minds*. For instance, I take it you're paying for this lunch?'

Remarkably, Burgess's steady elevation has never affected his appetite for routine journalistic work. 'I refuse no reasonable offer of work,' he wrote in 1978, 'and very few unreasonable ones.' His alarming energy perhaps has its source in a Lancastrian childhood which he now describes as 'poverty-stricken'. There is another reason why Burgess writes as if there's no tomorrow: for a period in his life, there *was* no tomorrow, or no very definite one. In 1959 he was invalided home from a teaching job in Malaya with a suspected brain tumour. He wrote five novels in a year (including *A Clockwork Orange*) to provide his widow with some security. Ironically, Burgess has long outlived his first wife; a prey to depression and drink, she died of sclerosis in her forties.

Much of Burgess's early career – as a musician, danceband arranger, teacher and tyro novelist – was frustrating and poorly rewarded. He speaks of those days with a touch of bitterness and even mild paranoia. 'Jobs were denied me', he says, 'because I hadn't been to Oxford. Manchester, you see. "Manchester." They didn't like that.' Similarly, Burgess still seems to be under the apprehension that he has never been taken seriously by that chimerical conglomerate, the London Literary World.

It is difficult to see how he has managed to stick to this impression. From quite early on, the critics asserted what is now generally acknowledged: that Burgess is one of the most intelligent, radical and adventurous of modern British writers. The list of titles on the inside page of *Earthly Powers* is a useful testimony to a talent of great richness – and, perhaps, of almost perilous facility. There is mainstream work like the Malayan Trilogy and the Enderby books, futuristic fantasies like *A Clockwork Orange* and *The Wanting Seed*, a 'biography' of Shakespeare written in Elizabethan English (*Nothing Like the Sun*), a novel about Napoleon written as a prose analogy to Beethoven's Eroica (*Napoleon Symphony*), a novel with verse appendices about the dying Keats (*Abba Abba*), an essay-come-projection on Orwellian themes (*1985*) – as well as a raft of translations, libretti, children's stories, verse collections, teaching guides, picture books, linguistics manuals . . . and now comes *Earthly Powers*, whose career-award reception should dispose of any lingering insecurities.

The book has the scope and intensity which we associate with the prose epics of Saul Bellow. At 600-odd pages, it also has something of a willed quality, like everything Burgess writes. 'I am very pleased to have written a long novel at last,' he says. Using the twentieth century as its canvas, *Earthly Powers* is about the powers of darkness, the way the non-human agency of evil finds its human forms: in the voodoo of a Malayan warlock, in the bestialities of Chicago gangsters, in Nazism and Mussolini's blackshirts – and, more obliquely, in the propagation of bad art, the artist's role being analagous to that of God. Burgess was brought up as an Augustinian Catholic and received his early education at the Xaverian College in Manchester. He is still a believer, though not a literalist.

'You've got to believe in something, in a moral order. I do believe in the forces of evil – I myself was subjected to black magic in Malaya. There is, for example, no A.J.P. Taylor-ish explanation for what happened in Nazi Germany. There's a very malign reality somewhere . . . Of course, you never know why God singles people out for special treatment. Take Lazarus – pissed every night, screwed everyone, slain in a tavern . . .'

For the time being, Burgess's life is like most writers' lives, beset by anxieties ranging from the metaphysical to the domestic. 'My first thought when I wake up every morning is – My God. The kitchen! My wife, you see, doesn't go in for that kind of thing. It's a constant battle – the kitchen, I mean.'

I had met Burgess before: as a child of six or seven, when he visited my parents with the first Mrs Burgess. I have a faint image of a jovial, talkative man, consistently out-decibelled by his wife. The second Mrs Burgess, the translator Liana (she is currently turning the Malayan Trilogy into her native

Italian) seems to be a woman of the same voluble genre. It is easy to imagine the babel of their apartment, where English and Italian vie for status as the international language.

At about five o'clock Burgess's son Andreas wandered into the restaurant. A heavy-lidded Latin, Andreas shook hands and addressed me in a piercing Scottish brogue. 'Well, Andreas,' said Burgess. 'The kitchen . . . How is it?' Andreas smiled and shook his head. Father and son made gestures of Neapolitan resignation and helplessness. Burgess shuddered. 'One more drink,' he said, 'and I'd better go and deal with it.'

Observer, 1980

Postscript: A few more words about that lunch. We began with gin-and-tonics (two each), followed by a tremendous amount of cheap red wine. I did my best to keep pace with Burgess, who, by five o'clock, was drinking double brandies as if against time: three swallows, and then the glass held up for more. At six he ordered a *gin-and-tonic*. This ended the session, though it seemed for a moment that we were about to repeat it, or relive it. I would go on to endure an authentically frightening hangover which lasted for half a week. At eight in the evening on the day after the day after, I was still sitting in an armchair with a hand on my brow and saying, 'Dear oh dear. Dear oh dear oh dear . . .' Whereas Burgess (I am sure) went home, did the kitchen, spring-cleaned the flat, wrote two book reviews, a flute concerto and a film treatment, knocked off his gardening column for *Pravda*, phoned in his surfing page to the *Sydney Morning Herald*, and then test-drove a kidney-machine for *El Pais* – before settling down to some serious work.

ROMAN POLANSKI

The interview took place in Paris in 1979. In 1978 Polanski fled America while awaiting trial on charges of raping a minor.

'When I was being driven to the police station from the hotel, the car radio was already talking about it. The newsmen were calling the police before I was arrested to see whether they can break the news. I couldn't *believe* ... I thought, you know, I was going to wake up from it. I realise, if I have *killed* somebody, it wouldn't have had so much appeal to the press, you see? But ... fucking, you see, and the young girls. Judges want to fuck young girls. Juries want to fuck young girls – *everyone* wants to fuck young girls! No, I knew then, this is going to be another big, big thing.'

'It could never happen to me' is the sort of remark that Roman Polanski will never have cause to utter. If strange things are going to happen, he is the kind of man they will happen to. Despite his reputation as a fixer, an ecstatic, thick-skinned bully-boy, he has, in many respects, always been fortune's fool. When he talks enthusiastically, and perhaps a little sentimentally, about all the promise, flair and freedom of the Sixties, it strikes you that there is no more conspicuous victim of the abysmal ironies of that decade. For him the Sixties were years of high energy and

246

achievement, ending (as, in a sense, they ended for everybody else) on 9 August 1969, with the bloody murder of his pregnant wife, Sharon Tate. His period of recovery was then marked by constant, and hatefully insulting, stories in the press, explaining how Mr and Mrs Polanski had opened the door to their own nemesis (by experimenting with drugs, decadence, weird rituals, etc). It wasn't his first experience of inordinate suffering, and inordinate humiliation. And now, ten years later, he finds himself in an altogether different kind of mess.

I went first to his airy, Hockneyesque, definitively bijou flat, between the Champs Elysées and the Seine. There can be few smarter apartment blocks in Paris: Marlene Dietrich used to have a floor of it, and so does some deserving member or other of the Pahlavi family. I waited for a few minutes in the bookless drawing-room, Polanski's agile manservant asking me if I would prefer my glass of beer with or without a head of foam. I went with the foam, and never regretted it. Then Polanski strolled promptly out of his bedroom, wearing tailored jeans and a monogrammed blue shirt. At five foot four, and with great liveliness of gait and gesture, he seems to be about sixteen years old. This impression didn't go away, even after several hours in his company. It occurred to me that his considerable and well-documented success with women has a lot to do with that fact. Contemplating little Roman, women wouldn't so much sense the appeal of being worked over by a priapic, trouble-shooting film-director; they would just want to take the poor waif upstairs and have him sob himself to sleep in their arms.

Looking sixteen, of course, does not entitle you to go to bed with adolescents. Despite what Polanski says – *contra* Polanski – not everyone wants to fuck young girls. One cannot hide behind a false universality: one cannot seek safety in numbers. Most people who do want to fuck young girls, moreover, don't fuck young girls. Not fucking apparently willing young girls is clearly more of a challenge. But even Humbert Humbert realised that young girls don't really know whether they are willing or not. The active paedophile is stealing childhoods. Polanski, you sense, has never even tried to understand this.

'You drinking *beer*?' he asked with routine incredulity. His voice is vaulting, declamatory, not only accented but heavily accentual in style.

'That's right,' I said. 'In his piece about you Kenneth Tynan says that you hardly drink at all. Is that –?'

'Ah Ken Tynan full of shit,' he said, turning and pacing round the room. 'I drink a lot of wine last night, as a matter of fact . . . But now I'm very *hungry*.'

We had lunch in a noisy German restaurant round the corner. Polanski eats as hectically as he talks. 'Here, have some harring – no harring, *herring* . . . This is lovely – you want some? . . . Here, I prepare you good little portion, some onion on top – there!' He is pointed at and murmured about by the other diners, and affectionately fawned on by the immaculate waiters. He is one of those people who can shout for service without giving offence: if he hollers for a beer it is because he must have that beer, and must have it now.

According to press reports, Polanski met with a cool reception in Paris after his escape from America in early 1978 ('I have not contacted him – and I'm not going to,' said Joseph Losey. 'A coward's way out. The ranks are closing against him,' said Robert Stack). Well aware of his catastrophe-prone nature, he is finding Paris a good place to keep out of harm's way. 'It's very grown-up here,' he says, adding, in one of the bursts of mangled eloquence that occasionally escape his rusty, staccato, always endearing English: 'I'm trying to extenuate those contrasts in my character that make me stick out as a sore thumb from my surroundings.' (Love that 'as'.) He is determined to return to America, despite the remote possibility of a 50-year jail sentence, for the alleged drugging and raping of the thirteen-year-old girl. 'But they have made me very welcome in Paris and I'm going to stay for some while. Unless something happens.'

After all, he was born here, in 1933.

The first few years of his life were relatively free of disaster. In 1936 his family returned to Cracow. As a child Polanski saw barricades being erected at the end of the street: the Nazis were closing off the ghetto. In 1941 both his parents were taken into concentration camps. Just before the ghetto was finally overrun, Polanski escaped through a gap in the barbed wire. 'One day, outside the ghetto, I saw people marching in a column, guarded by Germans. My father was among them. I walked alongside for a while but he gestured for me to run away. He survived four years in a camp – but that was the last time I saw him.' His mother died in Auschwitz.

Polanski's youth continued to be marked by near misses. He was brought up by Catholic peasants in the remote Polish countryside. Out blackberrying one day, he was casually shot at by German soldiers – 'like I am a squirrel or something'. Back in liberated Cracow in 1945, the only bomb dropped during one of the last German air-raids blew him through a lavatory door, injuring his left arm. At the age of sixteen, as an art student in Cracow, he was led into an underground bunker by a friend of a friend who proposed to sell the young Roman a racing bicycle. 'I always wanted a racing bicycle.' He described what followed very vividly, in his thoughtful anapests, leaning forward and parting his hair to show you the scars on his crown.

'I was walking in the tunnel, you know. He was behind me. He was behind me. I kept saying, "But where is the bicycle, sir?" Then I thought I get a sudden electric shock, thought I touch a cable or something – or I thought there was some other attacker down there. I couldn't *believe* the man was hitting me on the head.' But he was, with a rock, five times. Polanski's assailant, apprehended that day, had

already committed three murders. When he staggered out
of the bunker, Polanski had so much blood pouring from
him that he still feels a tremor of dread every time he steps
under a shower.

And, despite his multinational successes, Polanski's life has
never shaken free of the grotesque and calamitous. Over the
years at least half a dozen of his close friends and associates
have met with violent and unlikely deaths – suicides, strange
illnesses, a freak train accident. It is by now a cliché to say of
Polanski that his films, with their emphasis on terror, isolation and madness, seem no more than a demonic commentary
on his life. But such an impression is unavoidable in the light
of the atrocious events at Cielo Drive in 1969. Polanski, you'd
have thought, has endured enough for twenty lifetimes.

'Of course, my life has been very strange, full of strange
things. But it does not look like that to me, you know – from
my side. My life is just something I *live*, you see. Only when
I stand back do I see how strange it has been.'

At one ironic remove, this is the character Polanski plays
in his infrequent appearances in his own films. He has low
regard for actors ('the intelligent actor is a rarity, almost a
paradox') and has few pretensions about his own abilities
in front of the camera: 'I only use me because I'm cheap
and give no trouble. I'm so nice to work with, you know?
I always do what I tell me to.' In fact, he is an actor of
narrow range but perfect pitch: he has an unwavering feel
for the comedy and pathos of vulnerability. In his two most
memorable roles – as the jittery vampire-hunter in *Dance of
the Vampires*, and as the effaced, wide-open Polish clerk in
The Tenant – Polanski portrays, with authentic sympathy,
the little man to whom strange things happen. In those films
the little man half-expects strange things to happen to him,
and responds to them with obedient, uncomplaining horror
as long as they last. He seems to believe that if these strange
things weren't happening to him, then other strange things
would be happening to him instead.

I was reminded of this persona several times during lunch, most particularly when Polanski described his recent prison term in connection with the 'rape' case in Los Angeles. Reluctantly at first, later in a spirit of great hilarity, with painful whimpers of delighted recollection, he told me how his six-week incarceration began.

'When I arrived in the middle of the night, I couldn't get *in* to the goddamn prison! There were too many journalists and cameras there! And all the prisoners in yard because they hear it on the news, saying, "Hey, how y'doing, Planski!" But it was like a vacation, a sanctuary. It was terrific. I wouldn't mind to go back now, now I know what it's like. It is interesting to go on the other side, where bad people are. Full of in*cred*ible *mur*derers! There was someone who kill sixteen people!' He nods, adding more quietly, and with resignation, 'That is the trouble – you never know when people going to *stab* you, you know? That's the only problem, is that you can just get killed any time.'

The quality of resignation, of stretched stoicism, was perhaps what drew Polanski to the character of Tess of the d'Urbervilles. Called simply *Tess*, the latest Polanski offering opened in France late last year, with encouraging critical and commercial success. It is a respectful, perhaps over-faithful, certainly over-long and generally flawed piece of work. The difficulty of the film (as in another sense it is the difficulty of the book) concerns the character of Angel Clare, the supposedly adorable foil to Tess's swinish seducer, Alec d'Urberville. The point is that Hardy plays on these melodramatic contrasts (Angel strumming his harp in the attic, Alec glimpsed through flames carrying a pitchfork), while making it clear that Angel is more subtly despicable than Alec could ever be. Polanski was aware of the ambiguity, though I don't think he ever resolved it.

'Yes, let's talk about films. Films are my sector, my "cup of tea", as they say – in England.' He looks up in wonder. 'I think I'm going to have a cigar. You want one? . . . What drew me to the character of Tess was her incredible integrity combined with her – submission? No, submissiveness – and her fatalism. She never complains. All these very . . . *unfair* things happen to her, and she never complains until the end. The book is more morally complicated than you at first think. Alec had a cold, materialistic approach to life, but he is not too bad by today's standards.'

'And what do you think of Angel?'

'Oh, Angel to me is a complete shit. He represents to me very much the young man full of revolutionary ideals, but as soon as it affects him personally he turns out to be as hypocritical as everyone else.'

I was obliged to say at this point that the casting of Peter Firth as Angel seemed to be questionable. In fact it is disastrous. Angel must *appear* to have the attributes of a romantic lead. The vulgar truth is that Peter Firth would be fine if he looked more like Robert Redford and less like Jimmy Carter. Polanski shrugged and disagreed, showing no more than mild disappointment. But it was with shared relief that we went on to praise Nastassia Kinski's wonderfully steady performance as Tess. Polanski spoke of her with affectionate admiration – and with a little self-consequence: she is a protégée of his and, naturally, also an ex.

I asked him which of his films he liked most. 'Films are like women', I was informed (Polanski thinks quite a few things are like women). 'You always love the last most until the next one comes along.

'But of course there are films for which you have a special feeling. Some of my most praised films – *Rosemary's Baby, Repulsion, The Tenant* – were largely matters of convenience, done because of time or money or to accommodate a certain producer. I wouldn't have *choosen* them, you know? But my head tells me that *Cul de Sac* is my best film – it is the film that is the most self-contained. It only has meaning as a movie, as itself. My *heart* tells me that *The Vampire Killers* [an early title for *Dance of the Vampires*] is my favourite. I get more fond of that film every year. I suppose I am reliving my happiness at the time of making it. It was towards the end of the Sixties. Everyone was full of hope and good spirits. I was making a comedy with people I liked, and of course with Sharon ... But *Tess* is very dear to me now.'

It would be rash to try to make up your mind about someone like Polanski. He is something of a ranter, his speech dotted with show-biz clichés ('Jack Nicholson – he is a great professional') and self-consciously quotab'e tags ('I like food, I like women, and best of all I like women who like food' etc, etc). But there is a great deal that is generous, natural, even transparent, about him. His confidence, for example, is a real thing, and not the grinning shambles that often passes for confidence in the film world. Clearly he has sometimes gone too far into the gratifications that his fast-lane milieu offers him, as the case in California amply demonstrates. But he has survived an extraordinary life, and is still himself.

After lunch he invited me to his cutting-room in the Champs Elysées, where he is preparing *Tess* for the English and American versions. It was a gloomy flat, full of gloomy, Gitane-smoking Frenchmen. Polanski spent twenty minutes cutting half a second out of a reaction-shot to a fresh stage in Tess's doleful decline. I asked him if he was worried that the film might be mistakenly regarded as a blow for Women's Liberation.

'*What?* Tess responds appropriately to events, and as an individual. Women's Lib is an absurdity! A few just postulates do not make a movement just. How can one half of the species organise against the other half? There's not anyone who said at certain time, "That's the way women behave." Things are the way they are because of evolution! This is the way it is between monkeys, between dogs and between butterflies!'

'What about spiders?'

'Spiders, mm,' he said, nodding and looking serious. 'No, male spiders don't have a good time. Maybe they should get together and do something about it. I don't know.'

Tatler, 1980

MADONNA

Originally I came, not to review Madonna, but to interview her. Now, when you are circling round a star of this magnitude – stacked like a package tourist above her fogbound airport – you never negotiate with the star herself. You negotiate with her people or, in best post-modern style, with her people's people: her agent's agent, her assistant's secretary's assistant's secretary. The messages come back in a remote and cautious cipher. At first it looked as though Madonna had singled me out as someone she was especially keen to see. (Truman Capote, I remembered, gave the same impression, an impression gravely qualified towards the end of the interview when he abruptly addressed me as 'Tony'.) A few days later Madonna apparently decided that, on the contrary, she didn't want to see me at all. The reason she seemed to be giving was this: I was too famous. Madonna (I wanted to tell her), don't say another word. I completely understand.

Wearily I was envisioning my arrival at Kennedy Airport. As the Concorde taxied to a halt, its engines already outscreamed by the fans gathered on the terminal rooftop, my security guards would be patrolling the runway, using their infra-red binoculars to scan the skies for media helicopters. Paparazzi disguised as ground crew and maintenance men would vex my progress through immigration and customs.

The real trouble would begin in Arrivals. By this time the unconscious bodies of twelve-year-old Martin Amis look-alikes and wannabes would be heaped up by the improvised paramedical tents, as, with a slight movement of my left forefinger, I signalled to the police chief to start fire-hosing the crowds that besieged the waiting motorcade . . .

MAIMED BY MADONNA ran the *Sun* headline, after one of its reporters had managed to sprain his ankle in a Madonna crush (probably by throwing himself under her car). I had simply been Aimed by Madonna. But I went along anyway, out of aroused interest, and fellow feeling, to review Madonna – or more particularly Madonna's new book: *Sex*.

In the old, benighted, pre-modern days, a new book was normally sent to the reviewer, encased in a jiffy-bag or, under exceptionally glamorous circumstances, a Federal-Express wallet. But Madonna is perhaps the most post-modern personage on the planet, so in this case the reviewer was sent to the book, by supersonic aeroplane. The book lives under lock and key in the Sixth Avenue skyscraper of Time Warner, and in a few other hurriedly Fort-Knoxified locations. There have already been leaks and thefts, involving police investigations and, in one case, an FBI 'sting' operation. Most books submitted for review are top secret, in the sense that nobody knows anything about them. But Madonna always tends to do things the other way round.

The reviewer gets cleared and tagged, and gauntly rides the elevator to the tenth floor. He gives his name and sits waiting in a vestibule whose shelves are adorned with recent Time Warner offerings: rock biogs, real-life murder stories, accounts of financial delinquencies, mystery novels, fluff novels, novels written by two or more co-novelists. Summoned within, the reviewer sees on someone's desk a copy of a book – a whole book – called *Why Men Have Nipples*.

We're in the editor's actual office now. But before the

book is at last produced, the reviewer is obliged to sign a long and menacing legal agreement. 'You agree that Warner and/or Madonna', it says, among much else,

> shall be entitled to issuance of an *ex parte* temporary restraining order, and a preliminary and permanent injunction against you for any threatened or actual violation of this agreement, and shall not be required to post a bond to secure such relief.

The reviewer boldly signs. And then, in an atmosphere of laughable solemnity, the book is grimly shoved across the desk. When it eventually hits the shops, *Sex* will be swaddled in a kind of nuclear-hardened polythene sachet, unbreachable except by carving knife or chainsaw. (The sachet will bear a warning: This Book Contains Adult Material And Its Exterior Packaging Reflects The Controversial and Sensitive Nature Of What Is Inside. But the main angles, clearly, are to intensify suspense and to thwart the browser.) Here in the office, though, *Sex* stood proudly unsheathed, naked as nature intended, and massive, with its spiral binding and aluminium covers. The reviewer is suffered to sit with it for an hour on a sofa, monitored throughout. He is not allowed to discuss it with anyone afterwards. And he is not allowed to take notes.

Looking through a hundred-odd cardboard pages of Madonna and others in the nude and semi-nude was, as expected, no great hardship in terms of tedium, though to be frank (and there isn't much point, hereabouts, in being anything else) she hasn't done a damned thing for me physically since she went blonde and hardbody *circa* 1986. (The time I liked her was in the *Desperately Seeking Susan* period: 'the indolent, trampy goddess', as Pauline Kael described her.) I also reposed considerable trust in my own jadedness: Madonna might shock Middle America, but she wasn't about to shock this reviewer. And yet I will admit to being mildly disquieted by *Sex* – by its hostile iteration, by its latent anger and impatience, above all, perhaps (and to this I will return), by its palpable otherness.

The opening chunk of *Sex* is all hard-edged and black-and-white and predominantly gay and punk and sado-masochistic in its themes. Nothing here or elsewhere in the book is technically hard-core, but the milieu is in itself pornographic, and darkly pornographic: the heavy-gay, pre-AIDS sex-crypts of downtown Manhattan – one of which, I recollect, was undesigningly called The Toilet. The joint featured in *Sex*, anyway is called The Vault, a sooty basement furnished with lockers and urinals and, this being Madonna, religious knick-knacks like crosses and candles, before which she poses as if entombed or ready for sacrifice.

We also glimpse Madonna in mid-threesome with two girl skinheads covered in tattoos and with every stray protuberance pierced with pins and rings. In one photograph they hold a knife to Madonna's throat; in another, to her groin. The men on view here sport the half-dressed-policeman look of outdated career gaydom; in the elastic bands of their jockstraps Madonna's head is variously entangled. She is also often seen at the centre of a great press of gay-male flesh, in 'playful' gang-rape scenarios. The atmosphere recalls the intent, aggressive, leathery, specialist sexuality of the Seventies; the actors are a dedicated janitoriat in the venereal boiler-room.

After a while the book starts cooling down and brightening up. Many of the snaps that follow could be out of *Playboy* or *Penthouse* or even *Health and Efficiency*. There are some striking 'found' set-ups, where the dare element is simply a result of location: Madonna half-nude in a dumbstruck pizza parlour; Madonna on the kerbside in Miami, wearing only high heels, a handbag and a cigarette. The diversification in tone is accompanied by a diversification in personnel and 'preference'. Characteristically – indeed crucially – Madonna's bawdy house has many mansions: hardly

anyone who isn't already in jail need feel at all locked
out.

Apart from gays and sado-masochists, Hispanics and
blacks are of course represented in all inter-ethnic com-
binations. There are cross-dressers and androgynists. There
are posed encounters with the very old and the very young.
There is even a shot of Madonna looming over a belly-up
Alsatian with an expression of fond indulgence on her face.
And the book winds up with a solid reversion to hot-sheets
sleaze: an eight-page narrative of stills with paste-on speech
bubbles, depicting a fuddled orgy in a cheap hotel room,
during which a grimy rock musician has sex with, among
others (Madonna included), his sister. Then the acknowledg-
ments, in predictable style: private jocularity plus apocalyptic
gratitude.

Interspersed with the pictures are sections of scrawled
or printed prose from Madonna's own pen. These include
various bites of sexual advice, some of which might be seen as
contradictory. The now-familiar sloganising about condoms
('Safe sex saves lives') is soon followed by a paranthetical
few words about sodomy, hailed as 'the most pleasurable'
form of sex although it 'hurts the most too'. Not that *that's*
a contradiction, in these pages, where pain gets a consistently
good press (on bondage: 'Like when you were a baby your
mother strapped you to the car seat. You wanted to be safe
– it's an act of love').

Other prose sections include accounts of erotic dreams (too
boringly circumstantial to be anything but authentic), a series
of letters addressed to 'Johnny' (about how the authoress is
languidly toying with Ingrid while they thirst for Johnny's
return), sexual reverie or heightened reminiscence (trashily
generic, with such biological unlikelihoods as the Madonna
figure visibly 'gushing' in orgasm), dating tips ('The best way
to seduce someone is by making yourself unavailable. Don't
fuck them for the first five dates.'), cute panegyrics to her own
genitalia ('I love my pussy. I think it's a complete summation

of my life'), and a smattering of sexual slogans in praise of freedom, individual choice, lack of inhibition, and courage to explore your etc., etc. 'A lot of people are afraid to say what they want and so they don't get what they want.' But the book, remember, is presented as fantasy, a realm in which it is presumably okay to get what you want, even if it's your sister, or your dog.

Opinions on *Sex* will divide sharply, and will further subdivide when the book is dutifully processed by the innumerable interest – and target – groups that make up Madonna's mysteriously vast constituency. All the Middle-American, Dan-Quaylean moralistic objections can be concentrated as follows: if the identikit Madonna fan is still the thirteen-year-old lookalike and wannabe – then what? 'Let's face it,' as Madonna herself said recently, while complaining about the obsessed teens who camp outside her New York apartment, 'they're not that bright.' Any role model, in America today, must be ready for accusations of irresponsibility or even – to use the phrase unintentionally popularised by Woody Allen – 'abuse of trust'.

It is quite likely that *Sex* will scare up a political response on the national as well as the socio-sexual level. The Woody Allen story broke in August during the Republican Convention in Houston, where Pat Buchanan and Pat Robertson were somehow permitted to frame the party's recklessly militant 'family values' platform. The GOP is already backpedalling from its assaults on every domestic configuration that fell outside the traditional family – after it learned that the traditional family accounts for only 14 per cent of the American population. On the following day Woody Allen jokes were being freely tossed around the convention hall (Woody's upcoming projects, it was said, were *Close Encounters with the Third Grade* and *Honey, I Fucked the Kids*). There was even talk of 'the Woody Horton possibility': Allen might embarrass the Democrats just as Willie Horton – the black convict who violently recidivated on a

Dukakis-sponsored weekend furlough – had destroyed them in 1988.

Madonna would certainly be fair quarry in a campaign which finds single-parent TV-sitcom characters worthy of attack. Republican moralism is after all a blunt weapon (its intention here is simply to show that 'left-wing' sexuality can often look like a mess); and never mind, for now, the far-right video vicars who are regularly discovered on the floors of hot-sheets motel bedrooms, under a heap of hookers and forged tax-returns. For the sex that *Sex* celebrates is not only vigorously perverse but also highly conceptualised. The fact that Madonna regards the book as essentially *comic* – even the S/M poses are 'meant to be funny' – shows how overevolved and tangential her own sexuality has become. And although love gets a single approving mention, there is no suggestion that younger readers should get some corny erotic normality behind them, before delving into all this glazed and minatory aestheticism. More generally, and more personally, there is the feeling that *Sex* is no more than the desperate confection of an ageing scandal-addict who, with this book, merely confirms that she is exhausting her capacity to shock.

The defence will run as follows. Madonna's little clones have all grown up now, and have not been replaced by the current wave of teens – who, Time Warner suggests, will be adequately deterred anyway by the book's civic-minded price tag. Madonna's audience, like Madonna, has always been a shifting thing: teen girls, teen boys, gay men, and now young and not-so-young women in the twenty-forty range. And it is to this last group that *Sex* is apparently directed. As Warner's Nanscy Lieman appealingly puts it: 'The few men who have seen the book are definitely intrigued. But the women take one look and go [inhalation then exhalation]: "Sshh. Oooh." ' In this version, *Sex* streaks like a tracer bullet through the dark sky of female sexual fantasy. Erotica and pornography are male preserves, made by men for other men; there is nothing out there for women, except the joke beefcake of *Playgirl*, itself a crude transposition of a male idea. And here Madonna is, as always, on the crest of the contemporary: post-modern, post-feminist, she is the Woman of the Year of the Woman, incorporating Babe Power with the older, simpler Have It All credo of *Cosmopolitan*. This is womanhood without sisterhood. This is imaginative self-reliance.

Female sexual fantasy, or so men tend to believe, has always been a constrained and limited arena. Whereas the fierce specialisation of male erotica attests to a ridiculously detailed repertoire (a magazine shelf for every breast-size and leg-length), the female equivalent seems, or seemed, to be confined to variations on the theme of helplessness. In the staple, text-book example, the woman dreamed of abduction and rape (so that if she enjoyed it, it wasn't her fault), usually at the hands of some glistening exotic (who was therefore outside her own society). Such a story-line is clearly a relic – but where do we go from here? For the politically-correct, feminist-approved sexual reverie is just as obviously a contradiction in terms: person meets person on an equal-pay protest march; he is caring and respects her space; over a nut cutlet she frames the parameters of her erotic needs; he doesn't see a problem . . . Sshh. Oooh.

Half-unconsciously, gathering up all her pop-cultural ink-lings, Madonna may be on to something with *Sex* – on to something apart from more money and notoriety and everything else she already has to the point of boredom and embarrassment. The polymorphous perverse, the infantile mishmash of what can arouse us, may now be unprece-dentedly perverse but it is no longer polymorphous. It has exact and fixable shape (in two dimensions, anyway). It is made up of images. Take male homo-eroticism. The conven-tional notion used to be that the male liked thinking about two women together (the two women would, of course, drop everything if the male thinker actually appeared on stage), but the female didn't like thinking about two men together, because she more modestly assumed that she wasn't wanted or needed, and could not respond to something that seemed to exclude her. And the male-gay subculture felt darker, more hidden, more forbidding (and less legal) than its female counterpart. But this world, along with every other, is now part of our common currency of images and triggers, part of the visual babble we carry round in our heads. Sex is in the head. And the head has never been so crowded, or so hot, or so noisy.

From the start Madonna has included pornography in her unique array of cultural weaponry – because she understands its modern, industrial nature. In terms of dollar turnover, pornography in America is bigger than music and movies combined; it is bigger (and I don't know if I find this less or more amazing) than the motor industry. That she has utilised this huge and shadowy power is a tribute, not just to her flair for manipulation, but to her innate amorality – her talent for ruthlessness. The elements of the popular culture that she has melded together may look random and indiscriminate. In fact, they could have been assembled by a corporate computer: pornography, religion, multi-ethnicity, transsexuality, kitsch, camp, worldly power, self-parody and self-invention.

This last is perhaps the most important. Madonna's protean quality, her ability to redesign herself (evident in each new photo shoot: baby-doll, dominatrix, flower-child, vamp), represents an emphasis of will over talent. Not greatly gifted, not deeply beautiful, Madonna tells America that fame comes from *wanting* it badly enough. And everyone is terribly good at badly wanting things.

Alone among celebrities, she seldom talks about the real or private self that she supposedly reverts to when out of the public eye. A good deal of superstar neurosis is probably caused by such futile quests for the innocent original (though a psychotherapist has recently joined Madonna's entourage, maybe with a brief to root out this tiny phantom). Otherwise she is the self-sufficient post-modern phenomenon ('even her *publicity* gets publicity'), a masterpiece of controlled illusion. She has held nothing back. Her love life has long devolved into a mixture of adult soap and public relations. After this, it is no great wrench to detach your sexuality – your most intimate thoughts, your most delicate susceptibilities – and throw it into the mix.

Observer, 1992

V. S. PRITCHETT'S CENTURY

He meets you at the turn in the stairs, with an expression of mild apology and embarrassment. It's as if he expects the visitor to be astonished – even scandalised – by how well he is looking these days. He seems to say as much. And then he goes ahead and says it: 'I know. Yes, well, I had all my serious illnesses in late middle age. And now I'm just *stuck*, I'm afraid.' He stands there intact and entire. Time and gravity have merely made him look sculpted-downwards, out of wood. You might find this face on the totem pole of an Amerindian tribe, long-vanished, perhaps, but widely famed for its pacifism and its compelling cosmogony.

Urged on by Lady Pritchett, who manages everything (she is prodigiously handsome and vigorous), we moved into the sitting-room. The house was autumnal in light and tang – unlike many a furnace of the elderly – and the Pritchetts were recovering, or regrouping, after a three-week visit from Eudora Welty, who journeyed there from Jackson, Mississippi. This sounded like a scoop, or a literary fantasy. And did these two veteran heavyweights talk obsessively about the art they had both mastered, that of the short story? 'No,' said Dorothy Pritchett. 'They talked about everything but. They talked about the *Algonquin*.' V.S.P. resignedly concurs. Everyone calls him V.S.P. And Dorothy sometimes calls him 'Vsp'.

265

For a while we gossipped in our turn, children, grandchildren, then the illnesses and deaths of people much younger than V.S.P., including the ex-occupant of the next-but-one house along Regents Park Terrace, A.J. Ayer. Frances Partridge has said that this is one of the great consternations of longevity: how the deaths of your own generation are followed by the deaths of the generation that came after, while you remain. 'It's all the wrong way round,' said V.S.P., who admits to finding the prospect of a tenth decade 'very shocking'. Dorothy brought coffee and joined us for the interview. She is not his eyes or his ears or his arms and his legs, all of which he still has. She is his memory. 'It's in patches,' he says, and gives his fizzy laugh.

It would gratify me to claim that V.S.P. and I go back a way. But it can't seem very far back to him. I was twenty-five. He was seventy-five, and considered to be 'marvellous' for his age even then. This is what impressed and assailed me throughout our meeting: a sense of depth. Depth of genius, certainly, but first of all depth of time. The interview was taking place in the year 1990; yet Pritchett grew up in a London still recovering from Jack the Ripper. The title of his first volume of autobiography, *A Cab at the Door*, fully evokes his origins: improvisation, hurried departure, resolute gentility. Those peripatetic Pritchetts may be leaving a lot of unpaid bills, but they are making their exit via the front door, not the back, and by cab, not on foot. And the cab, of course, is horse-drawn.

The young Victor emerged from 'a set of story tellers and moralists' (and savage eccentrics); his mother was a superexpressive illiterate, his father a clothes-horse and debt-dodger: and his milieu was that of 'trade', whose antiquity is best expressed by its humble grammar: 'short jobs in the drapery', 'put into the millinery', 'had lately become shopwalker in Daniels'. Pritchett was obliged to leave school early, for the usual reasons. During the Great War he worked in a leather factory in Bermondsey. Nicknamed 'the Professor' at home, where he had the status of 'a tolerated joke', he left for Paris at the age of nineteen. And so Pritchett lit out for a life of mental travel, in which he was free to reinvent himself.

He now sports the settled persona of the refined, understated, omnicultured mid-century litterateur, with his heavily qualified speech ('rather', 'quite', 'slightly') and his reserved yet caressing good manners. The bitternesses associated with poverty, class, early turbulence and the autodidact's solitude have long been assimilated. And this aura of twinkly equanimity, of aged saintliness, has in my view tended to neutralise his reputation – which, although considerable, is inadequate and misemphasised. V.S.P. is a grand old man; he is marvellous; may he live to be a hundred! His reputation is a haven of elegance, civility and quiet. But the essential Pritchett isn't like that at all. It is noisy, dangerous and beautifully awkward. It is visionary.

One of the many hats or masks that Pritchett wears is that of our senior literary critic. Here as elsewhere, though, he is a rampant instinctivist. Innocent of theory, espousing no tradition, his criticism is always doing all the *don'ts*: it is a mixture of generous connoisseurship and inspired psychology. Travel-writer, biographer, novelist, essayist, as happy with P.G. Wodehouse as with Antoine de Saint-Exupery – Pritchett looks protean, but really his genius is indivisible. He is a teller of stories.

'I think I can hit upon a writer's voice quite well,' he said. 'Then I find myself inventing a story about the book. Which is itself a story.'

'And *your* stories – they're the main thing, aren't they?'

'Oh, the stories to me are absolutely everything. I can't write novels. I have written novels, but they're not good. But the stories I think are sometimes good.'

'Yes, I think they're sometimes good, too.'

Naturally, one was falling in with the Pritchett style:

one was putting it mildly. But at that point I was only beginning to establish a final sense of *how* good his stories are. Like many 'younger' readers (the word is used comparatively, and advisedly), I had picked up on Pritchett with the famous collections *Blind Love* (1969) and *The Camberwell Beauty* (1974). It quickly became clear to me that Pritchett was a writer of alarming clairvoyance: he had instant and unlimited access to the hearts and minds of so-called ordinary people. On the other hand there was a feeling that this genius was manageably minor, too febrile and amorphous, and somehow adrift in time and space: his was a shadowland of frumps and vamps, winking barmen, venomous valets, drunken matriarchs, venal quacks, lodgers, chamberpots, consumption and the smell of mouse.

This impression had survived the odd encounter with earlier stories in various Pritchett *Selected*s and *Collected*s and *Reader*s and *Best of*s. But now I was spending eight hours a day with *The Complete Short Stories*, and feeling the delightful pressure of its strength-in-depth. The book is hefty, practically cuboid (1,200 pages), and some reviewers have claimed difficulty in placing it on their laps. A better challenge would be to place it in world literature. In any case one is crushed by the weight of achievement. The volume, like the stories, comes up on you the other way: from a million little epiphanies Pritchett builds something vast. There may be half-a-dozen prose writers born in this century who could cobble together some kind of rival omnibus. But none of them is English.

A Pritchett story has two ways of announcing itself. The first way can only be described as thrillingly unpromising:

> It was the evening of the Annual Dinner. More than two hundred accountants were at that hour changing into evening clothes, in the flats, villas and hotel rooms of a large, wet, Midland city.

– where *wet* has never worked so hard, and done so much. Or the second way (more characteristic of the earlier work), with a glare of poetic revelation:

> The X-ray department of the hospital is reached by tepid corridors. A swing door admits the noises of the street and with a gulp swallows you and rejects them. You are cut off from the world. Stairways lead upwards to the regions of pain, six floors carefully labelled and distributed; yet, passing the open doors of laboratories, seeing instruments and retorts, smelling ether which excites the nostrils, the body begins to feel important. It is bringing its talent of pain to the total.

– where 'atmosphere' is suddenly condensed into a frightening truth. With a Pritchett story you are seldom going anywhere in a linear sense. Things happen; there are unitings and sunderings; deaths act as codas. You are not going anywhere but you are travelling mentally, and at speed. You are entering the writer's coherent version of reality.

It is a world lashed by weather and emotion. The city, in the blackout, where the siren sounds 'like all the dead cats of London restless beyond the grave'; or in fog, engulfed by 'moist horn-coloured vapour, with its core of weak pink or lilac light where the arc lamps hung. The corners of buildings were smudged and broken off in the upper air and, in the lower, the fog was like a damp sand, the vapour of a million individual breaths.' The rural winter, where 'the roads are like slugs', the horses move off 'like hairy yokels', and the frost has 'its teeth fast in the ground': 'Winter in England has the colourless, steaming look of a fried-fish shop-window.' Or the sea, sometimes 'as quiet as the licking of a cat's tongue', or else forming 'a loose tottering wall, green, wind-torn, sun-shot and riotous ... The lighthouse on the red spit eight miles across the bay seemed to be racing through the water like a periscope.'

Character is fixed by an adverb (the waiter comes forward, 'feebly averting his nose from the mess he was carrying on his dish'), by an adjective (' "I couldn't sleep – and when I can't sleep I scratch," said Margaret in her wronged voice'), or by the arrangement of epithets ('Frederick [the barman] stood upright, handsome, old, and stupid'). Like Auden, Pritchett loves to impact language, and run the cadences up the wrong way: 'He had a moustache of sweat, a hard, factory mouth, and blue, unwilling eyes.' Larger than life (and sometimes smaller, too), his creations never lose the delicacy of their lineaments. He is the heir of Dickens:

> Rogers and Mr Pocock had come together not because of their minds or tastes, but because of their bodies. They were drawn will-lessly together by the magnetic force of their phenomenal obesities. There is a loneliness in fat. Atlas met Atlas, astonished to find each saddened by the burden of a world. Rogers was short and had that douce, pleading melancholy of the enormous. His little blue eyes, above the bumps of fat on his cheek-bones, looked like sinking lights at sea; and he had the gentle and bewildered air of a man who watches himself daily getting uncontrollably and hopelessly fatter ... Mr Pocock's pathos was fiery and bitter. A pair of stiffly inflated balloons seemed to have been placed, one under and one above Mr Pocock's waist-line, and the load forced his short legs apart on either side of the chair, like the splayed speckled legs of a frog ... At night they met like lovers. They were religious drinkers. Whisky was Mr Pocock's religion, beer was the faith of Rogers. An active faith ranges widely. After the public-houses of the village there were two or three on the main road. The headlights of cars howling through the dark to the coast picked out two balloons in coats and trousers, bouncing and blowing down the road. Dramas halted them.
>
> 'What's that, old boy?'

'Rabbit.'
'No, old boy, not a rabbit. It was a fox. I know a fox.'
'I reckon it was a stoat.'
The point became intricate under the stars.

Nevertheless it is Pritchett's women who define the true
extent of his powers. For his sensibility is itself feminine,
undissociated, like Eliot's Metaphysicals: in him, thought
and feeling are congruent, not opposed. Pritchett's women
loom magical and multiform. 'Mrs Tagg jostled her various
selves together within her corsets and stared.' Or: 'She had
several chins. The small chin shook like a cup in its saucer.'
They 'swell with shame' and 'sit vast in nervous judgment'.
Crucially, Pritchett is a poet of female tears. This lady has
been drinking, and recalling a lost love: 'Mrs Forster's cheeks
and neck fattened amorously as she mewed and quietly cried
and held her handkerchief tight.' The warmth of the detail
(the gripped hanky) is delightful; and yet it is also pointing
beyond itself, to a larger mystery.
To something like this:

Gran's life was filled with guilt towards the living, whom
she looked at slyly, and her tears were not tears of sorrow,
but issued to conceal this guilt. She was guilty because she
forgot the living and neglected them in her absorption with
the dead.

And finally, at the end of the same story, to this:

And then [Aunt Gertrude] saw the crack in the mirror and
tears came into her eyes, large tears like the pearl buttons
in her blouse. To me they were not like the tears I had
seen before, for her common tears were hardly personal,
but a general oblation to the unexplainable coming and
going of woe in the world.

From this coming and going, this woeful rhythm, the male writer – the male himself – has long been excluded, or exiled. But it is always available to Pritchett, and deeply informs his universality.

'I found people were telling stories to themselves without knowing it,' he said, when I asked him about his habit of inwardness, his telepathic entry into ordinary minds. 'It seemed to me that people were living a sort of small sermon that they believed in, but at the same time it was a fairy tale. Selfish desires, along with one or two highly suspect elevated thoughts. They secretly regard themselves as works of art, valuable in themselves.'

'But in life they are silent. Until you come along . . .'

'Yes. I do think it is a kind of duty to speak for them.'

'He just *does* it,' said Dorothy. 'That story about the antique dealer. People think he did months of research. But all he did was go into an antique shop in Wiltshire and spend five minutes buying a dining-room chair.'

Morally Pritchett's people inhabit a Biblical world (displaced and of course vulgarised), a world of shame, pride, guilt, temptation, and fear of ruin. They may be weak or sinful, but they are never judged; Pritchett never arranges for their conversion or punishment. 'I'd much sooner they go on unpunished. I think the incurable side of human nature is what appeals to me.' ('He's like that', said Dorothy, ' – even about his own family. *I* can rage about them, but he never does.') Pritchett never judges, yet his style serves as a moral instrument. The slant of his prose and his comedy is a strict apportioner of guilt and innocence. He himself strikes you as innocent, and also terribly knowing.

Seen as a writing life, *The Complete Short Stories* describes the arc of ascension and inevitable decline. After the long crescendo, the long decrescendo. Formal artistry continues, but what it has to handle becomes less volatile. Now the cataract has become an unregarded mountain stream. It appears to be his only sadness.

'I haven't done anything for – how long? Several weeks?'

Dorothy: 'Several months. He's *longing* to write another short story.'

'I have jots of things which I think are no good. Start always again. Have another go at it . . . As one gets older one becomes very boring and longwinded to oneself. One's thoughts are longwinded, whereas before they were really rather nice and *agitated*. The story is a form of travel. As I go across the page my pen is travelling. Travelling through minds or situations which reveal their strangeness to you. Old age kills travel. Things don't come suddenly to you. You're mainly protecting yourself. Stories come up on you almost by accident. And now one tends to live a life in which there are no accidents . . . It's nothing to do with that really. It's just being older.'

Powers fail. But Pritchett's presence is still a testing one. I came away from Regents Park Terrace feeling heartened and relieved, as if after a psychiatric check-up; I had survived the stare of the benign basilisk. The great writers do something specific to their readers. They heighten and transfigure the world you see, for ever: 'like the clot of a spirit level to be steadily carried'. Parkway and Camden Town were busy and wet, entirely everyday in their anti-travel of errands and hurry. But Pritchett was filling these streets for me with theatre. He makes the world strange, humorous and dreadful, appallingly overpopulated with passions and fears. The queue at the bus-stop suddenly resembled the crowd at a stage door, their faces no longer vacant but full of fever and cunning. 'No two stories' – meaning no two people – 'are quite alike,' he had said. And 'I'm always anxious to speak the truth, you know.'

From 'The Upright Man', written sixty years ago:

Clerks flung their lives about and committed follies. One married to a voracious wife drank on Thursdays a glass of stout. One who copied weighing slips gave imitations

273

of the voice of the cashier. One who was bald put his hand down the blouse of his secretary and was slapped in the face. One would absent himself for twenty minutes in the morning to read the newspaper in the lavatory. One going deaf turned to an Oriental religion. One made use of the office telephone to communicate with a bookmaker. One told the Port of London Authority of an error in demurrage; it was his own. One staying after six lit his pipe.

And then later, after the War:

One who had come to suspect Divine Justice took to games of chance. One who was bald consummated love with a telephone operator and was presented with a clock on his marriage; one saddened by an adding machine took drugs which gave him visions; one moved into a town whose train service had been electrified; one who could imitate the voice of the cashier played in an orchestra; one sold his house at a profit; a typist given to the circulation of religious pamphlets had a week's leave to serve on a jury; many grew flowers and had newborn children.

Independent on Sunday, 1990

BY MARTIN AMIS
ALSO AVAILABLE IN VINTAGE

☐ Dead Babies	0099437333	£6.99
☐ Einstein's Monsters	0099768917	£6.99
☐ Experience	0099285827	£7.99
☐ Heavy Water	0099272660	£6.99
☐ Koba the Dread	009943802X	£7.99
☐ London Fields	0099748614	£7.99
☐ Money	0099461889	£7.99
☐ Night Train	0099748711	£6.99
☐ Other People	0099769018	£6.99
☐ Success	0099461854	£6.99
☐ Time's Arrow	0099455358	£6.99
☐ The War Against Cliché	0099422220	£8.99
☐ Yellow Dog	0099267594	£7.99

FREE POST AND PACKING
Overseas customers allow £2.00 per paperback

BY PHONE: 01624 677237

BY POST: Random House Books
C/o Bookpost, PO Box 29, Douglas
Isle of Man, IM99 1BQ

BY FAX: 01624 670923

BY EMAIL: bookshop@enterprise.net

Cheques (payable to Bookpost) and credit cards accepted

Prices and availability subject to change without notice.
Allow 28 days for delivery.
When placing your order, please mention if you do not wish to receive
any additional information.

www.randomhouse.co.uk/vintage